...hist Theory

ONE WEEK LOAN

Leisure and Feminist Theory

Betsy Wearing

SAGE Publications

London · Thousand Oaks · New Delhi

First published 1998

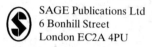

SAGE Publications Ltd
6 Bonhill Street
London EC2A 4PU

SAGE Publications Inc.
2455 Teller Road
Thousand Oaks, California 91320

SAGE Publications India Pvt Ltd
32, M-Block Market
Greater Kailash - I
New Delhi 110 048

British Library Cataloguing in Publication data

A catalogue record for this book is available from the British
Library

ISBN 0 8039 7536 8
ISBN 0 8039 7537 6 (pbk)

Library of Congress catalog card number 98-61180

Typeset by Type Study, Scarborough, North Yorkshire
Printed and bound in Great Britain by Athenaeum Press,
Gateshead

Contents

Acknowledgements

I would like to thank Chris Rojek for inviting me to write this book and for the light and encouraging hand he has kept on the helm during its production. His own openness to ideas which push the thinking further in the area of leisure has encouraged me to take some risks in my own writing. He may not agree with all of my feminist thinking, but he has allowed me the latitude to pursue my own ideas anyway.

Paul McCrohan and Kath Knowles acted as enthusiastic library researchers for the early chapters of the book as did Christine Wearing for later chapters. Stephen Wearing also gathered some of the material and we continued, as we have done for a number of years, to bounce around ideas which are new to both of us.

Ross Saunders has been an ever-helpful friend with computing and formatting, saving me many hours of tedious work.

My children, grandchildren, friends and colleagues have been tolerant of my lack of sociability at times when the book took over. My husband, Leslie, has at all times supported me through my academic endeavours and wonders now when I am really going to retire.

Introduction

Much sociological analysis of contemporary social systems founded on a capitalist economy, industrial and post-industrial production, urban dwelling and nation states has focused on the construction of the self through the disciplinary production-ethic (see Bell, 1978; Berman, 1983; Campbell, 1987; Featherstone, 1991). Such an ethic concentrates on discipline, control, work, 'clock time', deferred gratification, and calculative rationality and the related values commonly understood as the Protestant Ethic. More recently the pursuit of selfhood in such a society has been theorized as equally dependent on the complementary consumption-centred, hedonistic ethic that encourages the pursuit of selfhood through self-expression, leisure, consumer goods and pleasure (Moorhouse, 1983, 1989; Campbell, 1987). Both ethics, it appears, are necessary dynamics in the processes of contemporary capitalism and both contribute to the construction of the self. Leisure theory which surfaced in the arena of sociological analysis in the early 1970s, with a downturn in the productive sphere and an increase in non-work time, remained initially embedded in work-related frameworks but has progressively moved towards the sphere of consumption and pleasure where the multiplicity of postmodern selves are at play (see Rojek, 1985, 1989, 1993a, 1995).

Feminist analyses have critiqued the former excessive emphasis on the productive sphere and the work ethic as the basis of identity construction as a masculine perspective which ignores the everyday experiences of women. Women, they say, depend more heavily on the non-productive sphere of consumption and leisure as a source of some autonomy and sense of individual identity (Wearing, 1990a). Feminist leisure theorists began to shift the focus towards theories of leisure which recognized women's perspectives including unpaid labour, the domestic sphere, consumption and a more diffuse concept of the work/leisure dichotomy. The emergence of these feminist theories coincided with the shift in sociology generally away from work-centred models as convincing explanations for contemporary society. This book examines both feminist critiques of male-orientated leisure theories and the use that feminists have made of particular elements of these theories. There are as many feminist theoretical perspectives concerning leisure as there are sociological and feminist perspectives. Feminist theory here refers to those forms of analysis which seek to increase understanding of women's experiences in patriarchal, capitalist, modern and postmodern, Western and developing societies with a view to increasing the quality of life of both women and men. A recurring theme throughout the book is the relationship between the self or selves and leisure, where selves refer to both femininities and masculinities.

A second connecting theme which emerges as the book proceeds is that of space. Soja (1993) argues that academic study has, in the modern era, privileged time and history over space and geography. He claims, however, that,

> The material and intellectual contexts of modern critical social theory have begun to shift dramatically. In the 1980s, the hoary traditions of a space-blinkered historicism are being challenged with unprecedented explicitness by convergent calls for far-reaching spatialization of the critical imagination. A distinctly postmodern and critical human geography is taking shape, brashly reasserting the interpretive significance of space in the historically privileged confines of contemporary critical thought. (Soja, 1993: 137)

The feminist geographer, Massey, takes the argument a step further by suggesting that space in male-dominated thinking has been coded feminine and aligned with stasis, passivity and depoliticization. She wants to rescue space from this position and make clear the relationship between space, social relationships and identity, with all the implications of dynamism, multiplicity of meanings and power that this implies. The strategy she adopts is to rethink the concept of space in terms of relationships and identity (1994: 6–7).

This shift in thought is reflected in my own reconceptualization of leisure as social space or, in Foucault's (1986) terms, other spaces, 'heterotopias' which allow for constructions of the self which are different from those of the everyday constraints of our lives. The inevitable tension between freedom and constraint in leisure experience, and between individual resistance, negotiation and struggle and structural and cultural constraint, therefore also emerges as a recurring theme throughout the book. Feminist theory for a decade focused on the constraints on women's leisure, but more recently has also explored the possibilities that leisure offers for liberation.

In this book, as the various theoretical perspectives are presented and discussed, it will become obvious to the reader that theories arise in particular socio-political and cultural climates. There are two underlying assumptions in my presentation of the various theories. The first relies on Weber's (1970) notion of 'elective affinity' and Foucault's (1980) concept of 'discourse'. 'Elective affinity' refers to the notion that the ideas that are adopted and propagated at certain historical moments are those which are in the interests of powerful groups. By 'discourse' Foucault means an assemblage of statements arising in an ongoing conversation, mediated by texts, among speakers and hearers separated from each other in time and space which take on the credibility of 'truth' and which are constructed as knowledge by the powerful. Thus, my first assumption is that power, knowledge and theory are inextricably interlinked. The second assumption is that while no one theory has all the explanations for human behaviour or human selfhood, each has some insight to contribute. In hindsight it is possible then to observe some of the yawning gaps in the functionalism of the 1960s and 1970s, the Marxism of the 1980s and the Western, middle-class feminism of the late 1980s and early 1990s. But this is not to dismiss them – it is to recognize their relationship to power and knowledge and the blinkers thus imposed. It is also to value their contribution to the cumulative uncovering and understanding of, in this instance, the sphere of human endeavour called leisure.

It is my opinion that as sociologists we do a disservice to our discipline if we rigidly appropriate any one theoretical perspective in our analysis of any human phenomenon. Recent theorizing in the disciplines of physics, philosophy and theology suggest that both the cosmos and the individual human being do not obey the rules previously set down by their disciplines. There is a sense of nature and human nature being more than can be explained by rules. There is an element of wonder and surprise at happenings and behaviour (see O'Shea, 1995, for a more detailed discussion of these ideas). We, in the social sciences, must also be aware that human beings are more than our attempts to explain the patterns of their social behaviour. Individuals, groups, cultures, societies constantly surprise us – they will not fit neatly into our categorization. The current thinking in postmodernism concerning diversity, difference, complexity and eclecticism has reverberations in my own construction and presentation of the ideas in this book. As I have progressed through the various theoretical perspectives, I have taken what I see as valuable insights from each and ultimately developed them in my own way (not always strictly as the original theorist intended) into my own feminized version of leisure which I hope will add some further insights into our understanding of leisure as human experience in today's world. The structure of the book reflects my own thinking concerning leisure, and especially women's leisure, as I have moved from my socialist feminist beginnings (see my *Ideology of Motherhood*, 1984) to incorporate ideas relevant to leisure from feminist poststructuralist and postcolonial writings. The chapters dealing with these perspectives appear at the end of the book. Although this thinking has obviously influenced some of the critique and evaluation included in the earlier chapters, those chapters do not claim to have their bases in poststructuralist theorizing. Rather, there, I have presented the contribution that each perspective has made to leisure theory and some of its weaknesses.

The aim of this book is to provide a critical introduction to the leading positions in leisure theory and to guide the student through their strengths and weaknesses from feminist perspectives. The book is written to draw attention to the various leisure experiences that women encounter and construct in their everyday lives and the meanings that these experiences have for them. Insights that poststructuralist theories have contributed to the meanings of leisure are included. This means that the predominantly male theorists of the 1970s and the first wave of feminist theoretical reactions to such theorizing are examined from a perspective that takes into account poststructuralist ideas such as: multiple subjectivities of women and multiple femininities; the possibilities of resistance to and subversion of male domination through leisure; possibilities through leisure of rewriting masculine and feminine scripts; access through leisure to alternative discourses which challenge dominant discourses on gender; sites of leisure as culturally gendered enclaves which also offer opportunity for struggle and resistance to hegemonic masculinity; and the productive as well as the repressive aspects of power relations. Women in this work are portrayed not as passive victims of structured inequalities which favour males, but as active thinking beings who can and do challenge some aspects of male domination through leisure. Structural constraints on women's leisure are not ignored – they are placed in tension with opportunities for leisure which women carve out, even in oppressive circumstances. Thus, the selves which women construct in their own political, cultural and discursive spaces are not presented here as completely fragmented or as totally socially determined. To the extent that each woman has the ability to synthesize past and present selves into a cumulative whole, and to resist total domination, I believe that she has an ongoing, if changing, self. In this regard I differ from the poststructuralist feminists whose work I draw on in the book.

The book goes beyond previous leisure texts by providing a feminist critique of the variety of leisure theories based in masculine ways of viewing the world. It goes beyond previous feminist analyses of leisure by giving an overview of the diversity of feminist theoretical perspectives. In addition it applies, not uncritically, some of the insights of Foucault, French feminists and other poststructuralist and postcolonial feminists and masculinists to men's and women's leisure with a view to improving the quality of life of both.

The definition of leisure varies as the book progresses, as it is constructed differently within different theoretical perspectives. The methodology adopted by different perspectives also varies in accordance with the definition. For example, in functional theory, leisure is a category separate and different from work, and interpreted as non-work time and activity. Consequently the methodology for empirical research based on this definition relies on the ability on the researcher's part to categorize time spent and activities engaged in as non-work. Quantitative methods are used. In symbolic interaction theory, leisure is an experience, the meaning of which varies from individual to individual. Hence, in empirical research, data is collected concerning the subjective meanings attached to experiences defined by individuals as leisure. Qualitative methodology produces this data. In the final chapters of the book, where insights from poststructuralist and postcolonial feminist theory are the focus, leisure has been redefined as personal space, making room for the inclusion of a wider range of experiences, as well as a wider range of participants. Research conducted around this definition asks us to listen to the voices of those who do not belong to dominant groups or cultures and who previously have been invisible in leisure research. Here again qualitative methods are appropriate, with an emphasis on the speaking subject. Throughout the book, however, leisure remains a concept conceived around an element of relative freedom within the very many pressures, constraints and sites of power in contemporary society. It is a sometimes temporary respite or a different space (Foucault's 'heterotopia') within the demands of daily living.

As a feminist text, the author appears within the text, implicitly through the perspective adopted and, at times, explicitly through the incorporation of some of my own experiences and research. Finally I develop my own feminist perspective on leisure, looking to future possibilities for women and men to experience liberating leisure.

The book provides an overview of leisure theories with particular focus on their usefulness for understanding and improving women's leisure experiences. Men's leisure is also considered, in the light of feminist theorizing. As an educational tool this work encourages students to take what is useful from the theories presented and develop and apply the concepts to their own leisure experiences, those of the people they know and those they will encounter as professionals. In addition, it suggests some future directions for leisure research, leisure policy and professional practice.

My own interest in the sociology of leisure began with a study leave spent in Sweden in 1985. I was comparing Swedish and Australian social policy in an attempt to explain the greater convergence in Sweden of men's and women's incomes. The progressive Swedish policy of generous parental leave at the birth of a child and for the care of a sick child up to eight years of age, and the increase in availability of part-time jobs, enabled women to remain in the workforce during the child-rearing years. This was one reason for women's greater access to wages or salaries than in the Australian context. However, as Swedish women talked to me, they said, 'Betsy, by the time we are forty we are exhausted, we stay in the workforce and bear and rear our children and still do 80 per cent of the household work'. I began then to think about what happens to women's leisure under these circumstances. What costs are there for women in having greater access to economic independence?

Returning to Australia I began to read the leisure literature and with one of my sons wrote an article, '"All in a day's leisure": gender and the concept of leisure', which critiqued masculine views of leisure (Wearing and Wearing, 1988). I then embarked on an empirical study of the leisure of mothers of first babies (Wearing, 1990a and 1990b) which coincided with other feminist studies of women's leisure (see Deem, 1986; Wimbush and Talbot, 1988: Henderson et al., 1989). In 1991–2, I was seconded to the School of Leisure and Tourism Studies, University of Technology, Sydney, and began to transfer the application of my sociological knowledge from social work to the teaching of leisure theory and practice. This new area of study excited my interest and I perceived it as a more holistic, positive and preventative approach to the quality of human living than the problem-oriented approach of social work. At the same time my own socialist feminist theoretical concerns were being challenged by ideas from Foucault and poststructuralist feminism, so the two opened up new avenues of thinking for me. At this stage in my thinking I have tried to position the more optimistic perspectives of microsocial interactionist ideas on the self and poststructuralist ideas on capillary power and resistance within the constraints of the wider power structures of society. My geographical position in Australia influences my own perspective, as does my heterosexual sexual orientation. Through an educational system based largely on the British model, my thinking tends to be theoretical and critical, yet, as the reader will perceive, I have been much influenced by the pragmatism of American symbolic interactionism. Many of the examples in the book draw on the Australian situation and Chapter 8 is chiefly about Sydney, the city of my birth and upbringing. The literature, on the other hand, covers the relevant British, American, Canadian and Australian texts and those French feminisms which have been translated into English. In Chapter 9 there is a conscious attempt to let women of colour and women from developing countries speak for themselves in a book which may otherwise have excluded them. Where I write about the family and interactions in leisure between men and women, my own experience of forty-one years of heterosexual marriage has inevitably influenced my thinking.

The book is structured with an introductory and a concluding chapter and nine chapters which examine the various sociological theoretical perspectives that have been applied to leisure. For the sake of clarity, each chapter begins with an outline of the basic concepts of that particular theoretical approach. The leisure theorists who have drawn on those concepts are then discussed, including feminist theorists and applications. Finally some evaluation of the insights provided by this approach is given.

This introductory chapter has positioned this work within the development of sociological theory and, in particular, leisure theory from the 1970s to the present. In it I have presented my own interest in leisure and feminist theory, my approach to the topic and the underlying assumptions implicit in the book.

Chapter 1 examines functionalist theories. Within the functionalist tradition of Durkheim and Parsons, leisure is posited as an institution in society which performs a beneficial function for society and for individuals. Non-work time and activities provide a balance for workers, both rewarding hard labour and providing recuperation and a sense of well-being so that they can return to their labour refreshed. Theoretical works such as Parker (1983) and Roberts (1983), and empirical time and activity studies such as Szalai et al. (1972) and Veal (1987), adopting this approach, raised awareness of the importance and value of leisure for industrial society. However the (white and middle-class) male experience is assumed to be universal and where women appear they do so as 'other' to this male norm.

Analyses remain descriptive, gender power differentials are not addressed. Equilibrium in society is maintained by adaptations to change.

Chapter 2 explores Marxist and neo-Marxist theories. Based in the Marxian problematic of relationship to the means of production, these theorists analyse leisure time and leisure activity in terms of the profit motive, commodification, exploitation, alienation of labour, conflicts of class interests and an ideological superstructure based on an economic infrastructure. They emphasize constraints on individual leisure, inequalities in access to leisure and leisure as an ideology promulgating 'freedom' but obfuscating economic inequalities and class conflicts. The function of leisure in capitalist society is critiqued by theorists such as Coalter and Parry (1982), Clarke and Critcher (1985), Rojek (1985, 1986) and McKay (1990, 1991). For these writers class is generally prioritized. Where gender is included it is as an additional variable in the causal chain of leisure inequality. Socialist feminists such as Deem (1986) and Green et al. (1990) attempt to chart the control of women's leisure through the interaction of the structures of class and gender. There is an emphasis on women's common experience of oppression as a basis for solidarity and political action.

Chapter 3 is concerned with the implications of interactionist theories for the constraints and freedoms offered through leisure for the development of the self. Theorists such as Kelly (1983, 1987a, 1987b), drawing on the work of Mead, focus on the miscrosocial experiential aspects of leisure and on individuals as thinking actors (or agents) with an ability to construct leisure experiences which are both challenging and rewarding. The structures of power in wider society such as class and gender are not seen as completely deterministic. Feminist theorists who have adopted this approach, such as Shaw (1985), Samdahl (1988), Bella (1989), Henderson et al. (1989, 1996) and Wearing (1992a), show how the meaning of leisure in the everyday lives of men and women can be different, often (but not always) advantaging men. This approach allows for the development of the self through social space. It provides a foundation for hybrid constructions of the self beyond the structural determinants of gender, but has largely relied on social roles and socialization as explantions for gender differences.

Chapter 4 looks at cultural studies analyses of hegemonic struggles in leisure spaces and subcultures as well as in the media and the sporting arena. Cultural theories with their theoretical bases in Gramsci's civil society and cultural hegemony, rather than in ideological superstructure and economic infrastructure, were applied to working-class leisure subcultures through the Birmingham Centre for Cultural Studies (e.g. Hall and Jefferson, 1976). Williams's (1983) concept of culture as 'a whole way of life' has been applied to the analysis of cultural leisure spaces such as the beach, the pub and the shopping mall with a masculine bias (e.g. Fiske et al. 1987; Fiske, 1989), as well as to the dance (e.g. Walker, 1988). Feminists who write from this perspective show how girls' and women's experiences of these spaces are different from those of boys and men and involve greater constraint, but also some resistance to domination (e.g. McRobbie, 1978;

Roman, 1988). Hargreaves (1989, 1994), Bryson (1987, 1990) and Hall (1995) apply this perspective to women's sport and the domination of this area by the culture of 'hegemonic masculinity'. Yet here, too, leisure can be a space for struggle and negotiation for women to move beyond cultural prescriptions of femininity.

Chapter 5 turns to masculine experiences of leisure when analysed using insights gained from feminist theorizing. In response to the feminist theorizing of the 1970s which sought to document and explain women's oppression in patriarchal capitalist societies, masculinist literature seeks to raise men's awareness of the experience of being masculine in such societies, with an aim to liberate males. In the sporting arena, the work of Messner and Sabo (1990) has contributed to an understanding of some of the disadvantages for males of excessive emphasis on 'hegemonic masculinity' through sport. Kimmel (1996), on the other hand, demonstrates the impact of American culture over two centuries on the construction of a hegemonic masculinity which individual men must constantly prove to other men. The most sophisticated theoretical analysis of gender from a masculinist perspective has come from Connell (1987, 1995), with some acknowledgement of the differential power relations extant in gender differences and the cultural construction of hegemonic masculinity based on the inferiorization of women. Connell has also applied his ideas to men's sporting experiences. Nevertheless, this work succeeds in shifting the focus away from male dominance of women, to the dominance of hegemonic masculinity over other forms of masculinity as well as over all forms of femininity. I argue here for the need for some concepts from poststructuralist feminist theory concerning embodiment to restore the balance.

Chapter 6 applies recent sociological theorizing concerning the body and emotions to leisure. An interest in the social construction of the body has resulted in recent years in the emergence of sociological perspectives which place the body within a social and cultural context (e.g. Turner, 1984, 1996; Scott and Morgan, 1993). Implications for men's and women's leisure and sport in terms of aspirations and constraints have been touched on in the leisure literature (e.g. Hargreaves, 1987; Griffiths, 1988; Talbot, 1988; Hargreaves, 1989, 1994). This chapter develops these ideas further with regard to women's leisure. The constraints imposed on the use of the female body by its cultural definition are explored, as are ways of using leisure space to challenge and move beyond these constraints.

Similarly, an interest in the social construction of emotions has resulted in a growing body of literature on the sociology of emotions. Simmel (1978), Elias (1986a, 1986b) and Hochschild (1979) have each made significant contributions to an understanding of the constraints that civilization, living in the city and commodification of emotions place on an individual's emotional expression and ways that leisure may provide a space for emotional release.

Chapter 7 examines the contribution that urban sociology has made to the development of public leisure spaces in the city. For the most part, in urban sociology, women have remained invisible (Lynch, 1960; Castells, 1977; Harvey, 1985). Feminists such as Saegert (1980), Harman (1983) and Hayden (1984) have attempted to put women and their concerns into the picture. More recently, Sandercock and Forsyth (1992) and Watson and Gibson (1995) have turned their attention to the male world-views incorporated in the very foundations of urban theory. In this chapter the conceptualization of public places in the city as leisure venues for the male gaze of the 'flâneur' is critiqued. Instead I suggest the concept of 'chora' (Grosz, 1995a) as a safe space for social interaction and leisure experience which enhances the self and resists surveillance and control. The city of Sydney is used as an example.

Chapter 8 examines women's leisure from perspectives adapted from post-structuralist theories. To date there has been little attempt to apply ideas from poststructuralist theories to leisure, with a few exceptions such as Hargreaves (1987) and Rojek (1985, 1993a, 1995). In this chapter I develop a feminist perspective on leisure which incorporates ideas from symbolic interactionism and cultural theory, as well as Foucault's concepts of power, discourse, subjectivity and resistance. Ideas from the French feminists such as embodiment, multiple subjectivities, rewriting masculine and feminine scripts and desire and pleasure, and ideas from Australian feminist philosophers such as deconstruction of dichotomies and subversion of male dominance in theorizing as well as in practice, are included. The concept of leisure is rewritten as personal space. Leisure is posited as a potential site for resistance to and subversion of hegemonic masculinity, by men as well as by women, with possibilities also for some challenge to racism and ageism.

Chapter 9 extends the concept of leisure as personal and social space to the leisure experiences of women who do not conform to the theoretical analyses devised by white, educated, middle-class feminists. In postcolonial theory there is a critique of the domination of Eurocentric ideas and experiences as the basis for sociological analysis. Feminist theorists such as hooks (1984, 1989, 1993, 1996) and Spivak (1988a and 1988b) argue for their voices of 'others' to be heard, for their world-views to be incorporated into feminist theory. This chapter suggests some ways in which this may be done with regard to women's leisure experiences.

The concluding chapter draws together the ideas which have been developed throughout the book and makes suggestions for leisure research, leisure policy and professional practice. Recognition of the importance of leisure as a field of study arose in the political/economic context of the prospect of increased non-work time in advanced industrial societies in the early 1970s. In the thirty years or so since this upsurge of interest, various sociological theories have been applied to leisure. This book examines these theories and their usefulness for understanding gendered leisure. An argument is developed for the inclusion of insights from poststructuralist and postcolonialist feminist perspectives which open up possibilities for leisure as a sphere in which hegemonic masculinity can be challenged and the quality of life of both men and women enhanced.

1

Leisure is good for society and the individual: functionalist theories

With the prospect of increased non-work time in advanced industrial societies through the automation of industry, shorter working weeks, increased vacation time, flexitime, more part-time work, job-sharing and early retirement, in the early 1970s there was an upsurge of political interest in leisure. In 1975 the United Nations commissioned a report on world leisure and recreation. The report highlighted these factors and the growing importance of leisure in today's world. It claimed that:

> People cannot grow on the basis of physical sustenance alone: they need a cultural identity, a sense of social fulfilment, a regeneration of body and spirit which comes from various forms of recreation and leisure and makes their role one of growing importance on the world's agenda. (World Leisure and Recreation Association, 1975: 2)

Social scientists began to take leisure seriously and incorporated into their theoretical analyses the assumptions of functionalist theory evident in the above quote. That is, that leisure as an institution in industrial society is functional both for the smooth running of that society and for the mental and physical health of individuals within it. Functionalist theory with its origins in the classical sociology of Durkheim and its twentieth-century development by Parsons provided a useful description of relatively stable mid-century, post-war societies such as the USA and the UK where industry was booming and the nuclear family was seen to provide socialization for children and emotional stability for adults. It also provided a useful basis for an increasing emphasis on leisure as an important institution in contemporary society. In this chapter initially I outline some of the basic concepts and assumptions of functionalist theory as developed by Parsons. I then examine the works of leisure writers such as Parker, Roberts and Veal, empirical time and activity studies such as Szalai et al. (1972) and leisure benefits studies such as Driver (1990) where this approach is adopted. Others have criticized Parker and Roberts as purveyors of 'traditional' views (Rojek, 1985) and as blinkered to the domination revealed through class analysis (Clarke and Critcher, 1985: 16–44). I emphasize the contribution that this work makes to an understanding of leisure in contemporary society as well as critiquing the strengths and weaknesses of the functionalist assumptions underpinning the views presented. The gaps these works leave in understanding women's leisure are also explored. In relation to the latter, some feminist views of these works are explored.

Parsons's Functionalism

Talcott Parsons (1902–79) was a Harvard professor who incorporated ideas from classical European theorists such as Weber and Durkheim and from his own study of biology into a functionalist account of society as a viable system of interconnected institutions. His ideas remain implicit in much sociological, political, welfare and popular literature today.

The strategies of Parsons's approach are to identify the basic functional requirements of the society or system and to analyse the specific structures through which these functional requirements are fulfilled. The functional requirements include basic human needs such as food and shelter, socialization into the norms of the culture, allocation of scarce resources, social control and reinforcement of shared cultural values. The structures which ensure the fulfilment of these functional requirements include kinship structures, stratification, political organization, legal systems and religious institutions. Parsons likened to society the biological organism as a system made up of interrelated parts that function together to maintain the health and equilibrium of the organism. The concepts of equilibrium and integration of parts and the whole are essential to his theory.

Parsons postulated that in order for systems at all levels of society to operate smoothly there are certain basic functional prerequisites. These are: adaptation; goal attainment; integration; and latent tension management. Leisure, in this scheme, would be an institution whose chief function is tension management, but which also incorporates and reinforces shared cultural values and assists in integrating various types of action such as sport and recreation into the system. Thus leisure would involve values similar to those required in the educational and employment institutions of the society. In industrial society these include individual achievement and competition as well as fitness for work.

One basic assumption upon which structural functional theory depends is that in every society there is substantial agreement over shared moral values and codes. Consensus is the adhesive which binds the society together. The institutions of society, that is, the economic, political, legal, family, educational, health and welfare, religious and leisure systems, reinforce shared values such as honesty, reward for merit and hard work, competition and the right to free time. These basic values are translated into more specific directions to members of society through its norms, the 'oughts' or rules of that society. Status-roles assigned to individuals have a functional, that is, a goal or task objective, as well as a normative dimension which indicates how the task should or ought to be achieved. Status is the position the person holds in the structure. Role specifies the rules that the person holding that position should follow. Roles in this perspective are prescribed for the individual, not constructed individually in specific situations. Generally, in this view, the basic values of the society such as honesty and reward for hard work, remain unchanged, conflict is transitory, equilibrium is eventually re-established (Cuff and Payne, 1984: Chapter 2).

These ideas are exemplified in Parsons's influential analysis of gender roles in the family. According to Parsons the system of the nuclear family is made up of two sub-systems: husband/father, or 'instrumental' leader; and wife/mother, or 'expressive' carer. These sub-systems have assumed benefits for wider society and for individuals within the family. Each of the sub-systems has a part to play in preparing the child for its participation in society. In the early years it is the mother who has a special relationship to the child as emotional carer and supporter. However in due course the family also has a function in emancipating the child from dependency to take its part in the wider world. The occupational role of the father provides a role model for this. The mother as 'expressive' carer and 'helpmate' releases tension within the family and acts as a support for the father as provider. The father as 'instrumental' leader guides the family through the rocks and shoals of the world outside the family. Lack of competition between the two sub-systems is an important aspect of family solidarity (Parsons and Bales, 1955: 19–21).

Summarizing the basic assumptions of functionalist theory, Cohen (1968: 167) posits the following:

1 Norms and values are the basic elements of social life.
2 Social life involves commitments to agreed norms and values.
3 Societies are necessarily cohesive.
4 Social life depends on solidarity and generates harmony.
5 Social life is based upon reciprocity and co-operation.
6 Social systems rest on consensus.
7 Society recognizes power as legitimate authority.
8 Social systems are integrated and stable.
9 Social systems tend to persist – conflict is temporary until equilibrium is re-established. Change is functional adaptation.

Leisure, then, in this view, would reinforce the norms and values of the society as a whole, would include acceptable roles and generally contribute to the consensus, harmony, stability and equilibrium of the society as well as bring benefit to individual members. Caldwell (1977), for example, writing from this perspective about leisure in Australia in the 1970s describes Australian's chief leisure pursuits as sport, gambling, drinking and watching television, in line with the generally hedonistic and egalitarian values extant in Australian society. These pursuits are, according to him, generally open to all and enable Australians to enjoy both competition and

co-operation, the great outdoors as well the clubs, pubs and lounge rooms
that are available to them, and so contribute to individual satisfaction and
to the integration of Australian society. From the view of the 1990s, his
description appears rather utopian, to say the least.

Functionalist Leisure Analyses

In their analyses of leisure in industrial society, writers such as Parker
(Parker, 1983, 1988; Parker and Paddick, 1990), Roberts (Roberts, 1983,
1997; Roberts et al., 1991) and Veal (Veal, 1987, 1989, 1993; Cushman and
Veal, 1993; Lynch and Veal, 1996) have incorporated these ideas and have
demonstrated leisure's contribution to the functioning of modern industrial
society.

Parker

In *Leisure and Work* (1983), Parker added a sociological perspective to the
predominantly psychological writing on leisure at the time. He criticizes
psychologists and others who simply slot people into certain psychological
types and presents leisure as one situation through which people are
shaped, changed, developed or retarded. In functionalist fashion he presents the interrelation between the systems of work and leisure, and in the
tradition of male theory he sees leisure in relation to work (which for him
is paid labour) and generally defines leisure as non-obligatory time and activity 'chosen for its own sake' (1983: 10). At the time of writing the potential for increase in leisure time was constructed as the leisure 'problem';
people would not know how to use this time beneficially for themselves or
for society. So Parker addresses the 'problem of leisure'.

Parker sees the problem of leisure as also the problem of work; people
who are exploited in their work may find it hard to avoid being exploited in
their leisure and he sees the quantity of leisure time as increasing because
working time is getting less. He is concerned not that people may be ac-
quiring too much leisure but that leisure time may be unsatisfactory or of
sub-standard quality. This problem arises because people polarize their
work and leisure spheres in a physical sense and regard one as 'bad' and the
other as 'good'. At a metaphysical level he claims they remain naturally and
inextricably linked. For him, both 'work and leisure are necessary to a
healthy life and a healthy society' (1983: xi–xii). Successful socialization into
leisure roles will ensure that people know how to behave in leisure activity,
assist in the achievement of collective societal goals and maintain and
reproduce integration in the social system. Parker's model relies on a
work/leisure distinction which posits leisure as time and activity away from
paid labour, either as a compensation for labour or as an extension of some
of the satisfactions an individual gains from his labour. The male working
experience is posited as the norm, women's experience is 'other' to this. His

work has been criticized elsewhere for its exclusion of women's life experiences (e.g. Griffin et al., 1982), for its neglect of power in social relationships which allows the male norm to predominate and for its lack of possibilities for social change (Rojek, 1985: 95).

In an attempt to redress the former, Parker suggests that women at home 'constitute the polar opposite case to the full-time employed' (1983: 62). Although he acknowledges the socially held belief that married women do not need or even have the right to follow their own interests or to develop any kind of social life outside their family and are led to feel guilty about taking time off to pursue their own interests, he does not perceive gender per se or gender power differentials as significantly disadvantaging women's leisure time or activity. Rather, adopting a functionalist view of the complementarity of family roles, some women at home are able to develop 'values and cultures different from those of full-time employees and which benefit themselves and society'. Notably these are nurturing/caring activities such as 'the development of growing relationships within the whole family' (1983: 65). In line with the central position of paid work to his model, the biggest influence on women's leisure time and activity is perceived to be whether they have full-time work or not.

In a later paper (Parker, 1988) he addresses some of the criticisms of his work. In this paper he finds some common ground between his own ideas on leisure and those of critical theorists such as Rojek (1985) and Clarke and Critcher (1985) and feminists such as Deem (1986). Examples of the common ground are:

1   The need for leisure theory that begins neither with the individual nor society but with the multifaceted dynamic relations that people have with each other. Nevertheless Parker wishes to retain his functional tenet that society is more than 'relations' – 'it is also a set of institutions and associations ultimately composed of individuals in complex interrelations' (1988: 4).

2   Two sets of tensions which are the central contradictions of contemporary leisure. These are between the institutional control of leisure and the highly individualized model of leisure choice, and between change and continuity. These, he sees, along with Clarke and Critcher, as the forces within capitalism that determine the nature of contemporary leisure. Yet he retains the concept of adaptation to these forces so that even if change occurs equilibrium will be established. He does not tangle with asymmetric issues of power.

3   The significance of work in helping to determine the nature of leisure and the role of social structure in influencing leisure opportunities by restricting or providing access to necessary resources. He claims that work is but one of the influences on leisure maintaining a functionalist concept of the interrelatedness of the institutions of society. Yet his own work continues to prioritize work as the major influence on leisure and to include class and gender as secondary influences.

In applying his ideas to the Australian situation (Parker and Paddick,

1990), the assumptions of functionalism continue to surface. Parker again addresses the relationship between work and leisure, prioritizing work. He suggests the various ways in which work and leisure are related as: extension (work spills into leisure); recuperative (leisure as therapy); calculative (work as a means to leisure); and neutral (work and leisure as separate spheres of life) (1990: 2). In Chapter 1, 'Social changes and their consequences for leisure', the longest section deals with 'Work changes which affect leisure'. One of these is the vast increase of married women in the workforce, but the analysis remains at the level of 'For such women the world of work continually invades the stock of free time' (1990: 11). In spite of recognition of the limitations imposed on women's leisure by their responsibility for childcare and domestic work (even when in full-time employment) and their own feelings of guilt and selfishness if they take time out for themselves, there remains no discussion of the gender power relationships which make this possible.

Parker's functional assumptions concerning the complementarity of family roles continue to underpin the analysis of the leisure activities of men and women. In Chapter 2, national statistics and case study material are used to examine what Australians do in their leisure time. Here there is recognition that 'female recreation is clearly home and family based, especially while children reside in the home' (1990), but there is no questioning of unequal access to leisure space either at home or in the public sphere for these women compared with their partners. The case material furthers this perception. For example, Neville presents a very masculine example of the mix of sport and leisure,

> When I was young I was very active in sport as a form of leisure. I used to enjoy team sport – there was a sort of a bond, a spirit of unity in the team . . . I hope to play a few more years of football – I find it a great outlet, particularly because of the social side. I get to do exercise and enjoy myself in the sport, *my wife gets to meet people and socialize and it is good for my kid.* (Parker and Paddick, 1990: 30; added emphasis)

The authors comment: 'Neville enjoys his team sports, but it seems nowadays his enjoyment is derived more from the social and family aspects than from competition' (1990: 30).

On the other hand, three mothers are quoted:

> . . . we like to do things as a family and we spend our leisure time together.

> My main leisure is playing with the baby at the moment . . .

> I take my small son for bike rides, that is for his own leisure . . . sometimes it gets very boring because I have not got another adult to talk to. But still in a way I am enjoying it because I am watching my son having fun. (Parker and Paddick, 1990: 31)

The authors comment: 'All three mothers are saying that much of their own
1 ...tisfaction is derived from looking after and enjoying their own
1990: 32). Nurturing/caring is apparently for women, individual
...nent in the wider sphere for men, ensuring lack of competition
n the sexes and, presumably, harmony, consensus, stability and equi-
1 in the family and in wider society. The different but equal empha-
...guises any power differentials which may give men greater access to
leisure time and leisure activities. It ties in well with a functionalist solution,
that is, through education it is possible to make people aware of basic social
values such as 'freedom to choose' which will ensure leisure satisfaction: 'If
popular leisure activities are to be worthwhile, then the task is to create
individuals who, by their nature, choose activities freely' (1990: 87).

Similarly, Chapter 8, dealing with 'Policies for providing leisure', puts
forward policy solutions for the recreationally disadvantaged (i.e. the poor,
persons with young children, immigrants, the elderly) which are based
within a functionalist logic of self- or volunteer help. Ways in which power
operates through various discourses that exclude or devalue people are not
addressed. For example, in addressing the needs of isolated older women
the authors suggest quite stereotypically:

> Women who have been housewives all their lives do not see themselves as
> retired and it is good that places are coming to be called community centres
> rather than elderly citizen centres. Such women need some sort of interest and
> the company of other people. The challenge is to get volunteers to organize
> such groups. (1990: 99–100)

Or for ethnic groups:

> Ethnic people need to be given opportunities to organize their own activities
> but also to be introduced to other ways of getting the most out of their leisure.
> (1990: 99)

Parker's paradigm has raised the awareness of some of the important functions that leisure fulfils for societies where adult males are in full-time employment. His struggles with the work–leisure dichotomy have highlighted
the integration of these spheres in industrial society. When work is affected,
so is leisure and leisure can enhance the individual by complementing or by
continuing the satisfactions of the all-important sphere of paid employment. Thus it can contribute to the stability, harmony and consensus of such
a society and to 'the relaxation, entertainment and personal development'
of its individual members (1983: 41). Parker's arguments draw out the
strengths of the functionalist contribution to leisure theory: the interrelatedness of societal institutions such as work and leisure, the interrelatedness of the individual with these institutions and the prospect of
gradual change. They also demonstrate the weaknesses: the failure to deal
adequately with asymmetric power relations such as class and gender, and
the failure to incorporate into theoretical analysis the ideologies and

discourses which keep women in subordinate positions and inferiorized statuses both within and outside the workforce.

Roberts

In contrast to Parker, Roberts's work *Youth and Leisure* (1983) addresses in detail both class and gender in the context of youth cultures (that is, ways that young people use their leisure time and resources) and 'their consequences for different groups of young people, and the wider society' (1983: 5). Nevertheless, as we shall see, the basic assumptions set within the broader framework of cultural analysis are those of functionalism.

Roberts's work is to be commended because it raises many issues concerning class and gender differences in access to leisure. It documents the wider access of middle-class male youth to leisure time, activities and experience, compared with middle-class female youth and all working-class youth. It offers economic and patriarchal explanations and raises some issues concerning the social construction of gender. For example, he suggests that the two dominant features enduring within all youth cultures despite their adoption of different fads are class divisions and gender divisions. In particular class divisions are evident in 'divisions between the rough and respectable youth cultures of early school leavers, and the middle class youth styles nurtured by young people who continue to further and higher education' (1983: 31). He sees students in higher education as recreationally privileged due to their congregation on campuses giving solidarity and freedom from parental supervision; their grants and subsidized leisure facilities giving economic power; and their independence enabling them to defer employment, marriage and parenthood (1983: 58).

Roberts's work on 'engendered leisure' recognizes the important dimensions of gender and sexuality on the ways in which young people experience leisure. Roberts argues that 'the relationships between boys and girls at leisure are patriarchal rather than equal' (1983: 67). In particular he explores the ways girls' leisure is restricted and constrained as a result of gender inequality. For Roberts, gender divisions are evident in the male-led, post-war youth cultures where 'Girls have been invited to participate by dressing, dancing and otherwise acting to appeal to different types of male youth' (1983: 31). Moreover, 'Girls have less cash to spend, are subject to closer parental supervision, given a narrower choice and less freedom to select their own leisure interests' (1983: 62). And 'the sex act itself remains culturally defined in male terms, with the active male penetrating the female body. Sucking, absorbing and enveloping – words that emphasize women's control in copulation – are not equally acceptable in the public vocabulary of sexual intercourse' (1983: 67). Here Roberts dips a toe into the waters of gendered language and male power which a decade later is developed in much greater detail and with much greater force by French feminists such as Irigaray. (See Chapter 8 in this book for a discussion of these ideas.) He does recognize some of the feminist analysis of the 1980s,

notably Deem's (1986) work which documents women's objectively disadvantaged situation concerning leisure and the ways in which women
make the best of it by deriving leisure experiences from domestic roles and
by servicing husbands' and children's leisure. Very briefly he mentions the
≥ ·⸴ that is available to men to define leisure and to access a variety of
‥⸴‥⸴ activities for themselves which are compatible with the concept of
masculinity. Given the choice, he wonders if boys would give up this opportunity. His solutions are to make any alternatives more attractive to males
than traditional opportunities and to raise the status of feminine activities
(1983: 99 and 71).

Nevertheless, ultimately Roberts's answers are based in the functional
imperatives of socialization for adult sex roles in industrial society and in
the inherited nature of culture. The institution of leisure is seen to utilize
and, hence, perpetuate, reinforce and support the norms and values of the
family, the school, the workplace and the media. Change is cultural adaptation. He believes that, for adolescents, leisure is a site where conventional
gender roles are reproduced, not rejected (1983: 62). Novel recreations
merely reflect youths' statuses within their societies. In other words, in spite
of its emphasis on 'freedom' of choice, leisure contributes to the equilibrium of society.

A society's culture precedes individuals. It awaits newcomers as an external reality. But culture only exists in individuals' minds and actions.
Culture is 'absorbed' through socialization, but can also be 'used' to
respond to novel predicaments. Individuals and generations add to, modify
and sometimes lose aspects of their societies' cultures. Young people's ways
of life are not constructed solely from their own ingenuity. They use ma-
terials and ideas derived from families, schools, workplaces and media. But
young people do not become replicas of their parents. They can use the cultures they inherit to respond to new opportunities, like the growth of leisure
time, and to solve their own problems, like escaping from childhood restrictions. All leisure behaviour is cultural. This is why individuals can
'freely' choose and even design novel recreations in ways that clearly reflect
their statuses within societies.

Rebellion is illusionary or temporary. Negotiation, struggle, resistance
and transformation are defeated in the end by the socially transmitted heritage of culture; youth leisure is but part of the socializing process for conventional adulthoods.

> ... there is no way in which adolescent leisure might be harnessed to initiate
> radical changes – feminist or socialist, for example. Attempted rebellions are
> invariably unsuccessful, whether against class barriers, gender divisions or the
> law. Young people's resistance is transformed into accommodation. They are
> given just enough freedom to resist and establish independence from adults –
> parents, teachers, the police and employers, to allow them to acquire the very
> skills, including the art of treating other adults as equals, that are required for
> entry into established adult roles. Family backgrounds, educational attain-
> ments and job opportunities set young people apart, on masculine and

feminine, then separate social class trajectories, and youth cultures do not overwhelm but respect these boundaries, and assist in transporting young people to conventional adulthoods. (1983: 56–7)

Theoretically Roberts urges the necessity for a more diverse approach than functionalism in analysing youth cultures and leisure. For himself, he does find functionalism incomplete. Yet his own work merely touches on alternative theories, its basis remains firmly within a functionalist paradigm with its laudable descriptive ability but its inability to go beyond the status quo. The basic assumptions of leisure as functional in gender socialization for adult roles and for youth's adaptation to changes in wider society remain in his latest analysis of British youth cultures. Although 'youth cultural forms have changed in response to wider changes in young people's circumstances', 'the underlying functions of young people's leisure have remained unaltered' since the 1960s (Roberts, 1997: 7). Here he uses evidence from large scale pre-coded surveys and correlation analysis to provide evidence that subjective identities remain firmly rooted in and functional for the class, gender, age and ethnic structures of contemporary Britain. The methodology used and the evidence produced, as well as the argument presented, remain within the restrictions of functionalism and the positivistic research paradigm.

These strengths and weaknesses are further apparent in Roberts's own empirical work. For example, from a survey of the leisure activities of representative samples of 16–20-year-olds in Swindon and Liverpool between 1987 and 1989 (Roberts et al., 1991), we learn much about adaptation concerning leisure for unemployed youth and that leisure has a cushioning impact on the effects of unemployment. Swindon had higher rates of employment, higher paying jobs, higher personal incomes on average and higher levels of leisure spending. Yet young people in the high unemployment city of Liverpool

were able to maintain relatively high overall levels of leisure activity by drawing upon family resources, forgoing particularly expensive activities and purchases, and scaling down their spending on other leisure goods and occasions . . . the resilience of leisure among the age group and within the areas most affected by high unemployment can help to explain the absence of a strong, radical socio-political response to the predicament. (Roberts et al., 1991: 529)

This, surely, is an excellent example of Parsons's adaptation to change which maintains equilibrium. Families are reported to have absorbed some of the strain demonstrating the interrelationship between the two institutions of the family and leisure. Young people's leisure socialization in high unemployment areas is also seen to 'remain sufficiently rich that if the local economies were to recover in the population's lifetime leisure careers would be unlikely to bear permanent scars' (1991: 527). Here again the importance of socialization is stressed with its ability to maintain the status quo. Gender analysis remains rudimentary, being confined to the greater percentage of females than males in Liverpool who experienced sexual harassment or abuse (22 per cent cf. 4 per cent), and who would not feel safe at night in Liverpool city centre (54 per cent cf. 7 per cent) or in the area where they lived (21 per cent cf. 5 per cent).

Veal

Veal wrote *Leisure and the Future* (1987) in the context of the prediction of increased leisure time in Western post-industrialized societies where technology replaces manual labour and leisure consumption is ever-increasing. Leisure then will presumably take on increased importance in the everyday lives of individuals: '. . . while work and "bread and butter" issues dominate politics and public life, leisure has become a highly significant element of people's lives and of the economies of advanced industrial nations. In comparison with previous ages, we live in what is virtually a "society of leisure"' (Veal, 1987: 3). The non-work ethic which has always lurked in competition with the work ethic will burgeon. So Veal sees a future society where people will do less work, job-share and be more receptive to leisure. People will be able to spend more time with their families and domestic job-sharing is envisaged. There is therefore no gender breakdown in the numerous tables, charts and figures that he presents. There is no power analysis, so the changes in the workplace result in adaptation to and the re-establishment of an equilibrium based on unacknowledged male domination. Leisure is analysed as time, activity and consumption. Although the work/leisure dichotomy is seen as blurred, changes in leisure are still predicated on changes in the work sphere: '. . . the corollary of paid work is not necessarily leisure alone, it may include work for oneself or the community or general social/family interaction. It is potentially a realm of freedom of self-determined activity' (1987: 121). Concerning this freedom, Veal sees it constrained by the system. The status quo for individuals is hard to shift. There is little leeway for agency, or resistance, struggle and change from those in less privileged positions in Veal's homogeneous male, white, middle-class society, where consensus reigns, harmony is maintained and the functional prerequisites of the social system are fulfilled. 'People do want freedom, but the freedom they manage to obtain is based on privatized consumption which reinforces the system which is denying them, or from which they are not demanding genuine freedom' (1987: 122).

Veal's aim in this book is neither to 'advocate one point of view', nor to present a polemic. Rather it is to provide 'a guide and a source' (1987: i). And there are many thoughtful insights in the book, such as the discussion of the myth of the work ethic where he argues that workers have always found their own ways of getting around the system through 'sickies' and informal abrogation of the rules (1987: 73–7). Instead, the work adopts a common-sense approach which includes, as I have shown, some of the assumptions of functionalism. It is not, therefore, without a theoretical base, rather the theoretical position is unacknowledged. In a later article, Veal (1989) presents his own leisure theory which, I will argue, also falls within a functionalist framework.

In 'Leisure, lifestyle and status: a pluralist framework for analysis', Veal suggests that 'Weber's concepts of status, status groups and lifestyle offer a way forward for pluralist analyses' (1989: 141). Following Weber, Veal argues that the 'consumption of goods in the context of specific life-styles' adds another dimension to the one-dimensional Marxist view of class or economic dynamics. He sees leisure as a 'key contributor to lifestyle', thus linking leisure via lifestyle to the wider social order (1989: 143). Status groups are involved in constant struggles for control of the means of symbolic production as against classes who struggle for the control of the means of production. One example given concerns youth subcultures: 'it is very often the leisure-related symbols of youth life-style which are the source of conflict with parents and authority, whether this be drug taking, sexual activity, dress or music' (1989: 147).

The task for a pluralist analysis of leisure, according to Veal, 'is to explore the range of status/lifestyle groups: investigate what characterizes particular lifestyles, how lifestyles are achieved, sustained and protected and how and where groups conflict' (1989: 147). Thus he hopes to provide frameworks to understand the complexity of leisure lifestyles. Theoretically, Veal has begun the shift of sociological analysis of leisure away from its dependency and subordination to the work sphere, so evident in Parker's work. In post-industrial society, as he pointed out in *Leisure Futures*, leisure, the family and consumption occupy an increasing amount of time and attention in daily living and become less dependent on paid work. The concepts of status and lifestyle encapsulate some of the complexity of the prestige and symbolism attached to a great variety of leisure activities. Nevertheless his approach remains at a descriptive level. The struggles he describes are over symbols, they have no basis in power, conflicts of interest or unequal access to resources. Weber's own discussion of status was as one source of power, along with class and party, which enabled 'a man or a number of men to realize their own will in a communal action even against the resistance of others who are participating in the action' (Gerth and Mills, 1948: 180). There is no such analysis in Veal's work. In spite of struggles over symbols, he envisages an eventual peaceful co-existence or, at least, an equitable equilibrium – power is not included in his analysis. Veal's contribution to the text *Australian Leisure* maintains his pluralist stance (Lynch and Veal, 1996).

The pluralism Veal suggests remains very much within the harmony, consensus, stability, equilibrium model of functionalism. It is a functionalist pluralism and at odds with pluralism as it is generally understood in sociology. Giddens, for example, defines pluralist theories of democracy as: 'Theories which emphasize the role of diverse and competing interest groups in preventing too much power being accumulated in the hands of political leaders' (1989: 746). In Veal's version there is no mention of the conflicts of interests which drive the struggles between status groups, nor of power issues.

Others have critiqued the theoretical basis of Veal's 'theory' from a feminist perspective and from a neo-Marxist perspective. Scraton and Talbot (1989) take Veal to task for his omission of any gender analysis. He fails to take into account feminist critiques in sociological theory generally and in leisure theory particularly and sees 'the gender assumptions sur-rounding "productive" and "non-productive work" as entirely unproblem-atic'. Consequently he can ignore 'women's experience as irrelevant, marginal, invisible or aberrant to "mainstream" theory'. He also treats the family as a unified entity for both consumption and leisure, thus ignoring gendered consumer and social differences in power (Scraton and Talbot, 1989: 156). They conclude, as I do, that power is central to any meaningful lifestyle analysis: 'Lifestyle as a construct can be of use in understanding leisure only when it is considered in relation to the social construction of femininity and masculinity, employment, unemployment and unpaid work and racism; *power relations* are central, not peripheral to, this approach' (1989: 158; original emphasis).

Critcher also disagrees with Veal's use of Weber's concepts of *status* and *lifestyle* without any reference to power, without some questioning of the impact of class on them, without providing any motivation for status struggles and without Weber's use of *culture* as 'that elusive area where humans make and recognize meaning' (1989: 161).

In addition to these critiques, with which I agree, I suggest that the plu-ralist perspective presented by Veal is a profoundly functionalist version with its descriptive strengths and analytic weaknesses.

When Veal applies his ideas to empirical research, the same functionalist assumptions emerge. In 'The new generations of leisure survey – impli-cations for research on everyday life', Cushman and Veal argue that 'the design and analysis of recent leisure participation surveys ... have over-come many of the shortcomings of earlier surveys and that they do have a contribution to make in the study of the place of leisure in everyday life' (1993: 212). They base these claims on changes in leisure surveys so that the following issues are addressed: a wider range of leisure activities than sport and outdoor recreation are included; computer technology has enabled a wider availability of data from surveys for questioning and for secondary analysis; awareness of various theoretical perspectives and policy issues so that, for example, women's issues are addressed; use of surveys to examine the processes of social change, rather than merely presenting a static, de-scriptive picture; inclusion of non-participation and constraints on partici-pation; and the inclusion of direct measurement of health and fitness of the individual respondent.

They discuss the methodological question of weekly versus yearly record-ing of activities, the integration of quantitative and qualitative methods and the fact that the most frequently recorded constraint to leisure participation is lack of *time*. All this is done under the functionalist umbrella of so-called 'objective' collection of data concerning participation in allocated categories, with the ultimate assumption that as everybody has access to the same amount of *time* in a week, the individual is therefore responsible for the use of that time and so for participation in leisure. Where are Veal's claims to link leisure to wider society and its struggles and multiplicity of lifestyles and statuses here? In spite of the result of the Australian survey (Australian Bureau of Statistics, 1994) which showed that women who are in paid employment still perform most of the work in the house and are mostly responsible for the care of children and the domestic care of the frail, sick and disabled, there is no theoretical analysis of this clear inequality in time use. For all we know this is how it is, so it always will be. How exactly have 'new generation' surveys of leisure moved beyond gender differences in time use in order to fulfil societal needs, onwards to the awareness of various theoretical perspectives and policy issues so that women's issues are addressed? (Cushman and Veal, 1993: 213)

Similarly, Veal's chapters in *Australian Leisure* present much valuable data from national surveys which document the differential participation of age, gender and occupational groups in leisure activites and time and in leisure expenditure (e.g. Lynch and Veal, 1996: chs 5 and 6). The aim is to demonstrate the range and variety, in line with Veal's pluralist stance. Further analysis is left to the reader.

Leisure and the Life-cycle: Robert and Rhona Rapoport

Clarke and Critcher (1985: 30–6) have thoroughly evaluated the contribution that the Rapoports' work, *Leisure and the Family Life Cycle* (1975), has made to an understanding of leisure along the three planes of work, family and leisure, within the overarching influence of age. The Rapoports show how at each stage of the life-cycle, in line with Erikson's ideas of developmental tasks, leisure can contribute to identity formation, intimacy, establishment, integrity and generativity. Clarke and Critcher commend this work:

> there is an explicit recognition that existing stereotypes of sex roles within the family demand excessively damaging sacrifices for women. If the role of gender remains largely untheorized and never achieves more than the status of a variable within the life cycle, women are present in this book in a way rarely found in the sociology of leisure.
> . . . These emphases of the Rapoports – on leisure as related to other spheres of life, on the inadequacies of the consumer model, on variations and paradoxes in family life, on the costs of motherhood for women, on the unacknowledged problems of ageing – give their work a distinctive and positive quality. (Clarke and Critcher, 1985: 33)

I would agree here and also with their claim that, in this work, 'the key processes are being held to be biological and psychological: social determinants have vanished' (Clarke and Critcher, 1985: 35). In the context of this chapter, I would like to add to Clarke and Critcher's comments some critique of the functionalist framework of developmental approaches such as the Rapoports.

The major focus of the developmental approach is on the change in the process of internal family development viewed microanalytically. The more successfully each member of the family achieves and advances through certain role expectations called 'developmental tasks' at various stages of the life-cycle and the more closely the family accomplishes its group tasks the more successful is the development of the family. The normative values associated with family life in industrial societies are evident in studies of the family from this perspective. It is up to the individual and the family to adapt and develop in accordance with the constraints placed upon them by the salient tasks of each stage of the life-cycle (Rowe, 1966: 199–213).

For example, in the Rapoports' analysis of young people and leisure, they focus on their exploration of their environments looking for new experiences, in an attempt to 'crystallize their personal identities which will underpin a transition to greater independence' (Rapoport and Rapoport, 1975: 31). In the examples presented to illustrate their argument, they show how 'the person's individual make-up, family resources, the availability of specific provisions, the competence of mediators and so on, all affect the particular outcome, but they act on a similar set of developmental forces common to young people' (1975: 40). The objective is to reach a sense of identity which is satisfactory to the individual and to others involved and is seen to be achieved when it 'fits the requirements of the roles which he [sic] subsequently encounters at work, in heterosexual relationships and in community life generally' (1975: 34).

The example is given of Jenny, a middle-class girl who has gone through various adolescent phases from being a 'swot', to separating school (where she has always performed well) from her social life where she has tried the drug scene and various music groups, to settling down to a steady relationship with her boyfriend around whom her leisure activities now revolve. Her mother's one concern with Jenny at the moment is that she spends too much time with her boyfriend and that she won't complete a higher academic qualification and so will limit her choice of occupation. Her parents have tried to move flexibly with Jenny after being very strict with her older sister who joined the 'skinheads' and infringed all their ideals and has now been sent to the USA for a year to find herself. Both the family and the adolescent in this case, in contrast to the older sister's case, have generally achieved the societal norms and expectations for this stage of the life-cycle. Harmony, consensus, stability and equilibrium are established within and outside the family.

As one reads the Rapoports' work in a 1990s context, the whole life-cycle approach appears to be based on societal norms and assumptions which have a very narrow focus. These assumptions are that everyone will have a stable occupation, will form heterosexual relationships, get married, acquire accommodation and furnishings, have children, adjust to the 'empty nest' and retirement and to the problems of old age. People, such as Jenny's sister, who do not fit neatly into these norms are excluded or considered deviant. Leisure, in this view, has the potential to contribute to individual and family developmental tasks. If used judiciously, conflict can be overcome and one can conveniently ignore general differences between, as well as within, racial, ethnic and age groups, gender, class and sexuality divisions. Except at an individual level, sources and effects of power are ignored.

Time–Budget Studies

Neumeyer and Neumeyer (1958) and Brightbill (1960) have defined leisure as residual time and free or discretionary time and this definition has influenced many empirical studies of leisure. It has the advantage, in a society where the clock is essentially a dominant organizing factor in daily life, of making leisure quantifiable and comparable between groups. 'Time–budget' studies, such as the International Time Budget Study (Szalai et al., 1972), showed, for example, that across the 12 nations surveyed, an average of four and one-third hours per day were left as 'free time'. However, these free hours were distributed very differently for men and women across the weekly work cycle. Employed men on work days had 21 per cent of their waking hours as free time, employed women 15 per cent. On their days off, the proportions were 56 per cent and 40 per cent respectively. Housewives on weekdays had 25 per cent free time and on Sundays 30 per cent.

Work by Gershuny and Thomas (1980) in Britain, Samuel (1986) in France and Mercer (1985) in Australia has shown a general decline in the time allocated to paid work, an appreciable rise in 'free time' for most groups and some signs of a growing convergence between men's and women's 'free time' availability. Nevertheless Samuel's figures show that in France in 1975 urban working men spent an average of four hours, 27 minutes a day (Saturdays and Sundays included) on free-time activities and urban working women three hours, 25 minutes. Mercer's figures show a decline of 3 per cent for weekend 'free time' for employed Melbourne females, compared with an increase of 8 per cent for employed males and 14 per cent for non-earning females.

A later study in Australia (Bittman, 1991) questions the move towards greater equality between men's and women's 'free time'. Bittman claims that women have actually lost leisure time. His figures show that in the 13 years between 1974 and 1987, Australian men devoted (on average) five hours 36 minutes less to paid work activities. In the same period women increased the average time they devoted to paid work by four hours and 24 minutes per week. The corresponding reduction in women's unpaid work has only been 3.9 hours. The net result for women has been a loss of 'free time', from 36.4 hours per week in 1984 to 35.9 hours in 1987. For men there has been an increase from 36.2 hours per week in 1974 to 37.9 hours in 1987 (1991: 31–2).

It is obvious that these time–budget studies provide fuel for feminist analysis of gendered inequality in access to 'free-time'. As Bittman comments: 'Women have gone from a situation of near leisure time parity with men in 1974, to one of disadvantage by 1987. Feminist warnings about the prospects of women working the "double shift" – wage workers by day and homemakers by night – appear to be grounded in hard fact' (1991: 32). Where feminist analyses of discrepancies in male/female access to 'free time' have been carried out (see Deem, 1986, 1992; Green et al., 1990; McKay, 1990; Shaw, 1985, discussed in Chapters 2 and 3 of this book) the time–budget figures provide stark evidence for male power and privilege in the leisure area. However, in the time–budget literature, Bittman's sentence encapsulates the extent of feminist analysis. For the most part these studies have remained at a general level, indicating gradual change (albeit through struggle over rights as Samuel shows) in societal values from an overwhelming 'work ethic' to an increasing moral right to 'free time'. In addition, while leisure is conceptualized as 'free time' and quantified in hours or minutes, the differences in meanings attached to such 'free time' between men and women are obscured.

Recreation Benefits

The assumptions of functionalism that leisure, along with other institutions in society, serve a function which contributes to the harmony, consensus and stability of society and the well-being of its people underlie the plethora of recreation benefits studies which have surfaced since the early 1970s. In the functionalist paradigm, leisure has, in fact, the more specific function of recreation for bodies, minds and spirits through non-work time and activity. Those who make decisions concerning the provision of leisure services, both public and private, have a vested interest in both promoting and providing leisure that has economic, physical and mental benefits for individuals and for society. In recent times, in order to receive a share of scarce resources, leisure providers in the industry, in public policy and in the academic/educational sectors have needed to specify the benefits of leisure in the contemporary situation. In this section I argue that the documentation of such data contributes to the functional analysis of leisure in contemporary society, but unless adequately theorized, fails to address issues of inequality of access, the potential detrimental effects of certain leisure activities for health and the constraints of leisure.

From the beginning of interest in the area of leisure provision in Australia, there has been a focus on the relationship between sport and the fitness of Australians. In 1941 the National Fitness Act provided for a National Fitness Council to advise the Minister for the Commonwealth Department of Health on the promotion of national fitness in Australia. In

1972 the Commonwealth Department of Tourism and Recreation was established and a range of recreation initiatives was introduced, including a
programme of capital assistance for leisure facilities and the 'Life Be In It'
campaign which urged active participation in physical leisure activities. The
annual report of this department in June 1975 states that 'sport and physical recreation programmes recognize sport in its many forms, as the most
popular single facet of the Australian leisure environment and *that active
recreation has positive advantages for those involved*' (cited in Hamilton-
Smith and Robertson, 1981: 176; emphasis added).

In 1982 the Hawke government created the Department of Sport, Recreation and Tourism to provide a focus for activities in the recreation area. In
October 1985, the then minister for this department, John Brown, released
the statement 'Towards the Development of a Commonwealth Policy on
Recreation' as a first step in promoting 'leisure for all' (Brown, 1985). This
document emphasizes the increasing importance of leisure in advanced
capitalist society. Time for leisure is seen to be increasing for the majority
of Australians due to such factors as longer life and earlier retirement,
shorter working hours, flexitime, technological advances in the home and
decline in employment. It is suggested that in future years leisure may be
the main vehicle for achievement of feelings of worth and satisfaction
(Brown, 1985: 5). So the policy document posits several short- and medium-
term goals which emphasize 'the right of all Australians, regardless of
income, sex, place of residence or ethnic background, to the opportunities
to participate in recreational activities of their choosing' (13). There is some
recognition of disadvantaged groups: 'in a context of finite resources, those
who have been disadvantaged in terms of access to recreation require a
greater share of available support and resources' (14). Nevertheless the
general focus of the document is 'leisure for all', obscuring these divisions
with its emphasis on the general benefits of leisure, particularly sport, for
all. When the document was translated into the financial allocation of resources in the years immediately following its release, the basic assumptions
and biases were revealed. Mass sport and recreation received 7 per cent of
the total allocation of 24 million dollars, white-elite, male-dominated sport
received 93 per cent. In terms of Commonwealth-funded programmes
leisure means elite, national-level, competitive sport, whose participants
are likely to be fit young men (Wearing and Wearing, 1990).

Recreation benefits in this context, without some analysis of relationships
of power, merely reinforce the status quo – presumably the fit get fitter and
the unfit more unfit. The benefits of leisure do not get translated into
'leisure for all'. Hargreaves is similarly critical of 'sport for all' policies in
Great Britain, in spite of the concerted attempts of central and regional
Sports Councils to increase women's participation in sport (Hargreaves,
1994: 180–1).

Writing from a recreation benefit perspective, Driver (1990) examines
the Canadian and American experience, arguing that although most of the
current knowledge is largely intuitive and inferential 'past research does

indicate there are a wide variety of highly probable benefits of great magnitude' (1). For him leisure is best represented by human behaviours that fall on the right-hand side of the following equal weight bipolar continua:

Low sense of personal..................................High sense of personal
freedom/control   freedom/control

Extrinsically rewarding..............................Intrinsically rewarding

High sense of time......................................Low sense of time

Boundedness/Obligation

Such behaviours he perceives as benefitting:

> physical fitness; restoration from stress; social cohesion (of many types); enhanced self-concepts (such as through specific types of skill testing and competence building); promotion of a sense of place, a sense of continuity, and a sense of balance; learning of many specific types (including learning about natural ecosystems and about cultural/historical heritages); and therapeutic outcomes of varied specific types. (Driver, 1990: 13)

Thus leisure contributes to individual satisfaction and social cohesion, harmony, consensus, stability and equilibrium. Knowledge of leisure benefits would also be functional for management and for the profession. It would enhance rationality of resource allocation decisions; help promote optimal management; guide user fees; identify good service substitutes; enhance consumer and voter sovereignty; advance the leisure profession; increase support for the cause of leisure and promote pride in the profession (Driver, 1990: 13–17). From his review of the literature in the area, he concludes that the following categories of benefits are recognized: personal benefits (those that accrue to the individual); social benefits (benefits to groups of individuals, such as community stability); economic benefits (increased income and employment); benefits to the environment (contribution to environmental protection) (1990: 37). His overall conclusion is that 'the benefits of leisure are pervasive to all facets of human endeavour, and they contribute significantly to human welfare – more so than is commonly recognized' (1990: 49).

Not all recreation benefit studies concur with the functionalist assumptions of those cited above. For example, in the policy area, Galbally speaking on behalf of the Victorian Health Promotion Foundation questions 'the impact of recreation and leisure images which focus on the unattainable and undesirable perfect body image which will have a particularly serious negative effect on a community which promotes integration as opposed to segregation of aged and disabled people for their health' (1990: 6). Secondly, the Foundation is concerned to examine the negative health outcomes of the availability of recreation as a commodity for sale and to substitute healthy alternatives to commodities such as tobacco. Smoking as a leisure activity hardly fits into the recreation benefits paradigm suggested by Driver.

Hamilton-Smith critiques the consequences of a functionalist approach for research and policy:

> ... namely, the failure to look at the different benefits (or disbenefits) which accrue to people of different social class, gender, generation, ethnic or cultural background, or whatever. This arises not out of positivism per se, but rather out of its functionalist expression. In policy terms, it is perhaps one of the more dangerous research sicknesses – by failing to look at the differential impact of programs on different sectors of the population, so minorities are all too likely to be either ignored or subjected to totally inappropriate programs. (1990: 3)

He suggests we need to ask the question in recreation benefit studies, 'Which people receive which benefits or disbenefits from which aspects of defined recreation experiences?' (1990: 11).

Those who do look at recreation benefits from alternative perspectives such as symbolic interactionism (see Kelly, 1990; Scherl, 1990) seem able to include some of the personal and societal differentiation absent from functionalist approaches. My own work on mothers and health analyses the benefits of leisure through the lens of Foucault's concepts of 'discourse' and 'resistance'. In this view the leisure discourse which emphasizes a person's right to time and space for oneself allows for resistance to the dominant discourse of motherhood which stresses the needs of others over one's own needs (see Wearing, 1990a). Leisure is beneficial, but as opposition to societal norms, rather than in accordance with them.

Conclusion

Without the leisure studies conducted under the rubric of functionalism, our knowledge of time spent in leisure and the activities pursued would be poorer. These studies have highlighted the increasing access to leisure time and the emphasis on this sphere of life in advanced industrial societies in the second half of the twentieth century. Questions have been raised and studies conducted to examine how people actually use this time and in what ways leisure benefits the individual and the society. However, while analysis remains at the functionalist level, the contribution that these studies make to our understanding of leisure remains limited. Other theoretical orientations are needed to give the picture perspective.

In this chapter I have presented the important data which studies of leisure based on the assumptions of functionalism have produced. For example, Parker's studies raise awareness of some of the important functions that leisure fulfils for societies where adult males are in full-time employment, the interrelation of the institutions of work and leisure and the possibilities for gradual change without serious conflict. Roberts's studies go one step further and address in detail both class and gender differences in the context of youth culture. Veal also produces some 'hard' data to establish differences in participation in leisure activities, access to leisure time and expenditure on leisure for groups in society differentiated by class, gender and age. In his pluralist paradigm these differences impact on a variety of lifestyles which co-exist in contemporary societies such as Britain and Australia. Yet for these theorists the level of analysis, based as it is in the functionalist paradigm of harmony, consensus and stability, gradual change and adaptation which maintains societal equilibrium, does little to assist us in understanding the differences presented, or to suggest progressive policies to address any inequities in the status quo.

Developmental studies such as those of the Rapoports show how leisure can be integrated into the ways that nuclear families address developmental tasks across the life-cycle. Thus leisure is shown to be beneficial for individuals and for families. Yet the family model and the life-cycle examined have a very narrow focus, and those who do not conform to the norms of family or leisure practice are considered deviant. Conflict is temporary and to be sanctioned.

Both time–budget and leisure benefits studies again present us with much valuable information which is descriptive of current uses of leisure time and leisure activities. However, I would maintain that extensive data collection, however well intentioned, without some critical analysis merely serves the purpose of reinforcing the status quo and a societal equilibrium which disadvantages many people, including women.

It is not surprising that a post-war situation in which the economy was booming and there was a concerted attempt to re-establish families, communities and institutions which had been disrupted by war spawned structural functionalism. Its emphasis on equilibrium, harmony, stability, consensus over values and complementarity of roles fitted the aspirations of the period. Power, conflict of interests and inequality were minimized. The position of women in society as different from and complementary to men remained unquestioned in a period when women were being encouraged to reproduce and support their partners who had returned from war service and who needed the jobs held by women in their absence during the war. That this perspective has persisted through the demographic, social and cultural changes since the 1950s owes much, I think, to a desire for things to be as described in this approach. I do not think that it is a testament to its analytic power. In spite of the documentation of women's difference from men incorporated in studies based on the assumptions of functionalism, I do not consider it to be a feminist approach as there is no acknowledgement of gender power differentials.

Gaps that have been left by studies based in functionalism are those which deal with power, conflicts of interests and inequalities of access to leisure resources such as 'free time'. Thus, the control and subordination through leisure of various groups, including women, are obscured. These are the very concepts which form the focus of Marxist and neo-Marxist understandings of leisure, to which we will turn in Chapter 2.

2

Structure and Agency in Access to Leisure: Marxist and Neo-Marxist Theories

Based in the Marxian problematic of relationship to the means of production, these theories analyse leisure time and leisure activity in terms of the profit motive, commodification, exploitation, alienation of labour, conflicts of interest and an ideological superstructure based on an economic infrastructure. They emphasize constraints on individual leisure, inequalities in access to leisure and leisure as an ideology promulgating 'freedom' but obfuscating economic inequalities and class conflicts. The function of leisure in capitalist societies is critiqued by theorists such as Coalter and Parry (1982), Clarke and Critcher (1985), Gruneau (1983), Wilson (1988), Rojek (1985, 1986) and McKay (1990, 1991). For these writers class is generally prioritized. Where gender is included it is as an additional variable in the causal chain of leisure inequality. Socialist feminists such as Deem (1986) and Green et al. (1990) attempt to chart the control of women's leisure through the interaction of the structures of class and gender. Initially, in this chapter, I outline some of the interrelated concepts of Marxian theory. Then I examine the above theorists to explore how these ideas have informed analyses of leisure in capitalist societies and how they have advanced our understanding of class and gender divisions in leisure. Finally, I point out some gaps in this theoretical approach in its application to the study of leisure, especially women's leisure.

Marxist and Neo-Marxist Theories

For these theorists, human needs for autonomy and fulfilment, not functional requirements for maintaining the social system, are of prime importance. The ultimate aim of their critical analyses of society is to promote emancipation or liberation from various forms of domination, the economic and political as well as the internal domination of forms of consciousness. The resurgence of Marxian-based forms of critical analysis in the USA and the UK in the late 1960s went hand-in-hand with the human rights movement.

Whereas functional theories start from abstract social needs to explain how social practices and institutions such as leisure develop and function to meet these needs, conflict theorists ask the questions:

1 How do conflicting groups arise from the structure of society?
2 Whose interests are being served by the institutions, norms, values, rules and ideologies of society?
3 How does differential access to material resources affect everyday practices such as leisure?

Although Karl Marx died over 100 years ago, his work constitutes the main body of conceptual and theoretical work within conflict theory. Social reality for Marx consists of the forces of production and the social relations which arise from these in any society. In capitalist society, the forces of production depend on private ownership of the means of production. Those who own such means (the bourgeoisie) have power both to shape their own lives and the lives of those who have only their labour to sell in exchange for a wage (the proletariat). They also have the power to ensure that the norms and values of the society are those which serve their interests and legitimate their power. The beliefs incorporated in these norms and values then come to be accepted by all members of the society as 'natural' (ideology). The bourgeoisie form the dominant class with interests which conflict with those of the subordinate class whom they can exploit by means of the surplus value extracted from them through the work they perform over and above that for which they receive their subsistence. For example, the belief in the ideology of the work ethic benefits the owners of the means of production because they reap the profits from the work performed.

The other structures of society such as the religious, familial, political, educational and leisure institutions are shaped by the economic base. Stability in society is an uneasy peace, depending on the power of the dominant group to gain legitimation for their position through ideology. Change in society stems from the economic base or substructure. For Marx, men and women are essentially rational, intelligent and sensitive human beings who can bring about change. Nevertheless, for the most part their consciousness has been shaped by their historical, economic and social circumstances. These circumstances also constrain their daily lives and, according to critical leisure theorists, their leisure. In the Marxian problematic power resides with the owners of the means of production who can propagate ideologies or sets of beliefs which serve their interests but which are accepted by society as being in the interests of all. Thus ideas and ideologies form a superstructure which is dependent on an economic base (Cuff and Payne, 1984: Chapter 3).

Conflict theorists, following Marx, see leisure as a means of controlling conflicts of interests in society. Under the guise of a sphere of freedom, class and gender inequalities are perpetuated and conflict averted. Leisure is also seen as a sphere of consumerism which makes a profit for the owners and mangers of society. Marx felt that 'beer and circuses' would divert the working class from realizing their oppression.

Capitalism and Leisure: Clarke and Critcher

Whereas functionalist approaches to leisure emphasize freedom of individual choice in leisure and the benefits of leisure to society and to the individual, critical Marxian analysis, for example that by Coalter and Parry (1982), asked questions such as: 'Do the values incorporated into formally demonstrated leisure forms serve to exclude particular social groups?' They see leisure activities as reinforcing class boundaries, lifestyles and cultures.

Clarke and Critcher, in *The Devil Makes Work: Leisure in Capitalist Britain* (1985), offer the first extended attempt to understand the process of leisure in terms of the structural constraints of power present in capitalist society where access to material reward is unequally determined by the relationship to the means of production. Control is in the hands of the owners, the bourgeoisie. Access to leisure, along with access to other material rewards is restricted for workers. 'To garble a famous quotation from Marx – people make leisure, but not under circumstances of their own choosing' (1985: xiii). In this work they alert us to class, gender, age and racial inequalities in access to leisure as well as to its ideological justification for these inequalities and its commodification in capitalist societies. They argue that leisure is not a separate sphere from other social institutions, and that rather than being characterized by freedom and spontaneity it is marked by the social divisions extant in capitalist society, which affect both the material base and the ideological and cultural superstructure.

> Inequality of leisure opportunity has both a material and a cultural aspect. The material aspect includes access to key resources, essentially those of time and money. The cultural aspect includes the perception of what is appropriate leisure behaviour for a member of a particular social group. . . . Such definitions and expectations abound, distinguishing men from women, middle from working class, white from black, young from old. (Clarke and Critcher, 1985: 146)

In their analysis, a person's own relationship to paid work determines her/his access to leisure. For the working class, leisure is limited by lack of the ability to pay for access to private space, while public spaces such as museums, botanical gardens, sports centres are geared towards middle-class cultural values. For the old and the very young who are outside the productive system, access to leisure is also limited. For women at home, the expectations of the roles of wife and mother, as well as economic dependence on a man, restrict women's leisure both quantitatively and qualitatively: 'Women's leisure is quantitatively less than men's and qualitatively dependent on a narrow definition of the female role, especially within the family. Men dominate leisure physically and culturally, of which sport is the most transparent example' (Clarke and Critcher, 1985: 176). And:

> The sexual division of leisure clearly reflects the sexual division of labour. The commonplace observation that the experience of leisure cannot be divorced

from the experience of work is as central for domestic work as it is for the more visible case of paid labour. The qualitative and quantitative inferiority of women's leisure sharpens with the entry into the roles of wife and mother. Leisure has to be sacrificed in order to carry out these roles within existing social arrangements. Far from being the way in which women realize their leisure potential, the family curtails their leisure opportunities. (Clarke and Critcher, 1985: 224–5)

In Clarke and Critcher's view leisure serves the interests of capital by creating consumer needs which reflect the profit motive and limit consumer choice to those leisure activities and commodities which are saleable in the market-place. Leisure itself has become a commodity, controlled by capitalism and controlling individual choice under the guise or ideology of a social sphere for 'freedom of choice', spontaneity and self-enhancement: 'Choice has become the ideological validation of a system which in practice denies people the power to exercise control' (1985: 200). They give the example of the brewing industry which while introducing diversity in the decor and amusements of the traditional pub, in order to attract a younger and more affluent clientele, have become monopolized. Large corporations now own and control not only the brewing industry but also the production and sale of soft drinks and wines and spirits. They also own and control other associated leisure venues such as hotels, inns, bingo, casinos and betting shops. Clarke and Critcher see this monopoly structure as the dominant form of 'leisure capital' where diversity provides the appearance of consumer choice behind which stands a 'massive concentration of economic power' (1985: 106). They argue that real choice is largely illusory in capitalist societies.

For Clarke and Critcher leisure is not what it seems. It may be a contested arena, open to solidarity of action when conflicts of interests become apparent to certain groups, but in the main it is constrained by the structures of capitalist society such as class and gender and, to a lesser extent, age and ethnicity. Paid work remains the chief yardstick; those most deprived of work are also those with least access to leisure and class remains the principle mechanism through which inequality is perpetuated.

In a similar vein Gruneau (1983) analyses the development of Canadian sport in terms of 'a class-specific response to the pursuit of fun, achievement, and mastery in spheres outside of work and the management of public recreation and welfare' (1983: 144). The resource capacity of the bourgeoisie enables them to transform such a class-specific response into a broader 'shared cultural experience', resulting in class control of the structuring of sport and of its 'official' meanings. He shows how, in the development of Canadian sport, the bourgeoisie with access to capital and material resources have dominated all official sporting organizations and how these have become increasingly commodified. Yet this progression has seemed natural and inevitable, due to ideologies which promote sport and leisure as areas of 'free' choice. Money values in sport have thus been legitimized. Whereas once versatility and fair play were central to excellence in sport, its standards of excellence now include intense competition and single-minded commitment to the achievement of abstract standards, objectively defined (e.g. records). The intense commodification of sport, where the bourgeoisie reap the profits, have enabled them to control sport, its meaning and expression.

Nevertheless, in this work, Gruneau also grapples with the perennial sociological tension between agency and structure and sees in sport with its links to Huizinga's concept of play some possibilities for freedom of human expression, creativity and partial resistance to domination. Here he does mention the important intervention of the women's and black rights movements, but sees them as nothing more than mildly reformist strategies. For Gruneau, class dominates both men and women. Sport is an ideology which is partially true, offering freedom and creativity but constrained by class interests.

These seminal works directly challenged the harmony and consensus free choice model of leisure implicit in the functionalist writers. Links to power and ideology pointed the way for other critical writers such as Wilson (1988), Rojek (1985, 1986) and McKay (1990, 1991) to examine leisure in terms of its social, economic and political dimensions where under capitalism conflicts of interests, inequalities of access and commodification, as well as dominant ideologies and cultural hegemony, limit individuals' choices and experiences of leisure. These writers also include gender as an element in the power play or at least as a variable to be considered in conjunction with class. Socialist feminist writers such as Deem (1986) and Green et al. (1990) explore the structural gender dimension of leisure inequality in greater depth. I will look first at the male writers, who generally privilege class over gender, then at the feminist expansion of this perspective, where gender shares the spotlight.

Wilson emphasizes the political dimension of leisure. For him leisure is an arena of contestation with struggles over leisure time (e.g. Sunday) and leisure space (e.g. the streets) being linked to dominant and subordinate groups in society.

> Leisure is thus part of the struggle for the control of space and time in which social groups are continually engaged, a struggle in which the dominant group seeks to legitimate, through statute and administrative fiat, its understanding of the appropriate use of space and time, and the subordinate groups resist this control through individual rebellion and collective action. Increasingly, success in this struggle has depended on access to and control over the state. (Wilson, 1988: 12)

Groups involved in the development of the recreation movement beginning in the late nineteenth century viewed leisure as a social problem, but also as a potentially valuable aspect of personal growth in need of expert guidance and government support. However, as leisure became both professionalized and a welfare provision it also became increasingly controlled by elite groups and surveilled by the state. The dominant class propagated and controlled 'proper' or socially sanctioned leisure.

As with Clarke and Critcher, Wilson adds in gender domination to class domination. The structure of patriarchy or male dominance, he says, has shaped the political control not just of sexual conduct, but of women's leisure in general. He too is critical of the conventional, functionalist approach to leisure. He points out six ways in which such an approach is gender biased.

1   It assumes that work (against which leisure is contrasted) is paid work. Many women work, but are not in full-time employment and cannot therefore have leisure time.
2   In the conventional view work and leisure are separate locales, whereas for housewives their workplace and their leisure place are the same – leisure and work are intertwined.
3   Much of what men regard as leisure (e.g. eating), represents work for women. Women's work allows men to have leisure time.
4   Women's range of choices about the use of time is limited by their subordination to men and their 'free time' (e.g. dancing or drinking) is defined and controlled by men. Women are constructed as leisure by men, men's leisure often depending on female participation.
5   Leisure is seen as a reward for work, whereas women's housework is unrecognized or devalued as work, so they have not earned the right to leisure.
6   The idea of individual freedom is more meaningful for men than for women. Women are limited in the places they can freely and independently frequent, especially public leisure places such as pubs and saloons.

He concludes: 'There is, then, in the very meaning of leisure a powerful measure of political control by men over women' (Wilson, 1988: 51).

Rojek's wide-ranging works include a variety of theoretical approaches to leisure, some of which will be discussed in other sections of this book. In *Capitalism and Leisure Theory* (1985), he is critical of the failure of leisure theory and research to situate leisure relations in the context of the history and general power structure of capitalist society. He sets out to explore the 'submerged' tradition of leisure theory to be found in the classical sociological writings of Marx, Durkheim, Weber and Freud, as well as the theoretical innovations in relation to leisure to be found in poststructuralism and figurational sociology. He sees Marx's vital analytical insight for leisure theory as his recognition that under capitalism relations of leisure are tied to property relations.

Leisure time is not a thing in itself. It has to be demarcated and financed from the proceeds of the working day. The working class can have leisure only if it fulfils the production requirements of capital. The capitalist class can only maintain its leisure relations if it ensures that in the long run more surplus value is extracted at source, i.e. by intensifying the exploitation of labour. (Rojek, 1985: 46)

Rojek's own contribution to an analysis of leisure in contemporary capitalist society draws on aspects of Marxism along with concepts from other critical writers who see leisure embedded in the material power relations and ideologies of current capitalism. Rojek examines how leisure and leisure experiences reflect the capitalist framework. For Rojek, leisure and how it has evolved historically is a direct result of capitalist organization. As a result, the ways in which we produce and consume leisure is driven by the capitalist market. He differentiates four key tendencies: privatization; individuation; commercialization; and pacification. By privatization he means the emergence of the home as the prime site of leisure activity and the hold that possessive individualism exerts over capitalist societies. Activities such as watching television, reading alone in a quiet room, listening to music on one's personal stereo and home drinking, he claims, have priority over community leisure which is now relegated to the special occasion (1986: 15). Commercialization concerns the exploitation of the leisure market for profit. Leisure goods and services now constitute one of the main dynamics of capitalist production, turning even our living rooms into sales counters via television advertisements. Individuation in leisure relations means that under the guise of freedom of individual choice and uniqueness a perennial sameness is characteristic of the goods presented, especially those leisure commodities which are mass produced. Yet many are marketed as 'once-in-a-lifetime opportunities', such as foreign holidays, theatre, cinema and concert tickets, motor bikes, high fashion and luxury audio-visual equipment (1986: 16). Individuation, in fact, 'masks shared life conditions, and also marginalizes the whole question of how these conditions are materially produced and reproduced' (1985: 21). Pacification refers to the use of leisure as the outlet in a relatively safe context for intense emotions which have been comprehensively pacified in this historical period.

In all of these four structures Rojek (1985: 31) sees leisure as tied to systems of legitimation which regulate what is possible in leisure conduct. Rojek concludes that leisure relations are not relations of freedom at all: 'On the contrary, they are relations of power whose dynamics and subjective meaning reflect the historically structured economy of pleasure in society' (1985: 181). The ideology of leisure, which is predicated on the material relations of production in capitalist society, legitimates certain forms of pleasurable activity as leisure thus providing a rationale for material inequalities.

Although Rojek rejects a purely class-based model of such legitimation in favour of one which gives weight to nationalism, sexism and racism, he does not explore the implications of sexism in any depth. He does alert us to the fact that women's experience of leisure is significantly different from men's and that a mother's self-image of being at the beck and call of her spouse and children works against notions of having time off for leisure. He is critical of male domination of women's 'free' time and places this domination within 'the basic structural characteristics of leisure relations in capitalist society' (1985: 18). He posits the case of women's leisure to argue against the concept of free time as the basis for leisure theory and research. Nevertheless the work generally assumes the male experience of leisure to be universal.

In the Australian context McKay (1990) treats age, gender, income, level of educational attainment and marital status as independent variables affecting leisure participation. He claims that 'leisure features the same contradictions, conflicts and asymmetries that exist between dominant and subordinate groups in society at large' (149). Gender is one of the variables which constrain leisure pursuit in patriarchal–capitalist societies such as Australia. For example, he found that men had higher participation rates than women in all age groups and regardless of marital status and socio-economic status. In *No Pain, No Gain: Sport and Australian Culture* (1991), McKay extends his analysis, with particular reference to sport. He here specifically posits capitalism as the axis around which all other social relations revolve. Thus he proceeds to follow the historical and social development of mainly male sport in Australian society so that it benefits capital and excludes women, the aged and working-class people.

For example, using national surveys he shows that in 1986:

- whereas almost 38 per cent of those with incomes over $30,000 per year participated in informal sport, only 28 per cent of those with incomes under $10,000 did;
- 12 per cent of those who completed primary education participated in informal sport, while 41 per cent of those who were tertiary graduates did (McKay, 1991: 10).

In 1987:

- whereas almost 80 per cent of 14–19-year-old males and females participated in organized sport, only 10 per cent of those over 55 did;
- the rates for informal sport similarly declined, but men's involvement remained consistently above women's (McKay, 1991: 8).

In 1990:

- 65 national executive directors of sporting organizations were male and 12 were female;
- 58 national coaching directors were male and 14 were female (McKay, 1991: 13).

For women, McKay demonstrates that both economic and ideological constraints exist:

The tendency for women's bodies to be smaller and weaker than men's has been used to justify excluding women from vigorous physical activities and to legitimize the 'natural' superiority of men's bodies . . .

Women also have less access to sports than men because of oppressive economic and legal structures and because women's leisure in general is 'policed' by men. (1991: 53)

McKay's work effectively demolishes egalitarian myths concerning Australian society in the areas of sport and leisure. His ultimate aim is to remake sport as an 'important part of a larger pluralist socialist project of democratising culture and expanding human freedom' (1991: 178). Women, along with other subordinate groups, should benefit.

In these theorists gender is but one variable surrounding the axis of class-based capitalism. Gender is added in to the capitalist mix of materially based conflicts of interests; inequalities of access to valued resources and the concomitant legitimating ideologies; commodification and commercialization of the phenomenon of leisure and its products; the control of the state; and the centrality of the forces and relations of production where paid work dominates and determines individual lives, including leisure experiences.

Capitalism, Patriarchy and Leisure: Deem and Green, Hebron and Woodward

When feminists such as Rosemary Deem (1986, 1988, 1992) and Green et al. (1990) began to view women's leisure through the critical lens of a Marxian feminist analysis, gender could no longer be presented as an add-on variable to class. The influence of patriarchy in the construction and experience of women's leisure began to take centre stage.

Deem's (1986) introduction of a feminist approach to the study of leisure began with the empirical backing of her research of women's leisure in the newly developing British city of Milton Keynes. This study is overtly feminist, in that it 'places women at the forefront of its analysis and sees them as an oppressed group with certain experiences in common' (1986: 11). Although the women Deem observed and interviewed were diverse in terms of class, age, ethnicity, marital status and employment, she found common constraints on their participation in leisure. These stemmed from housework and the gendered division of labour; fragmented days; the need to define and construct leisure so that it fitted into the demands of caring for small children or of a seven-day working week; and the policing of women in public places by men. The women she researched are generally treated as unified subjects, experiencing a common world of women, in spite of differences. In Thatcher's Britain, where liberal individualism covered a multitude of social inequalities, there was a political imperative to demonstrate broad-based inequities in access to valued resources which were predicated on factors such as gender. The crucial factors which separated women whose leisure was least constrained from those whose leisure was very constrained were: having access to public transport; an independent source of money; some form of employment; a reasonably high degree of confidence in themselves and a determination to do what they wanted; a sense of a legitimate right to leisure; and a network of support from a friend or partner to a whole household or group of people (1986: 141).

This focus on women also revealed that women's leisure is not necessarily the same as men's leisure. Its own strengths included: solidarity with their own sex in a spirit of companionship rather than competition; an emphasis on caring and co-operation; a lack of aggression and selfishness; enjoyment of everyday things and happenings; an emphasis on the creative and aesthetic aspects of life; a willingness to include rather than exclude others; and greater detachment from consumerist values (1986: 148).

In her analysis, Deem links the 'personal' to the 'political'. Her theoretical contribution is the linking of the personal difficulties women experience in their everyday lives in getting access to leisure to the gender power relations of wider capitalist society. Where men are in positions of political power, power in the workplace, the community and the family they can control the political and economic agenda, as well as the ideologies of femininity which keep women out of public spaces and in serving positions in the home. She concludes that it is not in men's interests to give up political power to women, so that the structural changes to society which she sees as necessary for long-term benefits to women will be difficult to achieve (1986: 148). In this work, as in later papers (e.g. 1987, 1988, 1992), Deem, in the Marxian feminist tradition, is concerned with the structures and ideological forces which shape women's oppression and the ways in which women's subordination and oppression may be overcome by challenging patriarchal structures and ideologies (1988: 5). Women are either the same as, or different from, men and men hold the power. Although she has shifted the focus to women's leisure, men remain the reference point both politically and personally.

In a further theoretical development of some of these ideas, as well as the introduction of the idea of cultural domination through hegemony, Green et al. also draw our attention to the influence of patriarchy in the control of women's access to leisure. Their aim is 'to understand the relationship between leisure, both conceptually and experientially, and the maintenance of inequality between the sexes' (1990: 29). So they focus on concepts such as patriarchy, hegemony and ideology to examine the processes through which males in capitalist society gain and retain consent for their domination over women. Gramsci's concept of hegemony originally referred to the process by which a dominant class wins consent to their domination over a subordinate class, through civil society and cultural practices. These authors apply the concept to men's domination over women and go on to show how leisure itself acts as a means of cultural control of women's private and public lives. Drawing on Barrett's (1980) Marxist feminist use of the term ideology for the process by which meaning is produced, challenged, reproduced and transformed, Green et al. argue that leisure is a 'grossly ideological category based firmly on a male and relatively affluent experience' (1990: 31). Those who control the means of material production are also likely to control the means of mental production. Leisure in its social context is 'a social organisation which is predominantly patriarchal and fundamentally capitalist' (1990: 37). Into the feminist leisure literature they have introduced terms such as patriarchy, hegemony and ideology. In their sense, patriarchy means the power that men have over women due to their control of the means of production. Based on this material substructure are the beliefs, ideas and cultural practices through which male domination is legitimated and maintained (i.e. hegemony and ideology). The practices and beliefs become accepted by both women and men as the natural order determined by one's sex.

The term patriarchy has been criticized by feminists and also by male theorists. Marxist feminists such as Beechey (1979) and Barrett (1980) criticized the generality of the term and suggested that it should be grounded in specific historical periods with specific material conditions, such as patriarchal feudalism or patriarchal socialism. Thus they gave primacy to the mode of production rather than the kinship system. Eisenstein (1977), on the other hand, claimed that women have been subordinated in all time periods and under all modes of production so that there is a continuity in patriarchal history that is lacking in economic history. Of patriarchy, Eisenstein says: 'As we can see, patriarchy is cross cultural by definition though it is actualised differently in different societies via the institutionalisation of sexual hierarchy. The contours of sex may differ societally but power has and does reside with the male' (1977: 11).

The concept of 'patriarchy' which was intrinsic to 1970s feminist analyses of gender difference and inequality has been and remains the subject of debate. Walby (1990) argues that patriarchy can be criticized as a concept because it fails to deal with differences between women such as class and ethnicity. She argues for six structures which articulate different forms of patriarchy for different groups within society: paid work; housework; sexuality; culture; violence; and the state. In private patriarchy, she claims, the dominant structure is household production, in the public form, employment and the state, although in each case the other structures are also significant. In the private sphere the dominant mode of expropriation is individual, by the husband or father, while in the public it is collective, by men. In addition, hooks (1984) maintains that the focus on the family in feminist analysis of patriarchy as the major site of oppression does not always hold true for women of colour. In many instances, she claims, the family has been the site of resistance and solidarity for women against racism and thus is not so central to women's oppression.

The use of the term patriarchy by feminists in the 1970s served the theoretical purpose of highlighting gender differences in power which extend beyond unidimensional economic causes. Its weakness has been in its assumption of universal gender differences within one historical period. The deconstruction of 'patriarchy' in post-feminist analyses has served to remind us of cross-cutting issues of power within genders such as class, race, ethnicity, age and heterosexuality/homosexuality. Socialist feminist analyses such as Eisenstein's retain the term and attempt to integrate gender and class, capitalism and patriarchy. In this book I have retained the term as an umbrella to signify male dominance at all levels of society but with recognition of the many and varied forms that such dominance can take in societies where 'male' and 'female' are neither stable nor unified. With Walby (1992: 36), I consider there are 'sufficient common features and sufficient routinised connections for it to make sense to talk of patriarchy'.

Male theorists such as Waters (1989) and Turner (1996), who criticize the term, consider contemporary society to have moved beyond the dominance of men, either in the home (Waters) or in the public sphere (Turner). Waters critiques the concept as a family-based term and suggests instead 'viriarchy' for male control of the public arena. Turner (1996), on the other hand, critiques it as the public foundation of male power through law and politics which he sees as now being substantially eroded. He prefers instead 'patrism' to refer to the remaining prejudicial and paternalistic beliefs about the inferiority of women. I am rather suspicious of the desire of these male theorists who do not agree amongst themselves on the meaning of the term, to do away with it. Although there have been considerable advances made in women's economic and legal position in the family, law, politics and the workplace since the advent of the second wave of feminism, all structural obstacles have not yet been removed for the majority of women. Following Walby (1992), I value the emphasis that the term patriarchy places on the continuing maintenance of power that accrues to being male in current societies through men's institutional positions and relative access to economic resources, both in the family and in the public sphere. (For a more detailed explication of my own views on patriarchy, see Wearing, 1996: 21–3.) Turner's term 'patrism', as I see it, adds in the cultural dimension and so is helpful when discussing male hegemony, but, as yet, patriarchy has not been superseded.

From their empirical study of 700 women in Sheffield in England, Green, Hebron and Woodward demonstrated inequalities of women's access to leisure compared with men's access and men's social control of women's private and public leisure experiences. Some of the inequalities were: women have less time for leisure than men and a more limited range of possibilities; women's housework and childcare responsibilities generally render them 'on call'; leisure outside the home is problematic in terms of time, resources, childcare and respectable and acceptable femininity; women are generally financially poorer than men; and at home women are financially dependent on their husbands (Green and Woodward, 1990: 3–4). Male strategies for control over women's leisure varied between classes, being more direct in working-class families. For example, one working-class wife preferred to go out on her own because she found joint leisure, tailored to her husband's requirements, boring. He said:

> . . . well, if she wants to spend the same as me, she can go out every night with me if she wants, you know, I've no objection to that at all . . . I'd rather her go out with me and go to one of the places I like to go than stop her in. You know, I get a bit annoyed sometimes, if she won't come out and do things I want to do. (Green et al., 1987: 116)

A middle-class husband, on the other hand, commented that more frequent evenings out by his wife might be an indicator of marital dissatisfaction:

> I perhaps would not be unduly concerned about it . . . I wouldn't want to say, 'Well, you can't do that' or 'you shouldn't be doing that' but I would sort of say 'well', you know 'is there anything happening in our relationship', look at that way, 'which has occasioned it, perhaps' and that's the only reason I would see her doing that. (Green et al., 1987: 209)

Men and male power remain the reference point and women's friendships are seen as 'safety valves' for the expression of discontent but ineffective as a source of collective resistance to patriarchal controls (Woodward and Green, 1990). Structure predominates over agency.

This theoretical approach with its emphasis on male power stemming from a material base and legitimized through ideological and hegemonic processes informed other research concerning women's leisure in the 1980s. The constraints imposed on mothers of young children due to the ideology of motherhood were documented (Wimbush, 1988; Wearing, 1990b), as were those on adolescent working-class girls due to cultural expectations for these young women (McRobbie, 1978). Partners' constrictions of older married women's leisure were explored (Mason, 1988), and women's own acceptance of and collusion in male-defined leisure provision were demonstrated (Talbot, 1988a).

In a fifteen-year ethnographic study in an Australian rural town, Dempsey found that across the life-cycle where women were admitted to sporting and leisure activities outside the home, it was as supporters and facilitators of men's activities and 'virtually always as subordinates' (1989: 582). The following advertisement in the local newspaper for the Woman's Football Auxiliary at the commencement of the 1986 season illustrates the point: 'Ideal candidates would be mothers, wives or girl-friends of players . . . main activity throughout the season will be the stocking and manning [sic] of the canteen at the Smalltown Football Ground' (Dempsey, 1990: 39).

Dempsey concludes that the lynchpin in the ideological system which legitimates and facilitates the control of women in this community is the judgement on the relative merits of women's labour. Men's work is defined as superior to women's labour in the home because of its economic contribution to the future viability of the community. Men, he says, frequently joke about the many hours their wives have to slave over the microwave, the automatic washing machine and the dishwasher. The implication which is often made explicit is: 'They are on a great cop if only they would stop whingeing and recognize that they've got it made' (1990: 39). Women accepted the resulting inequalities in access to leisure as natural and inevitable. Strongly held ideologies of the family, femininity and women's place also ensured their compliance. Women who challenged the status quo were sanctioned and either conformed or left the town. Here again men's work in patriarchal capitalist society is the benchmark against which women's labour is measured and evaluated.

Similar results have been found in rural communities in Canada, especially in resource-industry towns to which families have moved because of the man's work in mining or forestry (Graveline, 1990; Dunk, 1991; Watkins, 1991; Hunter and Whitson, 1992). Hunter and Whitson found in their study of Cranbrook in the interior of British Columbia that there was a very strong male culture, based in the value of the men's work and carried over into leisure through the provision of facilities for ice hockey and pubs from which women were excluded. Community spirit for women was judged by their support for the men's sport and other local traditions such as the beauty pageant. They conclude that working men's towns 'are often places where patriarchal norms still set the tone of social life, and require women to adapt' (Hunter and Whitson, 1992: 235).

When applied specifically to the sporting scene, patriarchal domination has been shown to limit, define and trivialize women's sporting involvement (Hall, 1985; Bryson, 1987, 1990; Hargreaves, 1994). For Hall, sport is 'an ideological institution with enormous symbolic significance that contributes to and perpetuates cultural hegemony' (1985: 38). In sport the body is subject, sport depends on the body's capacities and skills in order to achieve. On the other hand, patriarchal culture defines woman as body–object, so that women have either been excluded from the symbols, practices and institutions of sport, or when included, what they do is not considered true sport or they are not considered to be true women.

For Bryson definitions of sport, direct control of women's sport, ignoring women's sport and trivialization of women in sport (especially in media presentations) coalesce to promote a maleness that is repeatedly linked with skill, strength, aggression and violence and which subjugates women. Thus, she says: 'We find boys from a very early age being schooled in the appropriate behaviour and sentiments at the same time that girls are learning that they are excluded' (1987: 358). Physical force and toughness, says Bryson, are woven into hegemonic masculinity which celebrates 'real men' as strong and tough. Such hegemony underscores the fact that men are in positions and have the right to dominate and this forms an irreducible dimension of power (1990: 70).

In an updated version of the socialist feminist position on women's leisure which takes into account the postmodern attack on universal categories such as gender, Scraton (1994, 1995) argues for the retention of the political agenda made possible by recognition of some of the commonalities of women's oppression under capitalist patriarchy. She argues that postmodern concerns with representation via the media and written texts have enabled the reality of the material disadvantages of working-class women to be minimalized. In addition, the focus on differences in women's subjectivities due to class, age, race, ethnicity, disability and sexual orientation have undermined the political possibilities of women's collective activity. Gender and class as bases of structural oppression have been marginalized. Yet, she says, the inequalities in leisure access and leisure experience still exist. For example, the findings of studies such as those of Deem and Green, Hebron and Woodward conducted in the 1970s under the banner of socialist feminism and with the aim of uncovering the founding cause of women's oppression remain relevant in the postmodern 1990s. There is still a material base of male power and control, in spite of the increasing numbers of married women who remain in the workforce or re-enter after the early childrearing years.

Scraton (1995: 12) points out that in Britain in the 1990s half of women's employment is in low-paid work. Few women make it past the 'glass ceiling' into the senior management – higher-paid positions and occupations, for the most part, remain gender differentiated, with women's jobs being inferior in status and pay. This means little disposable income for formal leisure activities or consumer goods. In the home the sexual division of labour remains. Whether they are in paid employment or not, women retain the primary responsibilities for childcare, cooking, cleaning and shopping. Thus those in full-time paid work have an estimated 10 hours less leisure time per week than similarly employed men. Childcare for the under-fives remains inadequate and women's responsibilities in the increasing number of women-headed one-parent families are even greater. Nor have the dominance of men in public spaces, the control imposed within the private sphere of the home and the threat and reality of men's violence shown any signs of diminishing since their documentation in the 1980s studies. Scraton concludes therefore that the material conditions of many women show little sign of change and that gender cannot be abandoned as a concept that retains political significance (1995: 12–13). She argues for the recognition of diversity amongst women but not at the expense of shared political aims and the recognition of material disadvantage and oppression. The aim remains 'equality for women and the right of all women to enjoy and define their own leisure choices' and such an aim necessitates a continued attack on the relationships of gender which are 'structured by dominant power relations of sexuality, "race", sex/gender, class and ability/disability' (1995: 14). Structure constrains agency.

There is some empirical evidence to support Scraton's claims. My own approach in this book has some similarities with Scraton's, but also some differences. There is indeed a very real danger in the poststructural emphasis on women's multiple identities and subjectivities of losing the concept of 'woman' with its political potential for collective action on the part of women. In my own writing (see Wearing, 1996), along with other feminist writers such as Walby (1992), I retain the concept as an umbrella term to recognize the similarities in women's position in society and their continuing oppression in spite of the very real advances made since the inception of the 1970s women's movement (especially for white, middle-class, educated women). I also recognize the continuing constraints on women's lives and leisure of patriarchal structures in capitalist society.

Nevertheless, one of the dangers of the socialist feminist position in the late 1980s was that such thorough documentation of women's oppression, theoretically linked to structural causes, implied that nothing that individual women could do would make any significant change in their lives. A pessimistic position, to say the least. And one which breeds a victim mentality. There was a shift from the 'victim blaming', 'bootstraps' approach of liberalism to the 'poor victim' approach of socialism. Yet in the everyday lives of the women I knew, and those I came to know through my research, women were continually constructing survival strategies, struggling, negotiating, contesting and sometimes transforming power relationships at an individual and group level. The feminist research described above includes many examples of such 'resistance'. For example, in McRobbie's (1978) study, the adolescent girls' control of their own leisure space, their bedrooms, enabled them to try on different identities and to challenge to some extent the dominant prescriptions of gender for them. In my own study of mothers (1990b), the idea of the right to time and space for oneself through leisure enabled some women to pursue activities as varied as horse-riding, oboe laying and surfboard riding, which conferred an identity outside motherhood and challenged some aspects of the ideology of motherhood. Yet socialist feminist theory did not appear to have room for this. Unless there was some form of solidarity which attacked the structures of class and gender, change did not seem possible. Power was top-down and repressive. Foucault's ideas on resistance and capillary power were, for me, a step forward in my understanding of the everyday lives and experiences of women. An examination of the strategies that women use to enlarge their own personal space and thus their experiences of leisure, and an exploration of sites of power such as the family, where many forces of power intersect to both give and receive pain and pleasure, have enabled me to move forward in my own thinking and my teaching concerning women's leisure. These ideas are discussed further in Chapter 8 of this book.

Conclusion

In the continuing sociological tension between agency and structure, it seems to me that both must be held in balance. In this chapter, I have referred to those masculinist and feminist theorists who have drawn substantially on neo-Marxist theories to examine the place of leisure in contemporary capitalism. Researchers who have incorporated these structuralist theories have been able to show the powerful impact of the structures of class and gender under the relations of production of industrial capitalism to constrain and construct the life options and life chances of men and women, in the area of leisure as in other areas of their lives. Feminist leisure researchers, such as Deem, Green, Hebron and Woodward and Scraton, have insisted on the centrality of patriarchal power in any analysis of women's lives and women's leisure and the inequalities of access to leisure which such an analysis reveals. In addition to the material inequities, these theorists have also emphasized the ideologies which gain acceptance without coercion to women's subordination and inequality. For these feminists, patriarchal power, derived primarily from economic power due to men's economic position in paid work, enables ideologies such as that of the family, motherhood and acceptable femininity to keep women in their place and deny them access to many leisure practices.

The concept of cultural hegemony, for these theorists, also legitimates the dominance of cultural practices which advantage dominant groups. Patrism and cultural male hegemony, according to them, go hand in hand to exclude women from access to leisure facilities and leisure resources. Leisure research has shown that, especially in rural towns, hegemonic masculinity excludes women from many aspects of sport and leisure and is based on continuing notions of women's supportive role to male breadwinners. Structures of power in patriarchal capitalism or capitalist patriarchy (depending on which is seen as fundamental) constrain and subordinate some men and all women in their leisure practices. Ideologies and cultural hegemony ensure the acceptance of such constraints without coercion. Taken to extreme, however, this theoretical perspective tends to place all women in the same corner, of being victims to the enormous weight of structural patriarchal power. The implication is that nothing an individual woman can do will alter the situation and the danger is to breed a victim mentality and a sense of equal powerlessness on the part of all women. My question then is: 'Where is the agency of individual women, in constructing leisure experiences for themselves which resist male domination?'

In the following chapter, the microsocial approach of symbolic interaction is examined in relation to leisure. In this approach both agency and process are prioritized over structure, with the strengths and weaknesses that such an approach has for understanding leisure experience.

3

The Self and Freedom and Constraint in Leisure: Interactionist Theories

In contrast to the macrosocial approaches of functionalist and Marxian theorists, interactionists turn their attention to the microsocial milieu of individual actors. The structures of power in wider society such as class and gender are not seen as deterministic within this framework. Theorists such as Kelly (1983, 1987a, 1994), drawing on the work of Mead, focus on the microsocial experiential aspects of leisure and on individuals as thinking actors (or agents) with ability to construct leisure experiences which are both challenging and rewarding. Feminist theorists who have adopted this approach, such as Shaw (1985), Samdahl (1988), Wimbush and Talbot (1988), Bella (1989), Henderson et al. (1989, 1996) and Wearing (1992), show how the meanings of leisure in the everyday lives of mainly middle-class white women can be different from their male counterparts. In this chapter, initially I outline some concepts of symbolic interactionism as they are applied by Mead to the individual and society. The contribution that Kelly's work has made to leisure theory by the application of these concepts to leisure experience is then discussed. Insights into women's experiences of leisure when viewed through the lens of feminist applications of symbolic interactionism in conjunction with social psychology are then explored and evaluated. Ideas from Goffman (1967, 1969) and MacCannell (1992) are included.

Symbolic Interactionism

In symbolic interactionism each individual is an active, thinking unit, capable of constructing a meaningful existence and a sense of 'self' from the social milieu in which s/he lives. This perspective calls attention to the detailed, person-centred processes that take place within the larger units of social life. Individual experience takes form from the meaning the actor places on her/his own acts and the acts of others. The act of interpretation gives interaction its symbolic character.

The ideas of George Herbert Mead, the American pragmatist philosopher (1863–1931), provided a conceptual foundation for theorists who follow this approach. In *Mind, Self and Society* (1972) he traced how social interaction, language and role taking create the human mind and the 'self', thus laying the conceptual foundations for social psychology. He attempted to explain how society gets into the individual, determines behaviour and becomes part of 'self'. The mind, for Mead, is a process through which individuals adapt to their environment; language and symbols give human beings a short cut to such adaptation which animals do not have. Through *language* the individual takes on and internalizes the attitudes of others towards both the environment and self. The young child internalizes the attitudes of those who are important to her/him such as mother and father (*significant others*). With maturity the individual learns to relate to *significant reference groups* and to a *generalized other*, that is, the community as a whole and its values conveyed through group activity and the media etcetera.

In Mead's terms, the individual need not and, in fact, cannot be totally controlled by the internalized attitudes of others, that is, by the *me* part of the self. The individual is also an *I*, someone who takes account of the 'me', but is not necessarily determined by it. The 'I' may act upon, influence and modify the social process; it represents the self insofar as it is free and has initiative, novelty and uniqueness. An individual's various 'me's', constructed in different situations, are seen by her/him not only as discrete objects but may also be perceived in a hierarchy according to which are most favoured. This perception of the individual as a whole person, Mead called the 'I' or self-conception. Essentially for Mead, the 'self' is formulated socially and varies with the situation, but it is the thinking person who does the constructing and integrates society into the individual identity (Cuff and Payne, 1984: 118–21).

Many of Mead's ideas have their origins in the writings of William James (1952). I refer here to these ideas since, in fact, we need to come back to them in the 1990s when sociologists are again considering the place of the body and emotions in reference both to social behaviour and a sense of self or rather multiplicity of selves. James posits the constituents of the self as: (i) the material self (the body and its manifestations such as clothes and style); (ii) the social self or selves (the 'me' or 'me's' and associated honours and esteem); (iii) the spiritual self (the thinking, reflective self); and (iv) the pure ego (the synthesized sense of personal identity which is 'out of time'). Self-feelings, self-seeking and self-preservation are the associated emotions. For James the 'me' is an empirical aggregate of things objectively known; the 'I' is neither an aggregate nor an unchanging metaphysical entity, rather a thought which constantly changes, but which incorporates past thoughts, feelings and experiences (James, 1952 : 188–259). I will return to these ideas later in the chapter in my discussion of feminist poststructural criticisms of the 'rational "I"' which forms the core of symbolic interactionism as well as the 'I'/'me' dichotomy and any sense of an inner fixed identity.

Criticisms of the ideas of Mead and symbolic interactionism are not confined, however, to the 1990s. Interactionism has had a tortured history in

American sociology. It has been criticized for its inability to deal with broader historical and structural issues, its repetition of a few general concepts with different empirical content, its middle- and upper-class American bias and its voyeurism of the powerless. Its end has been predicted several times. Yet, as Denzin points out (1992: xvii), it will not go away, it will not die. His own work in 1992 expands the horizons of the perspective to incorporate elements of postmodern theory such as the works of Foucault as well as the ideas of critical, feminist and cultural studies. Consequently he now includes considerations of 'the bedrock worlds of material existence that shape human consciousness' and 'local political resistance' in an attempt to 'assist those groups in which personal troubles are transformed into demands for a greater stake in the public good'. He has taken on board issues of power to the extent that 'those in power (the economic, political, and cultural elites) constantly define the personal in terms which further their own political agendas' (1992: 167–8) while yet endeavouring to capture the voices, emotions, meanings and actions of individuals.

When applied to leisure, symbolic interactionist approaches emphasize leisure as experience and the meaning given to leisure experiences by individual actors. These include the contribution that leisure makes to self and identity as well as the social interactions involved in leisure and the social meaning of leisure spaces. The balance between the social constraints imposed on leisure experience (through the 'me') and its potential as a space for freedom of action and self-development (through the 'I') remains one of the fundamental themes in leisure theory and leisure research having its origins in the premises of symbolic interactionist thought. The potential of leisure to reinforce or challenge traditional roles, including gender roles, was opened up through this approach. Feminists apply these ideas to freedom and constraint in women's leisure experiences.

Symbolic Interaction and Leisure

Kelly

In his book *Leisure Identities and Interactions*, Kelly (1983) provides the foundations for analysing leisure from an interactionist perspective. In this work he expanded the definition of leisure to encompass the subjective meaning given by individuals to leisure experience, and introduced the vital dynamics of freedom and constraint, and the individual and social interactions implicit in this experience. Leisure becomes a process, rather than a social structure or an institution of social control, social health or social liberty. Leisure has the potential for self-enhancement and self-development, but not unrestrainedly so. Nor is leisure restricted to ideas of non-work time or activity. These ideas have influenced and opened up the field of leisure research to new horizons and remain viable even in the rapidly changing 1990s. Their application by feminists such as Henderson, Bialeschki, Samdahl,

Shaw, Wimbush and Talbot and Wearing to women's leisure experiences has advanced the knowledge of the meanings that women give to this aspect of their lives beyond generalized male views. Symbolic interactionism with its recogition of the ongoing interaction between social selves and the cumulative 'I' allows for a more flexible approach to leisure and gender identities than structuralist approaches. Combined with poststructuralist feminist ideas on deconstruction, multiplicity of subjectivities and resistance, the way is opened for leisure to be a means for women to move beyond identities which are determined by class and gender and concomitant ideologies and cultural hegemonies.

Concerning the definition of leisure as freedom of choice of activity or use of time, Kelly points out that:

> Leisure is freely chosen because the activity or the companions or some combination of the two promise personal satisfaction. It is the personal and social orientation of the participant that makes an activity leisure – or something else. Leisure is defined by the use of time, not the time itself. It is distinguished by the meaning of the activity not its form. (1982: 7)

In *Leisure Identities and Interactions* (1983: 1–2), Kelly shows us how the meanings of leisure activities may differ for different individuals and over time. In leisure, he says, one activity may have many meanings. For example, for one young mother, her art class is primarily a social event, a release for two hours from home and childrearing, whereas for another young woman it is a demanding discipline focusing on the mastery of techniques and styles. Different activities may have the same meanings to participants, such as ceramics and squash if the focus is on mastery and skill. One event may also include many modes of behaviour, for example a party where organization, socializing, communication, new relationships and old relationships may be present for some or all of the participants. The same activity may have different meanings at different times, such as reading at home for escape or education.

Leisure, then, for Kelly, is both individual and social: it takes place not only in the mind, but also in the social world where it is a social space involving important face-to-face relationships and all kinds of social rules, conventions, definitions and expectations which may limit or expand the real options for leisure-related decisions. He includes here the position of women (1983: 5–9). His model of involvement and choice in leisure (1983: 11) incorporates the continuums, constraint and freedom, engagement and disengagement, pleasure and antipathy, and provides for the possibilities of institutional leisure, pure leisure, alienated and anomic leisure. It is a model which 'enables the sociologist to "bring freedom back in" to the social dialectic without discarding structural contexts' (1983: 199). It is not however a model which is concerned with power and inequalities of access to leisure resources according to macro-structures such as class, gender, race; it is concerned rather with the freedom and constraint open to individuals in their everyday experiences of leisure. The wider social context consists of social roles with their relevant statuses and expectations learned through socialization and generally adhered to through consensus in a particular society. The balance between freedom and constraint, individual and social/cultural norms and roles, is maintained throughout the work as identities, life-course, family leisure, leisure as social dialectic and leisure planning are discussed. The contribution of leisure to the ongoing construction of individual identity and the personal and social sense of self or selves remains one of the strengths of the work.

Leisure and Identity

For Kelly, 'Styles of leisure are not just combinations of activities, but are the stages on which we present our identities and receive feedback on our role identities' (1983: 93). Thus leisure not only provides a social space for expressivity and role reinforcement, but also a space for learning new roles, 'playing' with role identities and for developing individual identities apart from those associated with the family and/or work. There is, then, in leisure the possibility 'to be and become *ourselves*', to develop multidimensional personal identities in the ongoing process of becoming (1983: 94). There is also the possibility, of course, of damage. Nevertheless, Kelly's main focus is on the positive contribution that leisure can make to Mead's 'me', that is, the social self. Nor is the 'I' passive in this interaction, but has a creative, integrative and extremely personal function in this process:

> In this sense much leisure is both personal and social in meaning. We present ourselves in a role, develop and establish an identity, receive confirmation or correction on our performance and enjoy the process. We enjoy the experience of successful role enactment and find our self-concepts enhanced in the process. Some roles are quite central and others peripheral; some pervade many social settings and episodes and others are quite discrete and transitory. However, creating our portrayal of a role identity has its own satisfaction at the moment and in our building of selfhood. (Kelly, 1983: 119)

Identity, then, for Kelly, is the link, through roles, between the personal and the social in a process which develops and changes across the life-course, a process in which leisure has a significant part. In *Freedom to Be* he develops this idea (with considerable input from existential theory) to show how leisure is a dialectic between the actor and her/his environment with the possibility always of the freedom to create the 'not yet', the freedom yet 'to become', to expand and develop the self and identity in new ways (1987a: 227).

Kelly's own research reflects his concerns with freedom and constraint in leisure and the links with role identities and the self. For example, in *Peoria Winter* (1987b), interviews with 120 men and women over 40 years of age showed how leisure is a social space of relative freedom for expression, development, and community through the adult life-course and assists in 'successful' adaptation to later life. For these adults the investment in leisure activity provided a space for personal expression and self-enhancement and for positive interaction with and support from 'significant others' (Kelly et al., 1986: 536).

The example is given of 62-year-old Mary who has suffered two unsatisfactory marriages, one husband being mentally unstable and consistently unfaithful and the second an alcoholic who physically abused her. She has also undergone major surgery three times. Yet today she is a valued employee in an office with much younger women, is actively involved in her church and a dance club and shares close and warm relationships with her three adult children and her best friend of long standing. Leisure contexts provide times and places for personal sharing, interaction and enjoyable experiences. Kelly concludes:

> She has not just let life push her around. She has sought and found investments that have paid off in bringing balance and texture to her life. Somehow, all the context destroying events have not taken from her the self-acceptance and direction required to go on forming relationships that offer a sharing of both meaning and joy. (1987b: 6)

In a later paper (1994) Kelly addresses some of the criticisms of his symbolic interactionist approach to leisure and attempts to marry some of the further insights into leisure experience which have come from gender analyses, critical cultural studies and social constructionist theory to show how this perspective remains viable as a basis for leisure research in the 1990s. In this paper he recognizes his own emphasis on agency and freedom in leisure to the virtual exclusion of the power relationships of class, gender and culture which structure wider society and impose limits on the perceptions and actions of individuals. By setting the microsocial analysis of symbolic interactionism within the structural constraints of class, gender and cultural inscription, Kelly has restored some balance of agency/structure to his model of leisure. He maintains the value of the interactionist approach in focusing on reflexive interpretive practice, rather than on abstracted concepts, and argues that it can include discourse as well as action, culture as well as structure, and imposed as well as individually constructed meanings (1994: 94). That he is able to do this, in my opinion, demonstrates the flexibility of an interactionist perspective to bridge the personal/contextual, micro/macro, agency/structure divide. At the time of writing *Leisure Identities and Interactions*, this flexibility was certainly a needed balance to the more socially deterministic aspects of functionalism and Marxism. Today it also offers some balance to the more deterministic and pessimistic aspects of discourse analyses in which individual subjectivity may be swallowed up in dominating, subjecting and surveillant discourses. Like Denzin, Kelly recognizes his original explication glossed over power differentials in wider society which subordinated women's roles and female culture, as well as those of working-class people and racial and ethnic minorities. Set within a context which recognizes and incorporates societal power structures it retains some purchase by its focus on the possibilities for individuals to take some part in the construction and reconstruction of their own identities through leisure. In my opinion a move away from the focus on social roles and socialization, which rely on societal consensus and fixed notions of adult gender functions as the main mechanisms by which society becomes part of individual identity, would allow for a more fundamentally critical approach. The inclusion of concepts such as difference, cultural hegemony, dominant discourses and resistant subjectivities would, I think, add greater flexibility as well as greater explanatory power to Kelly's approach, especially where gender is concerned.

Nevertheless, the seminal ideas of freedom and constraint in leisure, the subjective meanings attached to leisure experience, the importance of interaction in leisure, the links to identity and the notion of leisure spaces which are both existential and social, which were present in Kelly's *Leisure Identities and Interactions*, have provided interesting and fruitful underpinnings to much feminist research into women's leisure in the 1980s and early 1990s. In application to women's leisure this approach also has the advantage of conceptualizing leisure as existential experience, not necessarily in its relationship to paid labour.

Freedom and Constraint in Women's Leisure: Henderson, Bialeschski, Shaw and Freysinger

When feminists apply the assumptions of an interactionist approach to women's leisure they bring with them a view of the situation which incorporates the meanings attached to leisure by the white, middle-class women whom they research. Thus they move the focus from the perceptions of white, middle-class males and challenge the assumption that these meanings represent the views of all. American feminists who use this approach within a social psychological framework focus on the constraints imposed on these women's leisure by gender roles and women's socialization but they also focus on freedom in the sense that leisure may contribute to 'the development of identities that can help women overcome issues of oppression in other aspects of their lives' (Henderson et al., 1989: 3). British feminists, on the other hand, set the 'relative freedoms' (Wimbush and Talbot, 1988) of women's leisure experiences and the meanings they attach to these within a framework of the structural, ideological and hegemonic constraints of patriarchy. In this section I discuss the issues of freedom and constraint in women's leisure which symbolic interactionist approaches have brought to the surface for theoretical and empirical examination.

In an explicit application of symbolic interactionist theory to perceived role constraint in an experience sampling study of 695 contexts with 18 men and women between the ages of 18 and 60, Samdahl (1988) found that the variables, role constraint and self-expression, explained 43 per cent of the variance in leisure. Constraint from this perspective is seen as the result of social interaction, 'an inherently restrictive process since actions are moulded and modified to fit the patterns of actions by others'. Because the cognitive self is enmeshed in anticipated judgements and evaluations, 'self-objectification typically restrains a more true expression of one's subjective self' (Samdahl, 1988: 29). In Mead's terms, the 'me' restrains the 'I'. On the other hand, 'a unique freedom characterizing the leisure context would be a reduction of interactive role modifications', 'reduced role constraint and reduced self-objectification', which 'should offer an increased opportunity for true self-expression' (1988: 29–30). Samdahl does not consider contexts of interaction where there may be support for the 'I'. Samdahl's results point to self-expression as the critical distinction between anomic free time and engaging leisure experience. Those, especially women, who were able to use leisure for their own self-expression were able to move beyond some of the role constraints of family and gender roles. For Samdahl (1992) leisure is an area where the socially learned role expectations of gender define behaviour, but it can also provide an area for expressions of self which move beyond these expectations. In this study the focus and assumptions are clearly enunciated, individual actors and their interaction within their immediate social milieu of social roles and socialization are the units of analysis and notions of the objective and subjective self provide the explanatory power.

The application of symbolic interaction to women's leisure experiences by Henderson et al. (1989), embedded as it is within a social psychological framework, is rather more implicit, although the logic is similar. In this work, *A Leisure of One's Own*, women are seen to be generally constrained in their lives and in many ways leisure reinforces traditional oppressive gender stereotypes. However, leisure as a form of freedom and self-expression 'could be a means of liberation from restrictive gender roles and social scripts, and thus, a means of empowerment'. The way forward is seen to be through the building through leisure of alternative self-definitions and identities to those developed through the restrictive social roles of wife, mother, housewife and daughter (1989: 8). The structure of the book follows the idea that leisure for women occurs in 'containers', that is, physical and social settings such as the family, the life-span, friendship and community groups. Some of the insights that such a focus produces include: the meaning of leisure to women; gender differences in leisure participation; and particular subjective constraints on women's leisure such as the 'ethic of care' and 'lack of entitlement'. The research interests of the four individual authors of the book provide some empirical evidence for the theoretical focus of the work.

Drawing on the work of Bella (1989), who examined the differences in men's and women's leisure experiences of Christmas, the authors suggest that men and women have different systems of reality, which extend to their subjective leisure experiences. Whereas androcentric views of leisure focus on quantity, activity, achievement and competition, the meaning of leisure to women is more likely to be quality, sociability, relationship and co-operation (Henderson et al., 1989: 53). The research of one of the authors (Shaw, 1985) into the self-defined leisure of 60 married women and their husbands across different daily activities revealed that most of the leisure experienced by the women was during free-time activities associated with social interactional settings and not associated with household tasks. Men, on the other hand, experienced more choice over involvement in household tasks and defined more of these as leisure for them. She concludes that, in the home setting, women's role responsibilities for household labour and for the emotional well-being of the family constrain, not only the time for leisure, but also the perception of leisure experience for women. The solution is not a change of attitude on the part of women, but a change in the constraints produced through gender roles, both in the workforce and in the family (Henderson et al., 1989: 66).

Such differences in the meaning of leisure for the men and women researched are further explored across the life-span through a developmental approach. The ideas of Chodorow (1978) and Gilligan (1982) are explored to show that men's identities from an early age are dependent on their breaking away from the mother and her femininity, resulting in task-focused, achievement orientation. Women's identities, on the other hand, remain within the relational orientation predominant in the mother/daughter dyad. 'These initial differences in childrearing and development are further supported by socialization processes which foster achievement and self-reliance in boys and nurturance and responsibility in girls' (Henderson et al., 1989: 81). When applied to leisure research such as that by Pfeiffer and Davis (1971), this approach showed that women spent more time socializing than men and that this activity increased with age for women. In adolescence, a crucial time in developmental theory for identity formation, Kleiber and Kane (1984) found that girls who exhibited playful, exuberant, self-expressive behaviour in leisure were able to move beyond cultural role prescriptions. They conclude that an individual who is willing to experiment with alternative styles and behaviours in leisure might become more self-actualized as a result. The authors suggest that this illustrates the developmental potential of leisure (Henderson et al., 1989: 75).

Research by two of the authors into women's leisure in friendship and community groups (Bialeschski, 1984; Henderson and Bialeschski, 1987) found that in the 'container' of women-only groups women can experience themselves and their abilities, while in mixed friendship groups men may have a tendency to 'take over'. Women, they claim, can participate and grow from a female environment whether it is a community club, a class, or an informal social gathering: 'women only groups are a way that women may experience recreation and leisure more freely because they are a less role-restricted environment' (Henderson et al., 1989: 103). This was particularly so in women-only outdoor groups where women were able to have a supportive environment while building their outdoor recreation skills (Henderson and Bialeschki, 1986).

Although volunteering has generally been referred to as 'work', Henderson (1983), along with other leisure theorists, such as Stebbins (1982, 1997) who placed voluntarism in the context of 'serious leisure', posits voluntarism as a site for personal fulfilment, identity enhancement and self-expression. Henderson, in her empirical research, found that volunteering provided women with an opportunity to interact with others, help people, express care and concern for others, maintain their personal growth, develop personal skills and to move from the private into the public sphere. At the other extreme, women's solitary activities or 'minute vacations' are suggested as a setting for leisure. Other areas suggested by the authors as 'containers' for women's self-expression and hence empowerment are education and sexual behaviour and intimacy. In Freysinger's (1988) research on the experience of leisure in adulthood, for example, a divorced mother of a teenager commented on her art classes as leisure: 'I've taken art classes, drawing, painting, which have helped me in my work but have also been a wonderful expression outlet. A lot of it is leisure and recreation but a lot of them have a dual function' (Freysinger, 1988: 132, quoted in Henderson et al., 1989: 111).

A balance to this optimistic look at some of the settings in which women can develop identities that go beyond their gender roles and socialization, and hence offer personal empowerment, is given in the penultimate chapter of *A Leisure of One's Own* (Henderson et al., 1989), entitled 'Constraints on women's leisure'. These restraints refer chiefly to subjective constraints such as 'the ethic of care' and 'lack of entitlement'. The 'ethic of care' is based on Gilligan's (1982) description as an activity of relationship, of seeing and responding to need, of taking care of the world by sustaining the web of connection so that no one is left alone. However, in our society where personal autonomy and maturity have been equated with individuation and individual achievement, this concern is often construed as a weakness rather than a strength. For a woman, especially in the family, taking care of others usually takes priority, limiting her 'freedom to' and 'freedom from' and hence her leisure. The concomitant notion is 'lack of entitlement', which as well as commitment to the 'ethic of care' also includes women's sense that they are inferior and do not deserve to have leisure. 'Leisure thus is constrained by psychological and social attitudes or guilt feelings that arise when a woman allows herself to "indulge" in leisure' (Henderson et al., 1989: 124). The book concludes that women must take an active role in forming their own futures through effort at both the micro- and macro-levels of society. The book itself has explicated both the constraints and opportunities that individual women (that is, white, middle-class women) have through leisure to take part in their own empowerment. In order to do so, the individual woman 'needs to be freed from constraints imposed by socialized roles to pursue experiences that are rewarding, self-defining and enjoyable' (Henderson et al., 1989: 151).

Nevertheless, in my opinion, socialization through gender roles as the constraining factor in women's lives and women's leisure remains an inadequate explanation for the position of women. Socialization needs to be seen as a product of the structural and cultural constraints placed on women's lives through patriarchal relationships of power which enable restrictive social norms that women internalize. In the update of the work (Henderson et al., 1996), more explicit attention is given to issues of power, in the notion of women's empowerment through leisure. While empowerment at an individual level through alternative identities which go beyond gender roles recognizes the agency of the individual, in the midst of personal constraints, it does nothing to address gender power relationships in the wider society, both material and ideological, which impact on the 'containers' the authors discuss. This work is grounded in the empirical studies on which it is based with the general exclusion of women other than those who are white and middle class, so that the empirical generalizations it produces cannot be assumed to apply to all women. For some women the space that they can make for any sense of 'I' may be extremely limited, due to their relatively powerless political position (see Yeatman, 1993, for a discussion of this position). Nevertheless, I maintain that all women, even those excluded from political processes and defined by the powerful as 'other' and 'inferior', do have an active 'I' with the ability at least to critique and hence resist such definition (for a discussion of poststructuralist, feminist philosophical debates in this area, see Nicholson, 1995b). My own preference is for a conceptualization of women as 'social subjects able to speak and act against domination' (Fraser, 1995: 160). Women, then, are able to resist and this leads on to a notion of leisure as resistance for women and other relatively powerless groups. It recognizes the weight of many different sources of social, cultural and institutional power against which they are practising the relative freedom of leisure. In other articles, Freysinger (Freysinger and Flannery, 1992) and Shaw (1994), while yet adhering to a social psychological perspective, use the term resistance in the sense that I mean it here.

In the British context, a book entitled *Relative Freedoms* (Wimbush and Talbot, 1988) suggests the freedoms provided by the sphere of leisure can result in greater autonomy for women, but are still constrained by powerful societal structures such as patriarchy, class, race, age and ethnicity. As the authors tell us:

> Moreover, women's time and choices are closely circumscribed, primarily by their gender, but also by their age, ethnic origin and class; these in turn shape their employment status, income levels and household circumstances. The autonomy which women have to enjoy personal leisure is relative to these overarching structures. Leisure is thus one of women's 'relative freedoms'. (Wimbush and Talbot, 1988: xiv)

Some of the authors included in the book, such as Deem, Green and Woodward, have been discussed in the previous chapter as their analyses draw more heavily on macroanalysis and the constraints on women's leisure produced by patriarchal structures. Others, however, posit the dialectic between women's agency and the constraints of patriarchy to show that women's leisure can enhance the self and challenge definitions of the feminine propagated through patriarchal gender power relationships. For example, Wimbush's study (Chapter 5) of young mothers showed how women whose time, money and mobility are constrained and fragmented by the routines and busy timetables of childcare are able to carve out spaces for themselves with other women who understood their situation and provided support and solidarity away from the domestic sphere. Dixey's study (Chapter 7) found that bingo provided a space for sociability and support for older working-class women: 'Many of the elderly women would arrive up to two hours before the afternoon session started, to eat, talk, knit, read or play cards.' The editors comment:

> 'Being safe' and comfortable in a public space is unusual for women, and bingo is one context which provides it. What is more, women as the consumer group control and regulate the social interaction within the bingo club – 'bingo is an opportunity which women have seized' – and bingo players have reconstructed a leisure activity which subverts the complex of constraints which operate on working class women. (Wimbush and Talbot, 1988: 88)

Similarly, Griffiths found in her study of young women and dance that women dancing with and for each other could be an open celebration of sensuality in a relatively safe context. Yet, as the editors point out, the disco dance competitions in which the girls participated 'also reify the stereotyped images of femininity which binds girls' behaviour and expectations' (Wimbush and Talbot, 1988: 88). In this work, the spectre of patriarchy looms large in the dialectic between women's freedom and autonomy in leisure and the constraints upon them. As the editors conclude, this work has given 'some insights into the *meanings and interactions* surrounding women's leisure in patriarchal society' (1988: 180; original emphasis).

At an empirical level, both of these feminist works show how women use leisure space to resist male definitions of women as wives, mothers, housewives and to enlarge their sense of self. At a theoretical level, the British book acknowledges the constraints imposed on women's sense of self and legitimate leisure activity by patriarchal structures and ideologies, whereas the American book, with its social psychological underpinning, focuses rather on women's own subjective attitudes and constraints within their socialized roles.

In the context of freedom and constraint in women's leisure, my own work also draws upon the concepts of symbolic interaction to examine how leisure may increase women's autonomy in lives which are constrained by patriarchal structures and cultural patrism. My theoretical analysis, however, focuses more directly on power at both individual and societal levels through Foucault's notions of discourse, power, subjectivity and resistance. In an early article with Stephen Wearing (Wearing and Wearing, 1988), we argued firstly that conceptualizing leisure as experience, rather than as time and/or activity, allowed for inclusion in the concept itself of the notions of freedom and constraint. Secondly, in applying Marxist, radical and socialist feminist theories to women's leisure, where power from both class and gender is top-down and seen to repress, oppress and control women, we could see little room for women to experience leisure. Rather we employed Foucault's notion of power in which there is the possibility for productivity and resistance as well as surveillance and control, subversion, negotiation and transformation at an individual as well as at the group and societal level. In a later paper (Wearing and Wearing, 1992), we argued that in the face of the current extensive commodification of leisure which tends to mass produce the experience of leisure and override its potential for the expression of individual identity there remains some purchase in Mead's concepts of the 'me' and the 'I'. We proposed that 'leisure in its decom-modified form offers possibilities for individual synthesis of identity which incorporates both the core of the individual (the "I") and the core of his/her communal culture (the "me") as represented by conflicting discourses on leisure' (Wearing and Wearing, 1992: 10). In conjunction with a view of power which recognizes the possibilities of resistance and negates power as a zero-sum game in which men always win, leisure space offers women room to move. The space created by contradictory discourses can be seen as an area for women where some inroads can be made into the constrain-ing powers of patriarchal structures and the attitudes of patrism.

In my own research I attempted to marry Foucault's ideas on power, sub-jectivity, discourse and resistance with the freedom and constraint implicit in interactionist theory. In Foucault, people are never just victims – they are free subjects with an ever-present possibility of alternatives through resist-ances. Individuals are encouraged not to *discover* who they are but to *refuse* what they are and to imagine and approach what they could be (Foucault, 1983). By resistance, he means the struggle against the form of power which pervades everyday life and constitutes individuals as subjects in the sense of being subject to somebody by control and dependence and subject to their own identity by a conscience or self-knowledge (Foucault, 1983). Gender in this notion can take many forms within the individual, within the life-cycle and between women. Contradictory discourses and subjectivities and oppositional positions of the relatively powerless in society allow space for resistance to dominant ways of thinking and speaking, surveillance and normalization (Wearing, 1992a: 326).

In three of my own empirical studies this approach produced insights into leisure as a site of contesting discourse and power relationships where there was room to challenge traditional stereotypes of passive, conforming, other-directed feminine subjectivities. The first study (Wearing, 1990a and 1990b) concerned the leisure of mothers of first babies. For the 30 middle-class and 30 working-class mothers interviewed, ideas and experiences of leisure both reinforced the identity of 'mother' and provided a sphere for resistance. Leisure for most of these mothers was family centred in activities such as resting, visiting friends and relatives, shopping, cooking, crafts, walking, gardening, aerobics, tennis, playing a musical instrument, mother's group, playing with the baby and holidays. Nevertheless, in this study a person's right to leisure is used by mothers to justify time and space for themselves. Access to an alternative discourse on leisure enabled some mothers to challenge the dominant selfless discourse on motherhood. As one mother put it: 'All people have a right to leisure and mothers are people, so they have a right to leisure.' This discourse gives permission for mothers to take time and space for themselves and to question their total responsibility for childcare. One mother asked: 'It takes two to make a baby, why is it one who always has to look after it?' Women in the study who were acting upon the leisure discourse which challenged total time commitment to selfless motherhood pursued activities as varied as horse-riding, oboe playing and surfboard riding, which conferred an identity outside that of motherhood. They used various strategies, including father's care of the baby for periods of time, sharing care with other mothers, friends or relatives and reduced input into housework and cooking, to resist the dominant discourse on motherhood. Thus they made spaces for themselves over which they had some autonomy to pursue leisure activities or non-activities, which were just for themselves and did not need to include the family. This study showed that where mothers are able to create time and space for themselves over which they have control to include or exclude whom they wish and in which they can pursue activities of their own choice, their mental health is significantly better (Wearing, 1990b).

A second study (Wearing, 1992a) explored the meanings attached to their leisure experiences in relation to their construction of gender identity, by a small sample (13 women, 7 men) of first-year students in two universities in Sydney. In one university the students had access to gender content in their first-year curriculum, in the other they did not. The data which emerged from the focus groups, individual interviews and diaries revealed a continuum from traditional to non-traditional male and female leisure experiences and subjectivities, with some elements of traditional stereotypes in all cases and varying degrees of challenge or resistance. Women and men with access to an alternative feminist discourse which encourages autonomy and individuality in leisure as well as in other areas of their lives had greater scope for challenging traditional femininity and masculinity.

For example, Jemma resists the dominant discourse on femininity. Leisure for her is doing something that she really wants to do, gets a lot of pleasure from and really enjoys, that is, competitive beach volley ball and the gym and beach training that goes with it. It means 'making a conscious effort, thinking you're going to make that time solely for yourself, for your own pleasure'. In spite of some ambivalence produced by the conflict between her athleticism and 'floating, wispy, femininity', Jemma has been able to move beyond traditional stereotypes and create a subjectivity which is forceful yet sensitive and shows a high degree of autonomy. She says of herself:

I am a strong, healthy, vibrant woman; I am happiest when my physical and mental faculties are utilized; I am responsible; I am always trying to understand how and why things are or aren't; I am striving for an academic career; I am striving for optimum performance in my sport; I am fortunate in that my friends and family support me . . . Leisure has provided me with the energy and confidence to pursue and live these choices and to express myself. (Wearing, 1992a: 332)

By focusing on leisure as an area where 'freedom' includes an opportunity for individual self-expression (Mead's 'I') within the constraints or encouragement of 'significant others' (family and friends), 'reference groups' and 'generalized other' or 'discourses' (Mead's 'me'), this research demonstrated that for some women resistance to the domination inherent in traditional passive, submissive feminine stereotypes is possible. Some autonomy of subjectivity or identity is possible. I would claim that the incorporation in this research of the microsocial concepts of Mead's 'I' and 'me' and poststructural concepts of subjectivity, resistance and power within a macrosocial framework of gender power allows for leisure to be seen as a process in which there is a creative balance between agency and structure, freedom and constraint (see Rojek, 1989).

In many senses leisure is a legitimate sphere for play, for spontaneity of action, for individuality, for the willing suspension of the rigours and beliefs of our everyday existences, for the expansion of the 'I' in spite of constraints which can be physical and mental as well as those of gender, class, age, race and ethnicity. In a third study of leisure and health amongst men and women over 55, I was able to show how leisure can act as a resisting force to dominant, constraining discourses on ageing (Wearing, 1995). In my own follow-up interviews with 39 of the 272 men and women over 55 surveyed in Sydney, I found some outstanding instances of resistant leisure behaviour amongst those with a high level of perceived general health. These included men as well as women. In this context I instance two women in vastly different circumstances who, through leisure, were able to expand the 'I' beyond gender and age constraints in one instance, and gender, age, class and disability constraints in the other.

Mrs Newton is a woman with many interests. She and her husband both retired a few years ago and are now in their early seventies. She has many interests. She enjoys gardening, she goes folk dancing once a week, she attends art class once a week and she is an active voluntary worker for a number of community organizations. She spends time with her children and grandchildren and shares her husband's interests in a number of social organizations. However, one of her main interests is bushwalking. She and a group of other women go bushwalking one day each week (six to eight hours), and a few times each year they undertake an extended walk over three to four days. As a highlight, over the last few years she has organized and led her group on 15-day treks in Nepal, Kashmir and the Himalayas, which were very successful. In her words, leisure for her age group is 'a chance to do things we didn't have a chance to do when we had families or work'.

Mrs Grant is aged 81. She is an invalid, having suffered a severe stroke several years ago. She lives in a bed-sitter unit rented from the Housing Commission in the Blacktown area. Her right side is paralysed, she walks with much difficulty and can barely look after herself, but her speech is un-affected. The living area is very bare and spartan. Chairs and other furni-ture are placed for convenience of movement. She is up and dressed each day, but spends much time resting on her bed which is placed facing the front door, so that she can see and talk to any callers.

She makes every effort to keep herself active and busy. Twice a week she goes to the Sydney City Mission activity centre for elderly people (four hours). A bus comes to pick her up. Once a week she goes to bingo at another senior citizens' club. Every few weeks she visits a friend in a nearby suburb; she has to take public transport to get there. At home she reads books which she borrows from the senior citizens' library (20–30 hours) and watches TV (20 hours). One or two neighbours come by several times each day 'to see if I'm all right'. Her daughter and family live interstate. Finan-cially, her resources are very limited. She would love to visit her family in Victoria but 'I can't afford it – a lot of my income has to be spent on med-icines'.

In spite of her material and physical constraints, her attitude to life is positive. She agrees strongly with the statements 'I don't mind getting older' and 'I look forward to getting older' and agrees mildly with the statements 'I am satisfied with my life', 'I feel better now than I ever have before', 'In the future I expect to have better health than other people I know' and 'Ac-cording to the doctors I've seen my health is now excellent'.

In absolute terms Mrs Grant is very constrained by material and physical resources, compared with Mrs Newton. However, within these constraints she resists in the sense of carving out a space for herself which gives her satisfaction. Hers is a triumph of spirit of no less magnitude than Mrs Newton's – indeed, perhaps it is greater.

Women's 'I' and 'Me'

My examination of the contribution to an understanding of the freedom and constraint in women's leisure made by concepts made available through interactionist theory brings us back once more to the perennial sociological debate concerning agency and structure. It is my opinion that symbolic interaction is most useful when its microsocial analyses of indi-vidual perceptions and negotiations of identity are placed within a macrosocial framework which acknowledges forces of power in wider society which structure social positions and ideas of legitimacy. Poststruc-turalist feminist theorists attempt to do this by challenging the very notion of a unified autonomous self, an inner fixed identity. This, they say, could very well be a male construction which, for women, is always 'other' to and inferior to masculine selves. Instead they posit a multiplicity of selves, open to change and 'becoming' with shifts in political and cultural discourses.

For example, Butler (1990) denies the essential, rational 'I' constructed by male theorists and the binary opposition of the objective and subjective concepts of the self. For her the self is a political construct and there are many subjectivities, many 'I's. She maintains subjectivity is a process of 'becoming' through repeated performative acts. She argues that gender is not a cultural inscription written on sexed bodies but a process through repeated performative acts which are culturally discursively constructed. She thus opens up possibilities for the self to grow and enlarge. This self may or may not conform to one's socially prescribed identity and may include a multiplicity of subjectivities. Subjectivities are politically constructed and possibilities exist for the subversion of the sex/gender dichotomy through the proliferation of cultural/discursive gender behaviours. In poststructuralist thought the subject is not a rational whole but a changing contradictory site, thus making possible a new politics of identity that can encompass gender, race, class and sexuality without a hierarchy of causation or political action. Butler's work remains ambiguous concerning the extent to which individuals have the ability to critique their own positions and thus differentiate positive from negative change and so move on from performative acts which are merely a repetition of previous ones. Without a notion of some form of individual agency, which I refer to as an 'I', it is difficult to see how relatively powerless women can make positive changes to their conceptions of themselves. While Butler's work holds out a hope for women to move beyond definition of the self which has been discursively constructed within dominant discourses, it remains somewhat deterministic (see Benhabib et al., 1995, for a more detailed discussion of this issue).

Writing with women's leisure in mind, McRobbie points out:

> Feminist postmodernism does not eliminate the subject or the self but finds it in operation as a series of bit parts in the concrete field of social relations. Politics must therefore imply subjectivities in process, interacting and debating
> . . .
> This might mean living with fragmentation, with the reality of inventing the self rather than endlessly searching for the self. (McRobbie, 1993: 138, 140)

McRobbie is suggesting that the 'real me' may, in fact, be a product of dominant discursive definitions of what it is to be a woman. She, along with other poststructural feminist writers, wishes to deconstruct such a self and open up possibilities for women to move outside these boundaries. Bock and James claim that we do not know at this time of any essence of woman which is independent of their past and present conditions and of their definition by others as being in some way inferior (1992: 6). I think these theorists, in effect, are enlarging the possibilities for Mead's 'me' beyond role prescriptions and socialization, so it is a step in a very positive direction for women. I, however, would like to ask the question raised by Kellner (1992): 'In postmodern conditions do we as individuals really dissolve into many droplets like oil on water?' In challenging the notion of the fixed and stable inner identity prevalent in modernity, poststructuralists are in danger of going to the other extreme, that is, deconstructing a sense of self, so that moment by moment it changes as it comes into contact with conflicting discourses. Thus, once again, as in Marxist analysis, it becomes the object of determination through powerful social forces. Foucault's idea (1983) of refusing what we are told we are and reaching towards what we could be remains for women an attractive alternative to an endless search for a 'real me' which in all probability has been prescribed by patriarchal notions of the 'feminine'. But the question remains, 'Who does this refusing and reaching?' In Giddens's terms (1984, 1991) human agency is based on the idea that an individual could always act otherwise, thus suggesting an 'I' who acts rather than merely reacts to societal inputs. Others who are grappling with the contradictions between the decentred, fragmented, multiple selves and subjectivities of postmodernity, and interactionist and phenomenological notions of self and identity, see, as I do, the possibilities of placing Mead's self in the context of poststructuralism and postmodernism. In their construction of a 'postmodern interactionism', for example, Jagtenberg and McKie claim that the reflexive self is able to move beyond prior definitions (1997: 149).

Nor do all poststructural feminists accept a purely discursively constructed subjectivity. Weedon (1987: 106) claims that in the battle for subjectivity and the supremacy of particular versions of meaning of which it is part, the individual is not merely the passive site of discursive struggle: 'The individual who has a memory and an already discursively constructed sense of identity may resist particular interpellations of or produce new versions of meaning from the conflicts and contradictions between existing discourses.' Smith (1988) argues for women to be conceptualized as active creative subjects rather than as the passive recipients of either structural forces or constraining discourses. These arguments suggest a cumulative 'I', not necessarily one that is rational, but one that reflects some spontaneity, originality and creativity. In any case, in order for individuals to grow and change, some sense of agency seems necessary. The 'I' that I retain from symbolic interactionism is a growing and changing one, a part of the self that retains some sense of agency, without being fixed. The present 'I' is a cumulative synthesis of past and present 'selves' which have been and are being constructed in the context of current discourses, with some reflexive ability to move in new directions.

In the light of poststructural feminist insights, James's (1952) concepts of the self retain some purchase, in spite of its male authorship. First, his concept includes embodied, emotional and spiritual dimensions as well as the rational and cognitive which came to be the principal components of Mead's and the social psychologists' development of the subjective self.

Secondly, his concept of the 'I' does not imply an inner fixed sense of identity, but a constantly changing sense of self which retains some continuity by its remembrance and recognition of past thoughts, feelings and experiences which reverberate with the current ones. Thus his 'self' retains some sense of agency and subjectivity and also the ability to change with changing experiences. Here again, however, if we are to retain a critical feminist analysis, we need to place such selves within a society which is politically gendered, as well as being subject to the powerful forces of race, colour, ethnicity, age and sexual orientation.

Conclusion

In this chapter I have examined some basic concepts of symbolic interaction theory, such as Mead's 'I' and 'me' and the meanings that individuals construct for themselves from societal input through those with whom they interact. I have suggested that these ideas underpin concepts of leisure which emphasize the personal experience of leisure and the freedom and constraint implicit in such experiences. Leisure theory owes a debt to Kelly for his ongoing theorization of leisure which incorporates these ideas. Feminist researchers, especially those who adopt social psychological approaches, have drawn on these ideas to research predominantly white, middle-class women's leisure as individual experience with a variety of meanings for women. The constraints of gender for the women researched have been shown to limit such experience. Nevertheless, the relative freedom of leisure has also opened up avenues for women to make some inroads into male definitions of what women are and should be. The space that leisure provides for these women offers the possibility of enlargement of self, however that self is theorized.

One of the limitations of symbolic interaction theory has been its reliance on social roles and socialization as the means by which society becomes part of the self. Lack of the recognition and critique of power differentials in wider society and, in particular, gender power differentials, in the construction and maintenance of these roles has tended to depoliticize this theoretical approach. Some insights from poststructuralist and feminist theory have been suggested to redress this balance, but not to the extent that the agency of the cumulative 'I' of interactionist theory is lost.

By concentrating on Mead and James, there is an important strand of interactionism which I have not addressed in this chapter, but which has something to add to our ideas about the self, and freedom and constraint in leisure. I refer to the ideas of Goffman (1967, 1969) whose insights into the interaction between individuals, their presentation of selves in everyday life and cultural constraints are as relevant and forward thinking today as they were when he wrote in the 1960s. They have been taken up more in the area of tourism than of leisure generally, and I cannot conclude this chapter without some reference to the insights they have produced. An early work by Cohen and Taylor (1976), for example, drew on Goffman's concern with the presentation of self in everyday life to argue that holidays are culturally sanctioned escape routes for Western *man*. One of the problems for modern *man*, they say, is to establish identity, a sense of personal individuality in the face of large anomic forces of a technological world. Holidays provide a free area, a mental and physical escape from the most immediate reality of pressures of the technological society. Thus holidays provide scope for the nurturance and cultivation of human identity. Cohen and Taylor argue that overseas holidays are structurally similar to leisure because one of their chief purposes is identity establishment and the cultivation of one's self-consciousness. The tourist, they claim, uses all aspects of *his* holiday for the manipulation of *his* well-being.These authors, like most male authors of the time, generalized from the white, middle-class male experience to the experience of all and did not recognize the power differentials between tourist and host culture, which has often resulted in cultural costs for the hosts. Nevertheless, they present the possibility of cross-cultural transformations of the self through tourism, which in some recent tourist enterprises has extended to conscious attempts to destabilize Eurocentric cultural domination and to institute a more democratized tourism. Host communities themselves have taken part in the construction and operation of such enterprises, and profits are then fed back into the local community (see Wearing and Wearing, 1996b and 1996c, for more details concerning some of these enterprises). The selves of host cultures under these circumstances expand, not only by renewed reference to their traditional heritage, but also through reference to cultures other than their own in a situation of power relationships in which they have a greater stake.

One author who has attempted to go beyond previous sociological analyses to open out the possibilities through tourism of widening culturally constructed identities, including gender, is MacCannell. He draws on Goffman's interactionism to emphasize the need for a sociology of interaction in conjunction with elements of deconstruction to 'gain access to the realm of contingency and determinism, and especially resistance to and struggles against [cultural] determinism' (MacCannell, 1992: 3). MacCannell sees the movement of peoples both to and from the Western world, through tourism, as an opportunity to form hybrid cultures which will be a precondition for inventiveness in creating subjectivities which resist cultural constraints. He claims that the neo-nomads of tourism in the postmodern era cross cultural boundaries, not as invaders, but as imaginative travellers who benefit from displaced self-understanding and the freedom to go beyond the limits that frontiers present. The 'true heroes ' of tourism, he claims, are those who know that 'their future will be made of dialogue with their fellow travelers and those they meet along the way'. His analysis, like mine, is grounded in 'human interactions' (1992: 7). The idea of hybrid subjectivities which move beyond the cultural constraints of gendered identities is as applicable to leisure spaces generally as it is to tourism. For women, it offers a way out of passive and dependent femininities while retaining what is valuable to them of traditional prescriptions. For men, the potential to move beyond aggressive competitive masculinities based on female inferiority may also be there. MacCannell suggests that rather than looking at face-to-face interactions for signs of oppression, we should be looking for 'creative opportunities to undo oppressive interactions' and to demonstrate our regard for the difference of the other (1992: 273). He gives several examples of such interactions between men and women. In Chapter 6, I argue that interaction between men and women in democratized leisure spaces may allow this to happen. In MacCannell's terms, the face-to-face interactions of tourists and hosts may provide some space for individuals to challenge the way culturally specific discourses construct the 'I' and 'you' of their culture in opposition to the 'he' of 'other' inferiorized ethnic cultures (1992: 125). In my terms, the interaction between men and women in the relative freedom of leisure spaces, may allow men to challenge and move beyond the 'I' and 'you' of their cultural construction of masculinity as superior and the 'she' of the 'other' as inferiorized femininities. It may then allow women space to move beyond oppressive interactions to self-enhancing ones. (For a more explicit application of these ideas in relation to tourism, see Wearing and Wearing, 1996a and 1996b.)

By concentrating on the micro-politics of interactionist theory in conjunction with some insights on power from poststructuralism, it has been shown in this chapter that interactions in leisure spaces have the potential to break down gendered cultural prescriptions, at least for some women. Empirical evidence supports this view for women who are privileged in many ways, that is, white, middle-class women. It has been tempting for the researchers in this area to universalize to all women. The theory itself has yet to be tested with women who do not belong to dominant groups. In allowing for individual difference and in positing an 'I' which is cumulative and reflexive, the theory does have the potential, at least, for a variety of women to resist the cross-cutting cultural impact of class, colour, race and ethnicity in a variety of relationships of power. No woman is entirely powerless. In the view being constructed here, leisure spaces provide relative freedom for women to move beyond situations in which power is a zero-sum game where men always appear superior and women inferior, in which men always dominate and women are subordinate and in which all women appear as the victims of structural and/or discursive oppression.

In the following chapter we move away again from the intensely personal scenarios of interactionism to the cultures and subcultures within which leisure and the spaces for leisure are experienced.

4

Hegemonic Struggles in Leisure Spaces: Cultural Studies

By studying leisure practices in the context of culture or 'the whole way of life' of people, cultural studies have added a dimension to the understanding of leisure which was not addressed by the uncritical theories of functionalism or the political/economic focus of Marxism. Cultural theories with their bases in Gramsci's civil society and cultural hegemony, rather than in ideological superstructure and economic infrastructure, have broadened the context of leisure to include the meaning-making institutions of wider society such as mass media, film, art, religion, politics, rituals, literature and rites of passage, as well as the meanings of leisure experiences for groups and individuals. Critical cultural studies have been most interested in how groups with the least power practically develop their own meanings of, and uses for cultural products, in fun, in resistance, or to articulate their own identity (During, 1993: 7). Feminists who write in this vein about girls' and women's leisure experiences and leisure spaces show how this is so for them. In this chapter, initially I outline some of the theoretical bases and development of cultural studies. Secondly, I examine some studies of leisure from this perspective. Thirdly, I explore the contribution that these studies may make to understanding gendered aspects of leisure, especially for women and girls.

Culture and Hegemony

When we think of culture we probably think of various ideas such as: high culture, that is, art, music, theatre, dance; popular culture such as football, surfing, barbecues, gambling, drinking, dress and style; popular traditions such as Christmas and Easter; or perhaps the culture of traditional groups such as the American Indian or the Australian Aboriginal people. All of these can be included in a formal definition of *culture*. Raymond Williams, a British sociologist who has been one of the key writers in this area, defines culture as:

(i) a general process of intellectual, spiritual and aesthetic development from the eighteenth century

(ii) a particular way of life, whether of a people, a period, a group, or humanity in general

(iii) the works and practices of intellectual and especially artistic activity. (1983: 90)

Culture, then, is both a macrosocial and a microsocial concept. At the macrosocial level it is a sphere which can be distinguished from the political and economic, but which is interrelated with them and changes as they change. At the microsocial level it encompasses the meanings that individuals give to symbols and everyday practices. The cultural studies approach to society blurs the Marxist distinction between the economic or material base of society (the emphasis on the means of production) and the ideological superstructure (ideas which propagate the interests of the powerful, the owners of the means of production). Rather it studies the relations between elements in a whole way of life, that is, the forms and relations of general social life in a field of mutually if also unevenly determining forces.

Economic determinism gives way to more general struggles over meanings and practices which are in process historically and across contemporary society. *Ideology*, with its emphasis on false consciousness, obscuring the reality of the relations of production which exploits the worker, gives way to Gramsci's (1985) more general term, *hegemony*. The hegemony of a political class meant for Gramsci that that class had succeeded in having its moral, political and cultural values accepted as applicable to all. Thus in civil society the agreement of the majority is achieved and this consensus is expressed through the so-called organs of public opinion, that is, newspapers, other media and associations.

Hegemony, then, is the control of consciousness by cultural dominance through the institutions of society. *Power* and *privilege* are maintained through cultural hegemony, but struggles over hegemonic control are inevitable. Subcultures are often formed which challenge dominant cultural forms. And, as Clarke and Critcher point out, leisure is integral to the struggle for hegemony. It is one of the areas of social life in which 'the cultural conflict over meanings, views of the world and social habits has been fought' and in which efforts have been made 'to repress and exclude "undesirable" uses of free time and . . . to replace them with leisure patterns which are civilising and profitable' (1985: 228).

Cultural Studies

The term cultural studies today encompasses a vast range of interdisciplinary theories and methods. Its emergence in post-war Britain in the 1950s had a foundation in the literary criticism of F.R. Leavis. Leavis wanted to use the educational system to distribute 'cultural capital' through literary knowledge and appreciation. He was concerned, however, with the 'great tradition' of English literature which developed the moral sensibilities of readers (e.g. Austen, George Eliot, James and Conrad), rather than so-called 'mass culture'. As developed by Hoggart and Williams, who were both involved in workers' education and who themselves came from working-class families, cultural studies lost its elitist focus. They adopted a perspective that argued that it is at the level of individual life that the cultural effects of social inequality are most apparent. With the establishment by Hoggart in 1964 of the Centre for Contemporary Cultural Studies (CCCS) in Birmingham, an intellectual and political tradition began which gradually expanded from the Marxist tradition of class analysis to incorporate ideas from semiotics, feminist and poststructuralist and postcolonialist theories. These have led to more dynamic and complex theoretical analyses which show how cultural products may be combined with new elements to produce different effects in different situations (During, 1993: 7).

Categorization by Stuart Hall (Hall and Jefferson, 1976) into dominant cultures, subcultures and counter-cultures provided a theoretical underpinning for early studies which emanated from the CCCS and were concerned with the leisure of post-war working-class youth. The *dominant culture* is perceived as that of the middle class, suited to production and profit making and emphasizing the work ethic, private ownership and consumption, individual achievement and competition, future rewards and educated taste. Dominant culture refers to the culture of the most powerful group in society. Its view of society, unless challenged, will stand as the most natural, all-embracing, universal culture. Working-class culture, which emphasizes solidarity, collective action, mass consumption and mass culture is seen as *subordinate culture*. *Subcultures* are sub-sets, smaller, more localized and differentiated structures within one or other of the larger networks. The post-war youth subcultures studied by the CCCS, such as the Teddy boys, the skinheads and the mods, focused around certain activities, values, material artefacts and territorial spaces used in leisure contexts to resist the dominant culture. Attempts at control by the powerful generally brought violent reaction (see Hall and Jefferson, 1976). *Counter-cultures* are the more diffuse, middle-class attempts to explore 'alternative institutions' to the central institutions of the dominant culture: new patterns of living, of family life, of work, of leisure. The 'hippy' cultures of the 1960s, the human rights, feminist and gay movements of the 1970s and the peace and environmental movements of the 1980s exemplify Hall's concept of counter-cultures.

This form of cultural analysis was heavily based on class power and initially assumed male experiences to be universal – girls and women were invisible. Angela McRobbie's work (1978) with working-class girls began to redress the balance and paved the way for issues of gender power relationships to be included. As the recognition and celebration of 'other' cultures has occurred, Hall's emphasis on the dominance of a white, Eurocentric dominant middle-class culture has also been diffused (see Wallace, 1993). MacCannell has introduced the term 'hybrid' cultures to signify new cultural forms which are being constructed as globalization blurs territorial boundaries between specific cultures (1992: 2). Nevertheless the idea of the leisure styles of subcultures as resistance to dominant cultures and the part of leisure activities, artefacts, music, art, dance, rituals and spaces in hegemonic struggles over meanings and values remains a strength of cultural studies analyses. Poststructuralist concern with the power of representation to control cultural images has been incorporated into cultural studies, so that much attention has been given in cultural studies to aural and visual media as well as to written texts.

In this chapter it is impossible to cover the vast area of cultural studies which has moved from its position within sociology to become a discipline in its own right. My concern here is with the contribution that cultural studies perspectives have made to leisure studies and, in particular, to feminist theorizing and analyses of leisure. First, I look at cultural studies of leisure spaces which demonstrate male dominance of such spaces and female resistance to this domination. Secondly, I look at the hegemonic struggle within the media, in particular magazines and television, over images of girls and women which subordinate or liberate them. Thirdly, sport as a cultural arena is examined. Finally, I assess the contribution that cultural studies have made to an understanding of gendered aspects of leisure for men and women.

Cultural Studies and Leisure Spaces

Space for leisure has long been an important aspect of the leisure experience. Physical spaces away from the site of everyday tasks have provided release and enjoyment for labourers since the industrial revolution. Such spaces enabled them time out, so that they could return to their labours refreshed and ready for further labour. Thus they encouraged conformity to the dominant culture of capitalist society. However, these spaces were also spaces for resistance to domination.

Efforts to control and restrain the leisure activities of the working classes at fairs and festivals by 'magistrates, millowners and Methodists' are documented in Thompson's *The Making of the English Working Class* (1980). The working man's leisure was seen as a distinct threat to developing capitalism in the nineteenth century. Leisure for labourers did, in fact, provide a space for resistance. For example, for the Derby framework knitters in 1845, the Shrovetide games holiday provided the opportunity for knitters from the region to gather to project a union to resist serious abatements in their earnings (Yeo and Yeo, 1981: 150). Wilson (1988) also points to the political potential for resistance through the use of leisure spaces. The home, friends and street gatherings, he claims, have long been spaces in which workers have been able to express values, ideas, projects and demands which do not conform to dominant social interests. In our own time we have the use of public spaces such as streets and parks in leisure time for demonstrations focused on the Vietnam War, Aboriginal land rights, gay rights, women's rights, environmental and peace issues. Cultural studies which have examined leisure spaces as relatively 'free places' where some of the rules of dominant culture are relaxed, reversed or resisted have generally documented the advantages of such spaces for men.

Fiske, for example, looks at the beach and the pub in the Australian context as such spaces. Urban beaches such as Manly and Bondi, says Fiske (Fiske et al., 1987), represent the Australian combination of the contradictions between free, natural, tough nature and urbanized culture and also the civilized/primitive and spiritual/physical contradictory paradigms. As the clothes of culture are shed on approaching the beach, so are some of the constraints of artificially constructed urban society. The beach is symbolic of freedom and challenge to daily work lives – a free space. However it is also a domain reached by the fingers of social control and the dominant culture. Social control is symbolized in the notices (e.g. no dogs, horses or vehicles allowed), flags, beach inspectors, surf lifeguards and designated areas for board riders, body surfers, and so on. Dominant culture is represented by jogging, walking, family groups, male gaze and commodified props, such as Bolle sunglasses and the latest swimwear. Its place is anomalous, a bridge between the city (culture) and the sea (nature), so it is also a place of challenge or resistance. It is a place where youth skylarking, topless and nude bathing are permitted and the pleasures of the senses and of the body accentuated. The freedom of the here and now opposes the disciplines of family, marriage and work. 'Society and its institutions exert a control that the pleasure of the senses resists' (Fiske et al., 1987: 71). Even topless and nude bathing, in this context, is seen primarily to be a source of pleasure for both sexes:

> Nude bathing is defiantly non-sexist; bodies are understood not as attractive for others, but as sources of pleasure for their owners. The topless sunbaker ignores or even challenges the male gaze (and wins when the man averts his eyes or pretends not to look). Shedding clothes and shedding culture deny the male role of looking and the female of being looked at. (Fiske et al., 1987: 63)

Fiske's analysis alerts us to the possibilities of such spaces for pleasurable leisure use as well as for reinforcement of and resistance to cultural control. However, the beach and its culture is presented as a leisure space of pleasure, control and resistance for men and women alike. There is no gender analysis here: the male experience is assumed to be equally applicable to males and females.

Yet, even a cursory glance at any one of Sydney's urban beaches reveals the territorial dominance of the surfboard riders. Apart from the specific area between the flags for body surfers, the best parts of the beach, in terms of the best waves, are occupied by surfboards and their male riders, and any non-board rider, incompetent rider or female rider who dares to enter this territory is immediately subjected to verbal and physical aggression. More detailed analyses of the surfing subculture (see Pearson, 1979; Young, 1994) show how, apart from a brief period in the early 1970s when women and gay men were admitted, the culture has become increasingly, competitive, aggressive and commodified. A recent analysis of the surfing magazine *Tracks* and surfing films over 25 years demonstrates the erosion of the initial resistance of the subculture to the traditional surf life-saving culture and the re-establishment of a hegemonic, heterosexual, macho subculture which has effectively reclaimed surfing as a male space which inferiorizes, trivializes and excludes women (Stedman, 1997).

In a similar vein, Fiske's cultural analysis of the Australian pub reveals the assumption that the male experience is universal. The public bar he sees as a 'free place' between work and home. 'The factory dehumanizes the worker, the pub restores his humanity and his masculinity' (Fiske et al., 1987: 10). If the boss joins in, it is as an almost equal, a mate sharing a common male humanity and values of mateship and equality. The 'shout', where each man takes his turn to buy the drinks, equalizes outside status differences between men. The pub decor, with its spartan tiles and high uncomfortable stools, contrasts with the comfort and display of the average suburban lounge. Pub values contrast with those of the home lounge – for example, the temporary relations of the pub versus the fixed and permanent relations of the home and the symmetrical versus the asymmetrical obligations of the nuclear family. Here again Fiske's finely textured description gives us an insight into a cultural leisure space which plays an important part in the daily leisure experience of many Australians. However, Fiske's analysis is decidedly masculine. He does recognize that the sexism of the workplace and the home are replicated in the pub and thus its critique of and transformation of the workplace is partial and incomplete. Yet, from a woman's perspective the Australian pub, in spite of more liberal attitudes to women's presence in the public bar as well as in the lounge, remains a predominantly male domain. A more detailed analysis of pool culture as a part of pub culture from a feminist perspective demonstrates this claim.

Using observation and interviews in an Australian university union bar where, presumably, middle-class educated males and females might be expected to share leisure activity, Broom et al. (1992) show how the culture of pool playing serves to confirm certain forms of masculinity and retain this leisure space as male territory. Sexual harassment and other forms of intimidating behaviour are used to exclude women from playing pool. Those women who *are* admitted to pool playing are accepted on terms (such as having a male sponsor) that minimize the intrusion and preserve male power and control over the space. The observers identified a small group of about ten women who were regular pool players. These women, in contrast to the many men who came and went over the 12-month period of the research, usually stuck together and played within the same group of people. Tactics used by the men to discredit women as pool players included ignoring them, treating games against them as less serious, scrutinizing, casting doubt on and commenting on their abilities. When a man was beaten by a woman or played badly in a game against a woman comments such as the following were made:

> 'Where are your balls mate?'
> 'Can't you handle being beaten by a skirt?'
> 'Who's the bird now?'
> 'You woman!' (a man's insult in response to unskilful play by a male partner)
> 'Gees mate . . . losing to a woman . . . can I get you a beer?'
> 'Try my cue sweetheart, it'll guarantee you a good game.' (Broom et al., 1992: 184–5)

Where a woman used this cultural leisure space to resist male domination, as did Daisy, who had played pool since she was eight years old and was extremely proficient, she was often the subject of male abuse. On one occasion, a group of tipsy males who had been unaware of her expertise, labelled her a 'communist lesbian' when she gained a considerable lead in the game. The authors conclude that 'A woman not only playing pool, but playing well undermines the masculinity-confirming properties of pool, and if she cannot be beaten, she must be discredited' (Broom et al., 1992: 184). If she persists, as did Daisy, she must do so on male terms and approximate as closely as possible the male pool hall rituals. She must 'become one of the boys' in terms of language and aggression. In response to the accusation of being a 'communist lesbian', Daisy grabbed the male by the shirt and placed the tip of her pool stick to the opening of his nostril, saying: 'Fucking bullshit! One more fucking rude remark out of you, mate, and this is going straight through your brain!' *Hegemonic masculinity* (i.e. the culturally dominant form of masculinity, which in Western culture is characterized by physical strength, toughness, aggressiveness, competitiveness and individual achievement) is difficult to shake, even in leisure spaces which may be expected to provide an arena for resistance to *masculine hegemony* (i.e. male cultural domination). Cultural studies from feminist perspectives highlight the specificity and control of women's experiences within leisure spaces. Where women resist, even with the power resource of expertise in the area, they are punished for it.

We might pause here to ask, 'What happens in cultural leisure spaces, such as shopping malls, which have been the traditional domain of women?' Wilson, for example, argues that in the nineteenth century the creation of the department store provided a space, half-private, half-public, which women were able to inhabit comfortably (1995: 68). Fiske's cultural analysis of shopping malls (Fiske et al., 1987; Fiske, 1989) presents these spaces as predominantly domains in which women experience some leisure away from their domestic work. They are an opportunity, he claims, for women to take an active part in the construction of their own identity through trying on different images of themselves by means of clothes, accessories and cosmetics. Although extensively commodified, he does not see the consumer as a passive recipient of the bombardment of advertising that meets her on entering this space.

Whatever the actual selections made, it is the opportunity given to the individual to use her imagination to create something new, something that will be uniquely hers, that confirms shopping as a leisure activity which is significantly opposed to work. The creative use of shopping by suburban housewives, as well as the popularity of shopping as a lunchtime activity among city workers, makes this structural opposition clear. Shopping whether it be actual purchasing or window-shopping is situated at the crucial interface between individual desire and social control; its special feature is that it gives *special precedence to individual desire.* (Fiske et al., 1987: 103; added emphasis)

Yet he also acknowledges that much of the female shopper's focus, whether browsing or buying, is concerned with the cultural construction of women as objects for the gaze of men: 'The "self" she constructs, according to this theory, defines the class and type of man she is competing with other women to attract by the "look", in both the word's senses – as an image and as a gaze' (Fiske et al., 1987: 99). So that even here, in a woman's domain, the shopper gives space to the male gaze and his desire. In a later article, Fiske uses shopping slogans such as 'When the going gets tough, the tough go shopping' to indicate that shopping for women can be seen 'as much a source of power as success in sport, war or business . . . an oppositional, competitive act, and as such as a source of achievement, self-esteem and power' (1989: 19). There is no acknowledgement here that gender power differentials in our culture mean that the status and prestige of success in sport, war or business will never be accorded to women's shopping activities. Quite the contrary, women's concern with fashion and looks is constantly constructed as trivial activity. Shopping malls may be a leisure space for women, but the cultural meanings attached to shopping as a leisure activity remain contested within the gender power differentials of wider society. A feminist cultural analysis of such a space is far more cautious:

> The semiotic space of the shopping mall is a conflictual space, where meanings are negotiated and projected through quite different formations of fantasy and need. This is to suggest a certain freedom, a function perhaps merely of the complexity of these interactions; but knowing how readily the appearance of freedom can itself be a ruse of power, a cultural studies critic is likely to be wary of positing any transcendental value for this ability to use public space. (Frow and Morris, 1993: xvi)

Another space which has been traditionally constructed as a public leisure space for women, especially adolescent women, is the dance. Cultural studies analyses of this leisure space show it also to be a contested space, which men have controlled, but which women may use to erode complete control and to construct identities which acknowledge, rather than subordinate their own sexuality.

Walker looks at the dance as leisure space from the perspective of high-school boys in his cultural analysis of his three-year study of an inner city boy's school. The following description of the boys' visit to the local girls'

high school for a school dance resonates with descriptions of similar occur-
rences in a middle-class, outer city environment recounted by my daughters
over a number of years, as well as with McRobbie's study of working-class
girls in Britain (1978).

> The evening began with males and females mostly separated – arriving and
> congregating in single-sex groups, which were also school groups since both
> schools were single sex. These groups were consolidated on the dance floor,
> dominated especially early in the evening, by the girls' expert dancing in twos,
> threes and sometimes larger groups and their enthusiastic singing of the
> numbers being played. The boys were, on invitation, invading this territory,
> intent on hunting down individual girls, thus splitting up their groups.
> Moreover, individual girls could, if necessary, be incorporated into the boys'
> groups . . .
>   Girls could be won over to an individual male, or could be lured into leaving
> the dance with a group of males, the male goal (or hope) being sexual activity
> . . . [G]irls have a broader agenda, partly structured by their own culture . . .
> going to a dance or disco can be very much a collective female activity in which
> girls gain excitement out of their own company . . . [and] out of believing they
> look sexy, desirable, good dancers and having boys stand around and 'ogle' and
> would sometimes prefer this to dancing with a male or joining male groups . . .
>   Thus if the girls decide to join the boys it will largely be on the boys' terms,
> notwithstanding that through dress and parading the girls have other ways of
> gaining a feeling of power in what is for them basically a relatively powerless
> situation. (Walker, 1988: 105–6)

When examined from the girls' views, the dance is seen also to be space
for resistance for girls, but the extent of this resistance is limited and often
subsumed under the interests of the males. Roman's (1988) study of middle-
and working-class girls' involvement in the punk slam dance shows both
male territoriality and male dominance from the very outset of the evening.
The all-male band leads and controls the dance through the music played.
Initially boys rush in and slam against each other and the girls remain
watching on the periphery, only becoming involved when slammed into.
Middle-class girls do venture into the dance when the bands play their
second sets and the boys are somewhat exhausted. Their resistance to their
subordination as females relies on becoming tough like the boys, showing
bravery and defensiveness and the free use of their bodies in ways that
would not be approved of at home, at school, or at work. They also with-
draw in pairs or trios to safe spaces, such as the 'cool off' room close to the
dance floor, the basement bathroom or the lighted area on the street. In
contrast, the working-class women attempt to challenge the male's use of
space either by assuming the positions of self-protected onlookers or by
inviting punks, especially band members, to their homes, thus moving the
interaction into domesticated space. Roman concludes that the punk slam
dance 'permitted very limited discursive spaces within which the young
women could experience intimate membership in the subculture and articulate their feminine sexualities' (1988: 179).

In her examination of the rave dance of the early 1990s, McRobbie also sees this subcultural leisure space as a place for some resistance to dominant gendered and romantic stereotypes for those who participate by the thousands in huge arenas. Rave DJs are also male and the dance is very much in their control. Nevertheless,

Rave dance legitimates pure physical abandon in the company of others without requiring the narratives of sex or romance. Rave favours groups and friends rather than couples or those in search of a partner. The culture is one of childhood, of a pre-sexual, pre-Oedipal stage. (McRobbie, 1993: 422)

For girls, McRobbie interprets this as the possibility for a more diffuse femininity than that which had the strong underpinning of the romantic discourse and the consequent dependence on a male. The rave dance provides a space for some empowerment outside the regulatory space of the home or school and the controlling and defining gaze of more powerful others such as teachers and parents. It is the perceived danger of this 'free' space together with its music and drugs which creates the fear and anxiety of the 'moral guardians' (1993: 424). On the Australian scene, the death of Anna Wood in 1995, supposedly from taking the drug Ecstasy at a rave dance, created months of moral outrage in national newspapers.

In a detailed ethnographic study of rave dances in Britain in the early 1990s, Thornton goes beyond the resistance/submission dichotomy extant in many studies of youth subcultures. Instead she looks at the 'subcultural' capital that the dance, music, dress and the use of space provide for youth by distinction from both mainstream cultures and other 'uncool' or 'unhip' subcultures. Following Bourdieu, she shows how cultural and subcultural capital are forms of power which can operate to confer statuses which cut across the economic lines of class. Thus cultural capital forms a basis of power for cultural hegemony and subcultures a basis of power for relatively powerless groups to rebel against mainstream cultural hegemony and make distinctions which create meanings in the service of power for themselves (1996: 10). Her study demonstrates the creativities and originalities of youth cultures, but also entanglements in micro-politics of domination and subordination where 'an alternative hierarchy in which the axes of gender, sexuality and race are all employed in order to keep the determinations of class, income and occupation at bay' (1996: 105). In her study the leisure space of the rave dance is but a temporary escape from the confines of home and school at an age when other routes to relative freedom are not accessible. Although girls predominate in this space and there is room here for fantasizing beyond identities tied to female roles, its subcultural capital does little to reduce inferiorization due to gender.

At an earlier period, pre-AIDS and before any specific challenge to the romantic discourse, jazz and the jazz dance can be seen, as in McRobbie's study, to shift women's subjectivities beyond the prevailing norms of the times. In this case it was the discourse of 'good' and 'bad' girls, the latter being those who wore make-up and dressed and behaved inappropriately in public places. And the moral guardians of the times held similar fears to those held today for rave. In Australia during the 1920s and 1930s, Matthews claims that all religious sects 'were appalled by jazz, the sensual and barbaric music, the voluptuous movements of the dances, the semi-nudity of female dancers and the paganising style of the whole entertainment' (1995: 84). Civic authorities and the medical profession also weighed in when several people were reported to have died from the Charleston dance – it was banned by suburban councils and doctors said it was undermining the health of those dancing it (quoted from *The Victorian Dance News*, 9 April 1936: 11, in Matthews, 1995: 84).

The leisure spaces examined here from cultural studies perspectives have been shown to be places for struggle, negotiation, challenge and resistance to hegemonic definitions of gender which subordinate and/or marginalize women. Resulting shifts in women's construction of subjectivies and definitions of femininity have eroded but not overthrown male power. Yet their potential to challenge the dominant culture has been recognized in the perception of such spaces as a threat by the powerful moral guardians of society whether they be the 'magistrates, millowners and Methodists' of the early Industrial Revolution or the parents, teachers or media moguls of today's society. I suggest that cultural spaces have been shown in the leisure literature to be spaces for male dominance and the reinforcement of male domination. Nevertheless they are also spaces for women to try out other subjectivities for themselves. These may be subjectivities which combine elements which they value from traditional notions of femininity with those which encompass more adventurous horizons.

Hegemonic Struggle in Media Space

Television watching, reading and listening to the radio are leisure activities with a high rate of participation. As purveyors of cultural practices their meanings impact on viewers' images of men and women, reflecting gender stereotypes and also providing spaces for less constrictive images. Where media portrayals of men continue to represent them as active, virile heroes who make decisions and get important jobs done, and women as good mothers, homemakers and moral gatekeepers or alternatively as sex objects, sirens and whores, the audience's images are likely to be similarly constrained.

> For it is here, from popular culture – soaps, sitcoms, the tabloid press, women's magazines, mass-produced fiction, pop music, etc – that most people in our society get their entertainment and their information. It is here that women (and men) are offered the culture's dominant definitions of themselves. (Gamman and Marshment, 1988: 2)

Early cultural studies analyses of the media produced strong evidence for the predominance of male cultural hegemony through traditional stereo-typing of males as strong and active and women as submissive, romantic, objects of the male gaze and generally inferior to men. With the introduc-tion of poststructural ideas concerning deconstruction, resistance, trans-formation, contradictory discourses and multiple meanings, the media as a source of pleasurable leisure is now perceived as a contested arena in which struggles over cultural gender hegemony are resulting in some destabiliza-tion of gendered dichotomies. The more recent inflection of postcolonial theory with its challenge to Eurocentrism, especially in feminist analysis, has added another dimension to cultural studies of the media and the mes-sages being received and constructed through this leisure activity (see Chapter 9 for a more detailed discussion of postcolonial theory). In this section I examine the contribution made to an understanding of women's leisure practices and their identities which has been made through cultural studies analyses of women's magazines and television.

Magazines

Changes in cultural hegemony have been reflected in the ways that women's magazines and books present their clients and feminist analyses of these representations have also shifted in focus. Angela McRobbie dis-cusses changes in both of these areas, using as example *Jackie*, the top-selling magazine in the UK among female adolescent readers during the 1980s, and *Just Seventeen*, the top seller in the 1990s. Feminist readings of girls' magazines, including her own of *Jackie*, she says 'concentrated on the seamless text of oppressive meanings held together by ideology, rather than on the disruptions and inconsistencies and spaces for negotiation within the magazines' (1993b: 415). In *Just Seventeen*, as opposed to *Jackie*, the girl is no longer the slave to romance; romance is an absent category. There is love, there is sex and there are boys, but the romance category, which McRobbie had argued created a neurotically dependent female subject, is absent. Having friends of both sexes is given prominence and girls are en-couraged to enjoy a more equal climate of sexual relations. Femininity emerges as a less rigid category, although still tied to bodily beauty, fashion consumption and the pursuit of happiness through harmonious relation-ships. 'Images of bold, assertive and ambitious girls leap out in their Doc Marten boots from the pages of the magazine' (1993b: 416). *Just Seventeen* is a marketable response of leisure reading for this age-group of women which reflects a new climate of confidence and self-esteem amongst them together with a sense of identity and well-being which is not dependent on boys. It presents a space for contesting the rigid boundaries of a femininity which continually seeks male approval.

Cultural studies analyses of women's magazines also show a shift in images of feminine identity, but see the struggle against male hegemonic control less optimistically than McRobbie. Winship, for example, writing in 1983 about the new British women's magazine *Options* shows how this journal draws on the ideology of superwoman to appeal to middle-class women. These are the women who are attempting to combine a career in a male-dominated workplace with homemaking in a male-dominated family situation. 'Options' for Winship are, in fact, choices concerning consumption which reinforce the idea of the successful career woman who is able to suppress her 'femininity' and sexuality in order to succeed in a man's world in the workforce and her 'masculinity' in order to succeed within marriage and family life as a 'feminine' woman. She gives an example from the June 1982 issue. June Daybell, who is an ex-beautician with a growing decorating business employing women only and accommodating to their family responsibilities, proudly asserts:

> I'm not a feminist. I can't wait to get out of my overalls and wash my hair after a hard day's decorating. My husband has a very time consuming job and he's away a lot. He gets up at dawn to go to work before I've got the kids up and out. His sherry and dinner are waiting for him when he comes home. Often he doesn't know I've been decorating. (Winship, 1983: 61)

Winship concludes that if feminism is there it is in addition to traditional femininity; women still care for nice homes and families, look beautiful and cook tasteful meals and make a success of being a career woman. Men's demands and their contribution to the home and family have not changed. 'What's so invidious,' she says, 'is the presentation of this overload as options' (1983: 63). Hegemonic struggle here has apparently resulted in a relatively minor shift in gendered subjectivity.

Other analyses from feminist perspectives of women's magazines also reinforce the persistence of male hegemonic cultural control (see, for example, Sheridan, 1995; Summers, 1994). One study which has actually looked at presentations of women and leisure in women's magazines points to the dominance of a cultural hegemony which presents female leisure as passive and male dependent. An examination of leisure advertisements in two Canadian women's magazines over a 24-year period revealed female leisure activity as sedentary and usually involving a male. Illustrations of physical activity peaked during 1974–8, then declined to a level similar to the 1960s. Although the depiction of women participating in leisure by themselves increased during the 1980s, the presence of men was still strong. The depiction of women participating in leisure with other women is rare. While acknowledging that women neither uniformly nor passively read the texts of magazines, the author concludes, somewhat pessimistically:

> Chatting with men, 'passive' physical activity, and lounging are the predominant illustrations of women's leisure. Analysis of the more than 1000 advertisements spanning 24 years failed to uncover a single example of a woman reading. Women's leisure appears highly sedentary, often mindless, and heavily dependent on men. As such, the media offer women limited examples of what their leisure options really are. The present study underscores the fact that we

may often assume that more advancements have occurred in the way society views and promotes women's lives than is actually the case. (Bolla, 1990: 251)

Male hegemonic control through the media is apparently hard to shake. How, then, does television fare when placed under the glare of feminist cultural studies analyses?

Television

Studies such as that by Mattelart (1986) assume that women are passive and uniform watchers of the box. For example, Mattelart traces the typical story of the 'soap opera' through its vicissitudes of suffering, temptation, conflict and obstructed love to a conclusion which rewards good and virtuous women and strong, heroic men, thus reinforcing 'the sacrifice, courage and self-denial of wives and mothers' by 'the return of the husband, the renewed gratitude of the son or the simple satisfaction that comes from doing one's duty' (1986: 69–70). Thus she sees these serials as countering the monotony and low status of household work by giving value to the realm of the private life and female world dominated by 'love and 'emotion'. In this sense they enter the realm of hegemonic struggle, but only by presenting love and romance as the panacea for individual unhappiness. They are not the material for the construction of alternative subjectivities for women.

Douglas, on the other hand, in her analysis of the American media's influences on women viewers from the 1950s to the 1990s emphasizes the contradictions presented and the possibilities for women of multiple subjectivities.

> Along with our parents, the mass media raised us, socialized us, entertained us, comforted us, deceived us, disciplined us, told us what we could do and what we couldn't. And they played a key role in turning each of us into not one woman but many women – a pastiche of all the good women and bad women that came to us through the printing presses, projectors, and airwaves of America. This has been one of the mass media's most important legacies for female consciousness: the erosion of anything resembling a unified self. (1995: 13)

There is here the suggestion of hegemonic struggle, in which there are gains and losses for women. Nevertheless there is also a suggestion that women are merely the products of the media, socialized by it, consumers who keep these contradictions in balance in their daily construction of what it means to be an American woman (1995: 20). The windows are there to wider fields, but there is no suggestion of the agency of individual women to use the spaces created by contradictory discourses to construct subjectivities which go beyond socialization to explore new and more powerful horizons.

A more sophisticated interpretation is provided by Gamman and Marshment. These feminists see aspects of female autonomy and control presented in dramas such as *Cagney and Lacey* and *A Woman of Substance* as creating spaces for disturbances of dominant meanings and thus shifting commonsense notions about women. They critique the idea that visual pleasure in cinema (and, by inference, TV) is predicated on a structure of male looking/female 'to-be-looked-at-ness' as presented by Mulvay (1975). Mulvay has assumed, they say, a (heterosexual) male protagonist and a (heterosexual) male spectator. They ask what happens when the protagonist is a successful business woman as in *A Woman of Substance*, or when there is a range of female looks as in the female police drama, *Cagney and Lacey*? They link the objectification of women, along with other groups such as aged, black, poor and homosexual people, in narrative fictions to the power relationships of wider society. They ask, 'Whose gaze is it and who controls the gaze?' Finally they urge feminists to be searching in the media, not for icons 'but for inroads to the cultural terrain that constitutes the "popular" and to the systems of power that shape and define the female subject' (Gamman and Marshment, 1988: 188). In this view the media presents the possibility for women to contest control of the gaze and to rearrange its meanings to break out of stereotypes which subordinate them.

Gamman and Marshment, along with other cultural studies analysts (e.g. Fiske, 1989), examine Madonna as the epitome of the current contradictions concerning femininity presented in the media. To these authors, Madonna is both the sexual object of the male gaze in exaggerated sexual poses of submission and also the more powerful looker, who gazes directly at the camera and the viewer, challenging their voyeurism. 'This parody of a classic pornographic peepshow,' say Gamman and Marshment, 'reveals the sophistication of a new young female audience that knows the difference between feeling powerful and feeling powerless' (1988: 184). Madonna, claims Fiske, wrests control from the male gaze and shows that women's control of the look is crucial to their gaining control over their meanings within patriarchy. One young woman's view of Madonna provides some evidence for this:

> There is also a sense of pleasure, at least for me and perhaps a large number of other women, in Madonna's defiant look or gaze. In 'Lucky Star' at one point in the sequence Madonna dances side on to the camera, looking provocative. For an instant we glimpse her tongue: the expectation is that she is about to lick her lips in a sexual invitation. The expectation is denied and Madonna appears to tuck her tongue back into her cheek. This, it seems, is how most of her dancing and grovelling in front of the camera is meant to be taken. She is setting up the sexual idolization of women. For a woman who has experienced this victimization, this setup is most enjoyable and pleasurable, while the position of voyeur is displaced into uncertainty. (Robyn Blair, 19-year-old fan, quoted in Fiske, 1989: 112)

Yet Madonna works with and within the materialism of commodified popular culture: she has contested some gender norms and provided raw material for alternative constructions of women's multiple subjectivities without overturning the power structures of the industry. The very complexity of her presentation, including homosexual as well as heterosexual images of women, has managed to destabilize notions of monolithic socialization for women through the media.

The question 'Who is looking at whom and how?' is extended to black women and television by Wallace (1993). The inflection of postcolonial theory into cultural studies has pointed to the domination of white cultural hegemony in television's representations of women. Wallace puts the black woman's perspective: 'Black feminism must insist upon a critical opposi-tional representation of the black female subject' (1993: 130). The use of television as a contested space for such representation is exemplified by Oprah Winfrey, who presents an image of a bubbly and carefree successful black woman on her popular daytime television talk show and that of fat, old, poor, downtrodden and unhappy Mattie in the mini-series *The Women of Brewster Place* at night. The latter, in contrast to the daytime presen-tation, 'turns black women into an unspeakable unknowable "other"' (Wallace, 1993: 126). And black women can more easily identify with this image than with the successful Oprah. The danger is that the underlying male, white discourse of television will subsume critical black female voices and continue to present alternative cultures as 'other' to and subordinate to the dominant culture.

Television watching by men and women is a leisure activity which invokes emotional identification and pleasure. Its representation of masculinities and femininities both reaffirms traditional divisions, but also provides space for contradictions, resistance and contestation of hegemonic cultural prac-tices. Feminist analyses have highlighted the dominance of hegemonic mas-culinities based on difference from and superiority to traditional femininities. Even such supposedly different programmes as soap opera (e.g. *Dallas*) and sport ('*Dallas* with balls') have been shown to tap into the traditional emotional interests of women and men and to reinforce power, control and autonomous activity for men and tolerance and passivity, clus-tering around the family, motherhood and romance for women (O'Connor and Boyle, 1993: 114).

Cultural studies analyses of the media have brought to the surface for critical examination, the messages concerning cultural norms which invade the everyday loungerooms of a variety of viewers through leisure activity. Cultural studies informed by feminist and postcolonial theories have been able to tease out some of the cultural prescriptions involved in gender rep-resentation through the media. Countervailing tendencies which challenge male prescriptions have created the media as an arena of contestation and struggle over meanings. The result has been a space which provides varie-gated threads with which women can construct the fabric of their lives and their subjectivities to challenge those which subordinate them to men and subject them to the male voyeuristic gaze. While the media has not been wrested from male control, its discourses have been challenged and de-stabilized. My own contention is that women today are not merely the passive recipients of the messages presented in this space. The function of the media is not simply one of socializing men and women into culturally specific gendered stereotypes. Women can and do use the contradictions the media presents to construct a variety of femininities, some of which remain dependent on male approval; others return the gaze of the male voyeur, turning *him* into a sex object. Others go further and creatively construct their own versions of femininities which are strong and independent yet self-reflective and sensitive. Here again, MacCannell's concept of *hybridity* allows for women to retain what they consider valuable from traditonal female culture and to combine these subjectivities with strong and independent subjectivities derived from traditional male culture. Television does offer a space for deconstruction and reconstruction of the female self and the male self. Along with images and icons which reinforce male hegemony in postmodern society, it also presents alternatives which can be elements in reconstruction. It can be a space for becoming.

Sport: a Contested Arena

Sporting prowess in most Western cultures is positively valued and associated with social acclaim and economic benefits. At a national level those who successfully compete in international competitions assume the status of heroes and heroines. Returning from the Olympics with a gold medal, for example, is regarded as one of the highest achievements for one's country and not to support one's national sporting heroes is tantamount to cultural heresy. Sporting achievement is rewarded from an early age along with academic achievement in the educational system. During adolescence, male competitive achievement in football of various codes, cricket, athletics and swimming within and between schools takes precedence in the informal school hierarchy of masculinity for boys, and often holds greater rewards for them than academic achievement at this stage of their lives. Boys are still taught that sport is a significant part of manliness. Along with various skills and a sense of superiority, they are taught the need to be tough and bear pain. Women are distanced and excluded by this process – it is the opposite of femininity and teams who do not play well are berated by coaches as playing like a pack of girls. To be better at sport is translatable into being better or more capable in other areas of life. Because women are deemed to be inferior at sport, by inference they are less capable in other areas of life. Such is the cultural control of male hegemony exercised through the arena of sport.

The media constantly reinforces the messages of hegemonic masculinity and gender domination being conveyed through sport. Three of the most influential commentators on Sydney radio dismissed the federal inquiry into equity for women in sport announced in November 1990 as a waste of time because men's superiority is a self-evident and immutable truth. Men are stronger, faster and tougher, so they must be better at sport than women. McKay's detailed analysis of Australian media coverage of sport shows the prevalence of hegemonic values which discredit and marginalize women's sporting achievements. These values include: 'innuendos about women athletes' lesbian tendencies; the view that women's sporting performances are inferior to men's; and the ability of some women to remain beautiful and heterosexual *despite* being athletes' (1991: 54). He cites incidents such as the following: comments on the 'little girl' attributes of successful international tennis player, 17-year-old Arantxa Sanchez, in the 1989 French Open, compared with the 'remarkable depth of stamina – mental, physical and spiritual' of Michael Chang, also 17; and the presentation of women such as tennis player Gabriela Sabatini as sexual objects for male gaze, as, for example, in the *Courier Mail* coverage of the 1989 Australian Open: 'Melbourne's "Uncle Mervs" were out in force for their first chance to gaze on the dark-eyed beauty from Argentina, who also strikes the fluffy yellow ball well enough to be ranked third in the world' (McKay, 1991: 105). McKay also points out that accounts of Lisa Curry's winning swimming performance in the 1990 Commonwealth Games focus on her maternal role, rather than on her swimming. He comments that men's paternal role, on the other hand, is rarely mentioned. He concludes that these comments assure readers and viewers that despite being athletes women can still be traditionally feminine, attractive and maternal. Missing, he says, are stories of the inferior facilities and second-rate equipment available to women; of women as athletes instead of 'dolly birds'; and of the extraordinary accomplishments by women in cycling, sailing, climbing and endurance swimming and riding. Rowe's analysis of sport as popular culture comes to a similar conclusion:

> The large scale absence of women's sport from 'serious' media coverage and the presence of sporting women's bodies as objects to be sexually appraised (as man-like/unattractive or woman/like attractive) is a significant reproduction in culture of persistent social and material inequalities. (1995: 134)

American studies of televised sport similarly reveal that women athletes, when they are reported on television at all, are likely to be overtly trivialized, infantilized and sexualized (Duncan et al., 1994). Media coverage of women's sport has been shown to endorse a hegemonic masculinity which disadvantages and inferiorizes women.

Bryson shows how this hegemonic masculinity achieved through sport for males (even those who do not reach the top in competitive physical competition) gains advantages for men in our society over women. Physical force and toughness, says Bryson, are woven into hegemonic masculinity – the celebration of 'real men' as strong and tough underscores the fact men are in positions and have the right to dominate and this physical force is an irreducible dimension of power (1990: 174). In Australia Bryson points out that historically both cricket and the various codes of football have had a huge following. In a national survey (Sweeney and Associates, 1986, quoted in Bryson, 1990: 174), 81 per cent of males over 16 years of age expressed an interest in football and 73 per cent in cricket. For women it was lower, but still substantial: 61 per cent and 59 per cent respectively. In Australia virtually all boys are introduced to cricket and the relevant code of football from a young age. Most houses have yards where these sports are played with strong endorsement from family and peers. These are also the basic sports pursued at school. Sport for boys and men, as participants and spectators and as a focus for socializing, remains a prime leisure activity throughout the life-cycle.

Women and the contrary skills of supportiveness, grace, gentleness and co-operation are thus inferiorized, masculinity and violence are endorsed, males gain in personal power, and sport assumes a strategic position in gender development. This constructed male superiority carries over into other spheres such as work. Bryson (1990: 176) gives the example of the 1978 Acapulco cliff-defying activity, in which the competitor dives from a great height into the sea. One of the male competitors complained about having to compete against finalist Barbara Mayer Winters, saying: 'This is a death defying activity – men are taking a great gamble to prove their courage. What would be the point if everyone saw that a woman could do the same?' For her 'protection' Winters was disqualified before the final dive.

Bryson maintains that definitions of sport, direct control of women's sport, ignoring women's sport and trivialization of women in sport (especially in media presentations) coalesce to promote a maleness that is repeatedly linked with skill, strength, aggression and violence and which subjugates women. Thus she says (Bryson, 1987: 358): 'we find boys from an early age being schooled in the appropriate behaviour and sentiments at the same time that girls are learning that they are excluded.' But, she goes on to point out, this is an arena where women can both challenge and resist dominant male definitions and control, not only by participating and seeking change, but also by taking up positions as commentators, reporters, administrators and coaches, and by promoting 'counter-hegemonic' sporting activities which involve neither aggression, violence nor excessive individual competition.

Other feminists also encourage women to contest the sporting arena as a male preserve. Oglesby (1990) argues for the recognition and strengthening of women's principles which have been historically present in sport for women. The 'feminine force' in sport characterized as passive, subordinate, co-operative, dependent, chaotic, non-violent and nurturant, she argues, is an antidote to the traditionally masculine in sport and the 'androgen poisoning' prevalent in today's world. Hargreaves (1994) documents the hegemonic control that men in Britain have exercised in sport from the nineteenth century to today, but emphasizes the inability of men to gain total control. She shows how women are taking action and producing new versions of sport for themselves so that there is the potential for women to transcend practical and symbolic forms of oppression in sport. She wishes also to incorporate men in the struggle:

> There is a need to examine more closely the lived complexities of men's as well
> as women's sporting experiences and the changing forms of masculinities and

femininities in sports which are linked to changing values. Although many men may be agents of oppression, they are not inherently oppressive and they have a primary role to play, with women, in the elimination of gender oppression in sports. (Hargreaves, 1994: 39)

These feminists go beyond traditional notions of power play in sport, in which men are always the winners and women the losers, to show how the contradictions of this contested space provide the conditions for struggle in which men sometimes triumph but women may sometimes shift meanings to their own advantage. The finely textured cultural analysis of a women's subculture in a sport which has traditionally been a male preserve provides some empirical evidence to support this approach.

Cultural studies analyses of the subculture of female body-building highlight the contradictions for women who challenge male hegemony by entering male sporting arenas. Hall (1995), using the example of Bev Francis, the Australian professional body-builder, shows how her entry into this arena transgressed the norms of femininity, but was quickly followed by resistance and then by compliance. She chronicles how her initial appearance as a woman in a 'man's body' lost her the 1983 Caesar World Cup Competition where she came last to the other seven finalists who were prettier, sexier, less bulky and more curvaceous. Yet four years later she won the Women's Pro World Championship, and from 1987 to 1991 was placed either second or third in the prestigious Ms Olympia contest. Her bulky size was considerably reduced to the right amount of muscularity and symmetry, she wore make-up and fluffed her bleached blonde hair, had cosmetic surgery on her nose and wore sexy bikinis and spandex outfits. Thus she was 'tamed' and, like other professional female body-builders, she was pulled back towards a normalizing regime. Hall comments: 'Their heterosexuality and heterosexual desirability are secured; their muscle is rephrased as "flex appeal" and only shows when "pumped up"; and their bodies are positioned as the site of heterosexual pleasure, romance, youth and fun, and beauty' (1995: 27). Here again male hegemony seems to have triumphed.

This is not, however, the end of the story. Hall goes on to show that feminist cultural studies of female body-building subcultures by people such as Schulze (1990) and Miller and Penz (1991) tease out a more complex struggle over this space and its relationship to feminine identity. Schulze points out the possibilities of destabilizing the male/female dichotomy through body-building: 'The deliberately muscular woman disturbs dominant notions of sex, gender, and sexuality, and any discursive field that includes her risks opening up a site of contest and conflict, anxiety and ambiguity' (1990: 71). Miller and Penz's study demonstrates how women body-builders attempt to disentitle men's claim to the field by asserting that certain male uses of body-building such as ego-building are inappropriate. Their own use, which has to do with managing their appearance, is one in which women excel. This body work is not necessarily in the service of male interests but can be put to good use in the service of female mastery and control. They claim to be the best at body work and are thus able to stake a new claim for themselves in a formerly masculine preserve. By making a strength of their difference they have made a shift in meaning to their own advantage.

In her comparison of women ballet dancers, body-builders and weight-lifters, Brace-Govan (1997) found that women who used these spaces to increase their bodily strength also had an increase in self-confidence. Those furthest from 'hegemonic femininity' in bodily appearance, that is the body-builders, experienced the greatest sense of subjective empowerment, albeit at some cost to their sense of heterosexual attractiveness in interactive situations. Nevertheless, at least one woman was able to move beyond her dependence on the opinion of others to gain a subjectivity which she saw as autonomous. And, as a whole, these women were able to shift to some degree the acceptable shape for female body-builders. The woman in the study, however, who most threatened male hegemonic control was a weight-lifter who was able to lift world-class weight in a meditative, personally centred fashion with no recourse to masculine discourses of aggression or violence and without male sanction (1997: 316).

I would argue that cultural studies analyses of women's sport have opened our eyes to the warp and weft of women's attempts to shift inferiorizing definitions of femininity without homogenizing men and women, that is, without trying to be equal by becoming the same. Women can retain a concept of difference while engaging in activities which have previously been used to shore up a sense of masculinity, based on their physical superiority over women. When women do take on body-building or other traditionally male activities, they do it in a different way from men and are not completely overcome by male hegemony. These ideas have ramifications when we come to discuss the masculinist response to feminism in the next chapter. Will men, when they do get in touch with their emotions, necessarily need to express them in the same way that women do, for example through tears? Is it necessary in equalizing power relationships between genders to make them the same?

Sport in its professionalized, amateur, organized and informal forms creates spaces for the transmission *and* confrontation of cultural values, especially with regard to gender. Its commodification as big business ensures that it will take up space in the media and thus remain constantly before our eyes. Feminist cultural studies analyses of sport have demonstrated the power that male hegemony holds in this arena, but also the possibilities for women to contest this space in ways that will both enhance their own enjoyment of their leisure and possibly shift the goalposts slightly in their favour.

Conclusion

In this chapter I have examined from a cultural studies perspective physical leisure spaces such as the beach, the pub and the dance, as well as the more generalized spaces of the media and sport. These leisure spaces have been shown to incorporate dominant cultural practices which advantage those with power, but also to be open to challenge and resistance from less powerful subcultures. The concept of hegemony which signifies taken-for-granted dominant and dominating cultural practices, as well as the possibilities of struggle, destabilization and reformulation, has remained a predominant theme through changes in the theoretical perspectives incorporated into this form of social analysis. The term itself has been criticized by Rojek (1993b, 1995) as being imprecise, generalizing processes of coercion, consent and resistance to the levels of culture and politics. Its neglect of the body and treatment of psychic pleasure as a reflection of the political structure add to its imprecision (1993b: 283). Nevertheless, says Rojek, it has highlighted how leisure meanings are imposed and challenged and enables people's subjective perceptions and accounts of leisure practices to be taken into account. It also allows for the emancipatory potential of leisure (1995: 24).

In the development of a concept of leisure which adequately accounts for women's experiences and the potential for women's use of leisure to shift the goalposts of male cultural domination, it is the latter aspect which interests me in this book. The concept of hegemony, as applied to cultural spaces and male domination, has been shown, in this chapter, to allow for contestation of exclusionary male practices by women. The potential for poststructural recombination of multiple elements into hybrid cultures which do not necessarily inferiorize women is there, at least in the media and sport. In my opinion, one of the strengths of the cultural studies focus on hegemony has been to move away from economic determinism and to recognize the importance of cultural practices for the social control of individuals, as well as the possibilities of social change through contestation of these practices. The weakness has been the consequent focus on the effects of relationships of power, without some analysis of the sources of power. Economic power remains a source of power for the construction and struggle over hegemonic cultural control. But other sources of power such as status, age, gender, race, ethnicity and sexual orientation also exist. In addition, as has been shown in this chapter, cultural and subcultural capital can create meaning in the service of power. In the gender struggle over male hegemony, having a male body engenders power, especially in the arena of sport, as does rational control of the emotions and individual competition. Subsequent chapters in this book will address these sources of male power in the hegemonic struggle over leisure spaces.

I retain the concept of hegemony as a useful way of describing the way that many cultural practices, which may or may not be dependent upon an economic power-base, have been taken for granted by subordinate as well as dominant groups. The term, when referring to gender power relationships, conveys the idea of the blanketing effect of masculinized cultural practices which inferiorize women and which women accept as natural and taken for granted. This chapter has shown that such male hegemony in leisure spaces is hard to shake. Nevertheless the term also conveys the possibility, without an essential political, economic or social revolution, of struggle, negotiation, destabilization and reconstruction which responds to challenges by subcultures. The construction of hybrid cultures which retain some worthwhile aspects of previous dominant and subordinate cultures may result. The concept of hegemony suggests that leisure spaces where cultural practices such as surfing, drinking, dancing, television watching and sport tend to reinforce masculine territoriality and masculine dominance of values and world-views are also spaces for contestation by inferiorized groups such as women. These spaces, in spite of considerable personal costs, can be spaces for becoming selves which go beyond those previously inscribed through male hegemonic control.

Struggles over male hegemonic control of leisure spaces such as the beach, the pub and the dance, as well as the media and sport, have been shown in this chapter to result in challenges to traditional gender stereotypes which inferiorize women. Although the power to propagate the myths of male superiority has not been transferred to women in the process, traditional ideas have been destabilized by women's pleasurable uses of these leisure spaces. There is here, then, the potential for further shifts in cultural practices in favour of women. Feminist cultural studies of these leisure spaces have shown through the finely textured analyses of texts and experiences that women in the postmodern era are not passive recipients of cultural messages but creative agents of shifts in meanings in their favour. Men's 'natural' right to leisure space and 'natural' physical superiority which were taken for granted by men and women for so long are now being challenged by some women. Women's leisure is one site of this challenge. Feminist analyses from this perspective have been able to draw out both the costs and the benefits for women of struggles over leisure spaces.

In the following chapter, masculinist responses to the feminisms of the second wave of feminism since the 1970s are discussed in relationship to leisure spaces, leisure practices and leisure experiences.

5

Leisure and Masculinities

One of the impacts on social theory of feminist theorizations since the 1970s has been the recognition that previous theories have posited male perspectives and experiences as universal. For example, Marxian analysis centred on the relationships of production in the market-place which posited male experience in the market-place as the lynchpin of power with its social consequences for men and women alike. Women's experience in the family was virtually invisible. Feminist theorization since the 1970s has made visible the subjective experiences of women and the validity of the personal as an entry into understanding and critiquing political, economic and social gender inequalities. During the 1980s male responses to such critiques have resulted in various men's studies which have focused on the specificity of what it means to be male in capitalist and patriarchal societies as against the acceptance of male experience as the norm for all men and all women. Studies of the construction of masculinities and the powerful place that hegemonic masculinity occupies in contemporary societies have ranged over many social arenas including the family, politics, the workplace, religion, education, medicine, sexuality and leisure. Leisure features in this literature as a site both for the construction of hegemonic masculinity and its reinforcement and also as a space where fissures in such hegemony occur, a place where traditional masculinity may be challenged and validity attributed to alternative forms of masculinities.

In this chapter initially I explore masculinist responses to feminism in terms of social psychological, cultural and poststructural perspectives and the implications that these ideas have for understanding the place that leisure has in men's lives. Each perspective throws light on the ways in which sport and leisure shore up hegemonic masculinity and contribute to male hegemony while disadvantaging many men. At the same time most forms of sport and leisure reinforce dominant forms of masculinity which are based in opposition to, distancing from and inferiorization of traditional forms of femininity. The place of leisure in the necessary process for men of proving their masculinity and defending it against the ridicule of other men and the perceived loss of women's admiration is discussed. Finally, leisure as a space for men to reconstruct masculinities which may combine a variety of subjectivities, including those which are deliberately anti-sexist but which are not the same as women's subjectivities, is suggested.

Masculinist Responses to Feminism

In order to understand the construction of masculinity within patriarchal capitalist society, the study of men has needed to go beyond the previous sociological invisibility of women and the concomitant assumption that the male experience is the universal one. Masculinism or the 'new' study of men is essentially a response to the issues raised by the feminist theories of the 1970s and 1980s. Without this basis the new studies of men would merely be reinforcing the importance and value of being male in our society. As Kauffman comments: 'The mere attempt to explore various masculine archetypes or to celebrate men's lives does not a new men's studies make' (1990: 14). In this new approach, he claims, 'we are studying human relationships or human perceptions of nature that are shaped by the conceptions of power and agency that are hegemonic in patriarchal societies' (1990: 14).

It is clear that any fresh sociological examination of the position and subjectivity of men in patriarchal society will need to take account of power, agency and hegemony. Power will include macrosocial structural sources such as class and gender which generally endow men with resources which can be effectively used for dominance in gender relationships. It will also include institutional power, that is, the power available to those (generally males) in top positions in the institutions of our society such as politics, education, religion and medicine. In addition, ideologies such as those of the family, motherhood, femininity and masculinity keep individual women believing in the naturalness and inevitability of their subordinate status. This combination of structural, institutional and ideological power enables hegemonic control through a masculine culture which valorizes and rewards physically aggressive, competitive, task-focused, achievement oriented masculinity and inferiorizes all forms of femininity (Carrigan et al., 1985). Much of the sociological literature in the masculinist response to feminism draws on this concept of hegemonic masculinity which Connell describes and defines as follows:

> The concept of 'hegemony', deriving from Antonio Gramsci's analysis of class relations, refers to the cultural dynamic by which a group claims and sustains a leading position in social life. At any given time, one form of masculinity rather than others is exalted. Hegemonic masculinity can be defined as the configuration of gender practice which embodies the currently accepted answer to the problem of the legitimacy of patriarchy, which guarantees (or is taken to guarantee) the dominant position of men and the subordination of women. (1995: 77)

Such hegemony gains acceptance throughout society by being rewarded in the market-place, as well as by its representation in civil society, culture and the media and its enactment in the everyday practices of men and women, so that it is seen as the normal and natural way of behaving. Challenges to it are generally constructed as deviant and sanctioned accordingly. Nevertheless it is a historically mobile relation, subject to struggle and reformulation. In this struggle, the insights from poststructuralist ideas have suggested the importance of agency both in the construction of a variety of masculinities and femininities and in resistance to dominant forms of gendered subjectivities. Poststructuralist feminism posits a relationship between embodiment or the cultural construction of male and female bodies as a vital source of male power in contemporary Western society. In addition, poststructuralism suggests the deconstruction of hierarchical dichotomies such as culture/nature, rationality/emotionality, objectivity/subjectivity, public/private and male/female, and the construction for each gender of multiple subjectivities which allow for recombinations of gendered identities. Where these concepts have been incorporated into the masculinist studies of gender, the rewards have been new insights into men's lived experiences in capitalist, patriarchal societies and the possibilities for change, at an individual level as well as in wider society.

It seems obvious that there are aspects of male subjectivity that women cannot tap into, just as there are aspects of female subjectivity that males could not tap into, but which have been enlightened by feminist analysis. So that, theoretically, the inclusion of masculine perspectives will complement insights gained from feminist analysis of gender difference. In addition it can be invaluable for men in coming to grips with an idealized masculinity which has been socially constructed and which in practice is the perfect fit for very few men. Hearn suggests that in terms of men's material self-interest, in everyday life as well as in the academic study of men, there are the following benefits for men in the study of masculinities:

> 1. the increased possibilities of love, emotional support and care for and from others, particularly other men;
> 2. the privilege and emotional development that may come from increased contact and work with children;
> 3. the possibility of improved health, the reduction of certain illnesses, and the extension of life;
> 4. the creation of the conditions for the transformation of the capitalist mode of production (that being inherently gendered) to more liberating productive relations;
> 5. the avoidance of other men's violence and of the fear of men, of killing, of being killed; and most importantly,
> 6. the reduction of the likelihood of nuclear annihilation, the grimmest legacy of patriarchy. (1987: 185)

It does not follow that men who grasp the new men's studies will then necessarily be more sympathetic to female versions of socially constructed gender, nor may they be willing to relinquish some of their gender power, as the histories of some of the therapeutic men's groups demonstrates (see

Connell, 1995: 206–11 for a discussion of these groups). Nevertheless an exploration of masculinist responses to feminism can increase our understanding of gender differences and the advantages and disadvantages that rigid male and female stereotypes have for men as well as for women. It may also lead on to suggest ways that men might use leisure spaces to enlarge their own subjectivities beyond the 'tight pants of masculinity', as described by Kauffman (1990: 14).

Masculinist responses to feminism vary in theoretical approach from the incorporation of the social psychological and psychoanalytic analyses of Gilligan and Chodorow (e.g. Messner, 1992a and 1992b), to cultural studies (e.g. Kimmel, 1996), and a combination of these with poststructural insights (e.g. Connell, 1995). Each has something to contribute to an understanding of leisure and masculinities, so I will briefly overview these authors and draw from them their contribution to understandings of leisure. I will also show that, for the most part, they remain within masculine perceptions of social and personal situations.

Before discussing Messner's contribution based on insights concerning psychosexual development provided by Gilligan and Chodorow, it is necessary to critique the use of leisure in the therapeutic work of men such as Bly. Robert Bly's *Iron John: A Book About Men* (1991) is an amalgam of anthropology, myth, poetry, psychology and autobiography which emphasizes men's separation from their fathers as a source of emotional damage for them. While acknowledging women's oppression by men, he also in some ways blames women for men's loss of a sense of inner manliness. His solution amounts to a therapy for manliness where men use their leisure to go out into the woods, in groups, at weekends to rediscover the Wild Man within and to reinforce a strong tough hegemonic masculinity. In so doing, claims Bly, men are able to counteract the erosion of true manliness brought about by the everyday circumstances of men's contemporary living in civilized society. Connell (1995: 209) terms this type of masculism the 'mythopoetic men's movement' and shows how even those such as Farrell (1974, 1993), who began by examining men's lives in the light of feminist insights through the use of men's groups, moved more and more towards a defensiveness of traditional masculinity and hostility to feminist critiques of this. As we shall see in this chapter, it is not unusual for men to use their leisure to prove manhood, especially at times when it is threatened, but as an enlightened response to the insights of feminism, mythopoetic male therapy through leisure groups serves rather to reinforce patriarchal power than to move gender relationships into a less hierarchical configuration.

Messner: Sport and Hegemonic Masculinity

Messner's articles (1987, 1990, 1992a, 1992b) draw on the insights of Nancy Chodorow's (1978) and Carol Gilligan's (1982) feminist analyses, which he applies to boys' experiences of sport. For Messner sport is part of boys' establishment of their masculinity by forming boundaries around their identity in the break away from the mother and femininity. Men's sense of self is henceforth generally solidified through separation from others. Sport is seen as an avenue for male identity through task orientation and achievement and male-governed behaviour:

> For the boy who both seeks and fears attachment with others, the rule-bound structure of organized sports can promise to be a safe place in which to seek non-intimate attachment with others within a context that maintains clear boundaries, distance and separation. (Messner, 1992a: 168)

But the emphasis changes from participation to winning as he learns that in order to receive the attention that he craves he must be successful. The conscious striving for successful achievement becomes the primary means of connection and a sense of self-worth is conditional upon being a 'winner' (1992a: 169). The catch is that success comes to only a few, even in primary school. On leaving school the opportunities to participate in competitive sport are diminished, even fewer males are successful and the audience has diminished. Then what happens to those few, once the physical prowess necessary for the majority of competitive sports attenuates with age?

Young men, claims Messner (1987: 203), often feel comfortable exploring close friendships and intimate relationships only after they have established their separate work-related (or sports-related) positional identity. Relationships are likely to become more problematic than ever during disengagement from sports. For those who are successful at sport it provides an ego boundary, the distancing and sense of achievement necessary for a strong sense of masculinity in our society. But its promise of intimacy with others is never fulfilled. It acts rather as a barrier to intimacy for many because of its competitiveness and ultimately exacerbates men's difficulties in constructing intimate relationships with others (1990: 439). For those who are unsuccessful it provides only a sense of uncertainty and failure, not one of strong masculinity (1992a: 170).

Messner points out that young men from varied socio-economic backgrounds all experience similar exposure to organized sports and the 'joys of receiving attention and acceptance among family and peers for early success in sports'. However, in the course of development the young male from a high-status background makes a conscious shift towards educational and non-athletic career goals. Young males from lower-status backgrounds, on the other hand, tend to develop higher levels of commitment to sports careers as their perceptions of real life options become narrower. Messner claims 'the immediate rewards (fun, status, attention), along with the constricted (non sports) structure of opportunity attract disproportionately large numbers of boys from lower-status backgrounds to athletic careers as their major means of constructing a masculine identity' (1992a: 173).

Yet their rate of success is severely limited. Class and race intersect to limit success through sport and thus the promise of a strong sense of male identity. For middle-class boys there may be other routes. Nevertheless

Messner's general message is that of the majority of males whose sense of masculinity is extremely fragile and constantly under threat. Not only does fear of failure ('you're only as good as your last game' (1987: 199)) pose a threat, but so also do changing gender power relationships in wider society.

Where male power is under threat, the institution of sport is used to re-establish male superiority and the inferiorization of women. For Messner (1992b: 16), 'The dominant structures and values of sport came to reflect the fears and needs of a threatened masculinity'. Dunning (1986: 274) suggests that some men responded to the growing power of women in the mid-nineteenth century 'by developing rugby football – as a male preserve where they could bolster their threatened masculinity and, at the same time, mock, vilify and objectify women, the principle source of threat'. His analysis of rugby songs such as 'Eskimo Nell' and 'Mexican Pete', for example, shows how they embody a hostile and brutal, but at the same time fearful, attitude towards women who were seen as powerful and sexually demanding. Sport is seen in the accounts of Messner and Dunning as a means of resisting an increase in female power, a regrouping of men to exclude and inferiorize women. Here again men are the vulnerable ones. Power is acknowledged, not as power over women, but as power to resist the threat of female domination.

This critique of the role of competitive sport in the construction of masculinity presents a sophisticated argument in the mode of masculism based on a psychosexual development which requires boys to break away from the femininity of their mothers by forming strong boundaries around their sense of self, inhibiting intimacy and focusing masculinity on achievement and success. Its strength is in an understanding of some of the disadvantages to males of male subjectivity constructed under the conditions of patriarchal society which require women to be the primary parent during a child's early years. Men's need for intimacy is distorted and it is difficult for males to establish the balance between separation and attachment. The fragility of maintaining a *macho* image and a strong masculine identity is also demonstrated while at the same time its importance for male dominance and its resilience under threat become obvious. These insights into male experiences of subjectivity would not have been possible without feminist questioning of traditional forms of masculinity and critique of societal demands for women's responsibility for parenting with its consequences for male and female subjectivities. Messner's work tends to reinforce universalistic notions of gender divisions, so that one concludes that *all* males behave in this way and *all* females in a different way. In my opinion, however, the insights that his work has given to an understanding of how many males construct identities should not be ruled out on this score. In some senses any theory which relies on theories of psychosexual development are essentialist and universalistic in terms of gender. Both Kimmel's (1996) and Connell's (1995) work, which are discussed later in this chapter, also make use of psychoanalytic theory. Yet these insights assist in understanding some important issues for many men. The danger in pre-feminist uses of these theories has been to construct the male as the norm and women as different from men, deficient in some way and inferior to the male. While one must also question the appropriateness of application of these theories in a similar way to all males and all females, irrespective of the relationships of power between them and between each other, important insights would be lost if one were to dismiss their validity purely on the grounds that they are generally interpreted in universalistic terms.

Others writing in this mode, such as Seidler (1989), also address the issue in patriarchal society of males' lack of ability to be in touch with and express their emotions (except anger) and their consequent difficulty in forming strong and stable emotional relationships with other men and with women. His argument is reminiscent of Lloyd's (1989) feminist claim that males have appropriated rationality and logic as their preserve and dichotomized, feminized and inferiorized intuition and emotion. Whereas Lloyd shows how this situation disadvantages women, Seidler focuses on how this division disadvantages males.

> When we think about masculinity and the identification of male identity with reason we see that this has historically involved a process of separation from our natures. We discover that our notions of 'reason' have been developed in fundamental opposition to nature, to emotions and desires. For men this has meant an attenuated sense of our lived experience as we discover we have been systematically estranged from our emotional lives. It is as if we exist as disembodied minds able to produce arguments for our behaviour, but unable to share what we feel and experience about a situation. (1989: 189)

Seidler recounts the conflicts and changes, sense of enlargement and freedom which he experienced in his life when he began to challenge, through his work, leisure and relationships, the male focus on reason to the exclusion of emotions and relationships. He shows how male lives are truncated by their gendered construction in our society and advocates the advantages for males in transforming such construction. In his later work (1994), Seidler develops these ideas within a wider critique of masculine power embedded in the control of social theory through male appropriation of and valorization of rationality since the Enlightenment.

The work of Messner and others who follow this line of argument have contributed enormously to an understanding of the place of sport and leisure in men's individual struggle to establish a strong sense of masculinity which conforms to the hegemonic mode. It also demonstrates the disadvantages that this has for the majority of men. From my own experiences of teaching, especially male human movement students, these ideas have thrown light on some of their own predicaments and, in some instances, have acted as a catalyst for rewarding change in the focus of their identity. Nevertheless, the weaknesses of this approach lie in the lack of recognition of the multiple subjectivities of both males and females and, more importantly, the wider issue of the power of male identities associated with hegemonic masculinity. As Segal (1990: 82) observes, traditional masculinity is 'the exciting identity, linked with success, power and dominance in every social sphere ... it becomes an issue precisely because it is so valued and desirable'.

When this is recognized, as in Bryson's (1990) analysis of sport from a wider sociological perspective, the argument concerning sport as individual, social psychological detriment for males carries much less weight. Bryson shows how 'hegemonic masculinity' achieved through sport for males (even those who do not reach the top in competitive physical competition) gains advantages for men in our society over women. Physical force and toughness, says Bryson, are woven into hegemonic masculinity – the celebration of 'real men' as strong and tough underscores the fact men are in positions and have the right to dominate and this physical force is an irreducible dimension of power (1990: 174).

Women and the contrary skills of supportiveness, grace, gentleness and co-operation are thus inferiorized; masculinity and violence are endorsed; males gain in personal power; and sport assumes a strategic position in gender development. This constructed male superiority carries over into other spheres such as work. Bryson introduces the term 'male hegemony' to refer to the overarching superiority attributed to males (even those who don't participate in sport) due to their supposedly biologically based superiority at sport and the societal power that this accrues for them.

> To be better at sport (by implication even for those men who do not participate in athletics) is symbolically translatable into being better or more capable in other areas of life. Through a dialectical process, women who are culturally defined and perceived as incapable of equaling men at sport, are refered to as inferior and, by inference, less capable in many areas of life. (1990: 173)

Whereas in the sporting arena the masculinist literature concentrates on the disadvantages for many men of hegemonic masculinity, the feminist counterpart sees the sporting contribution to hegemonic masculinity as an important source of male hegemony and male control of society.

Kimmel: Proving Manhood through Leisure

In his detailed examination of manhood in the USA from 1776 to the present day, Kimmel (1996) posits hegemonic masculinity as the 'ideal' version of masculinity against which every male must measure himself. He quotes Goffman:

> In an important sense there is only one complete unblushing male in America: a young, married, white, urban, northern, heterosexual, Protestant, father, of college education, fully employed, of good complexion, weight, and height, and a recent record in sports ... Any male who fails to qualify in any one of these ways is likely to view himself – during moments at least – as unworthy, incomplete, and inferior. (Goffman, 1963: 128)

Although this ideal varies historically, its demands on men continue to exact behaviour from men to prove a manhood which is, in fact, fragile and constantly under threat. Along with the dominating form of masculinity are the parallel and competing versions that co-exist with it and vary according to class, race, ethnicity, age, sexual orientation and region of the country. His book explores the 'tension between the multiplicity of masculinities that collectively define American men's actual experiences and this singular "hegemonic" masculinity that is prescribed as the norm' (Kimmel, 1996: 6).

Kimmel, like Messner, draws on psychosocial accounts which posit an individual male's sense of masculinity as being dependent upon separation from his mother and a constant distancing throughout life from the feminine. However he places this individuality within the culturally specific framework of American society as it has developed over the last two centuries. Manhood, for him, is created in culture – it is neither static nor timeless, it is socially constructed. Although men's masculinity is constructed in opposition to womanhood, it is not specific women who provide the reference point. Rather it is an abstract conceptualization of femininity and it is other men, not women, he claims, whom men seek to impress with their manhood and whose ridicule they fear. Women themselves have such low status in America, he says, that their approval doesn't really count. Women often serve as a kind of currency that men use to improve their ranking with other men, but it is other men's approval that they seek, 'from fathers and boyhood friends to teachers, coworkers, and bosses, the evaluative eyes of other men are always upon us, watching, judging' (Kimmel, 1996: 7).

It is in this context that Kimmel places the relationship between men's leisure and masculinity. It was at times when hegemonic masculinity was most threatened, as at the beginning of the twentieth century when working life no longer provided a firm footing for masculinity, that men turned to leisure pursuits to shore up and prove their manhood. In previous eras, a sense of inner strength and confidence had radiated out into a 'sturdy and muscular frame from years of hard labour' (1996: 120). With the increase in indoor factory, office and retail work, the body now needed to be worked on through sports and gyms to demonstrate the appearance of masculine strength, and the feminine needed to be excluded or escaped by the provision of male-only spaces and fictional heroes who celebrated traditional masculinity. It was in this period that the term 'manhood' was replaced gradually by the term 'masculinity'. Masculinity, according to Kimmel, referred to 'a set of behavioural traits and attitudes that were contrasted now with a new opposite, *femininity*. Masculinity was something that had to be constantly demonstrated, the attainment of which was forever in question – lest the man be undone by a perception of being too feminine' (1996: 120).

Kimmel discusses the place of sports, gyms, athletic fields, men-only clubs, drinking and the reading of the exploits of tough heroes such as Tarzan and various cowboys, as ways in which men countered the perceived feminization of culture. In the USA in the early twentieth century there was a dramatic increase in bicycling, tennis, golf, weightlifting, boxing, football, basketball and baseball. Sports were seen as character building, promoting the moral virtues of courage, manliness and self-control, substituting 'hardiness for effeminacy and dexterity for luxurious indolence' (1996: 137). Together with gyms, this form of defending masculinity is termed by Kimmel, 'self-control'.

The second form, which he terms 'exclusion', is an attempt to distance and exclude femininity through all men's clubs and societies. He details the rise of the Boy Scout movement in Britain and the USA as an example and also discusses all male fraternities in universities and men's business clubs as examples. For all groups of men, he sees drinking together as a means of cementing manly solidarity when 'traditional artisanal conviviality was superseded in impersonal factories' and women gained increased control and feminization of the home (1996: 124).

The third form of shoring up a threatened masculinity through leisure, Kimmel terms 'escape'. Here he discusses the role of literature which 'could help promote savagery in even the most timid man's breast'. From the biographies of the highway robber Jesse James and the tough-minded military general, Custer, to the mythic heroes of cowboy fame, American literature of the early twentieth century celebrated hegemonic masculinity. For example, the cowboy is fierce and brave taming the wilderness for women, children and emasculated civilized men – a man of action, moving in a world of men, in which daring, bravery and skill are his constant companions. He lives by physical strength and rational calculation and forms no lasting emotional bonds with anyone (1996: 150). By mid-century the focus had somewhat changed from the tough hero conquering the forces of nature to the sexually powerful male who, in fantasy, conquers 'large-breasted women', epitomized in the rise of magazines such as *Playboy*. Kimmel comments, as the title suggests, men now experienced their manhood most profoundly 'when they were boys at play, not men at work' (1996: 254–5). So the shift to leisure seems complete?

Ultimately, however, none of these forms of re-establishing an idealized form of hegemonic masculinity in an increasingly feminized culture is successful. Kimmel concludes that the battle to prove manhood is a battle that can never be won. For the muscular man, there is always someone stronger working out in the next gym. Propping up manhood by exclusion has never brought men the security and comfort of a stable gender identity. Respite through escape is only temporary and must be renewed constantly. The answer, he claims, is in renouncing the battle and joining in the battle of others for their share of the sun – renouncing exclusion, while embracing diversity and equality for women, people of colour, gay men and lesbians. He says men must wrest their identities away from the arena of competition, domination and power, and re-anchor them in the arena of accountability, responsibility and hope. There must be a masculinity aligned with a commitment to act ethically, with controlled aggression, self-reliance and dependability coupled with the newer masculine virtues of compassion, nurturing and a fierce egalitarianism. He does not want men to be the same as women, but to recombine what was best from the older traditions of honour and trust with a newer enlargement of masculinities to encompass men's relationality, emotionality and caring (1996: 333–5). A tall order indeed! There is a need, then, to think how men's leisure may contribute to such reformulated masculinities, of the costs along the way and of changes in cultural emphases and power which may allow this to happen.

In Kimmel's analysis, leisure becomes a major factor in men's attempts to measure up to the idealized form of masculinity which is hegemonic at a particular historical period. Yet, even as the ideal varies, it remains unattainable for most men and makes their individual sense of masculinity vulnerable. On the other hand, each variation incorporates a toughness and strength, whether physical or sexual, which is deemed superior to women's gentleness and passivity, so that male power is protected and perpetuated. While Kimmel does not explore the overall implications of this power for men, as he focuses rather on the fragility of masculinity for most men, it does provide insights into the construction of masculinity in a patriarchal society. It has needed feminism and masculinist responses such as Kimmel's to place such collusion in the wider cultural context and to ask men to examine for themselves their own part in the perpetuation of hegemonic masculinity. The strength of Kimmel's analysis in relationship to leisure is to position men's sport and leisure as a means of shoring up a cultural construction of masculinity which is by no means inviolable. By inference, leisure may then also be a space for men to challenge such hegemony and to recombine some of the real strengths of traditional masculinity with some of the affirming aspects of traditional femininity. Such hybridity, it seems, would advantage both men and women at a personal level.

The weakness of Kimmel's approach is his failure to go beyond a nominal acknowledgement of the power that accrues to men in patriarchies through hegemonic masculinity. While he reminds us in the introduction that we need to make gender visible to men in order to critique male-governed military exploits, policy decisions, scientific experiments and writing styles, he does not pursue these results of male power. The main thrust of his work is to engage our sympathy for individual males caught up in a culture which valorizes and idealizes a certain type of masculinity and which leaves men in constant fear of exposure to vulnerability in the eyes of other men. A more thoroughgoing critique of the construction of hegemonic masculinity in patriarchal capitalist societies is left to Connell, whose work consciously attempts to place masculinities within the context of the structures of power in such societies.

Connell: Masculinities, Multiple Subjectivities and Cultural Reconfiguration

By far the most theoretically sophisticated analysis of gender from a masculinist perspective has come from Connell and those who have worked with him in a genuine attempt to acknowledge the asymmetry of power relations between men and women in patriarchal society. In a seminal article,

Carrigan et al. (1985) critiqued sex-role theory and socialization as explanations for male/female differences. As long as these explanations are adhered to, they claim, the status quo of male dominance/female subordination will be not be dislodged. Sex-role theory enshrines the categories of male and female within a functionalist logic – what is has to be, because it is functional for the industrial society in which we live. The male, instrumental, breadwinner, leadership role requires aggressive, competitive, competent men and it is the function of the family, the education system, church, peer groups, sport and the workforce, to socialize males from an early age into these characteristics. Those who do not conform are deviant, and various attempts are made to re-socialize them for correct fit. The female, nurturing, caring, expressive role requires women who are gentle, passive, conciliatory, self-effacing and supportive. Socialization through explicit and implicit sanctions, as for males, is the means by which these characteristics are internalized and come to be accepted as normal and natural. Without some acknowledgement of the gender power differentials that such socialization draws upon and creates, and without some critique of the inevitability of adult male and female sex-roles, little is gained from sex-role theory for an understanding of the lived experience of gender difference and male dominance in industrial patriarchal society. Carrigan, Connell and Lee provided such a critique by showing the ways in which men are advantaged by this socialization, while at the same time addressing some of the restrictive aspects such as emotional poverty for men.

Included in this critique are the insights gained from the burgeoning literature arising from the gay movement, that is, from those men who were also disadvantaged by not fitting into the dominant form of heterosexual masculinity implicit in sex-role theory (see Mieli, 1980; Walter, 1980; Bayer, 1981). There are also ideas from poststructuralists such as Foucault (1979a, 1979b, 1983, 1984), who focus on the deconstruction of rigidly gendered subjectivities. There is an emphasis in the argument on the variety of masculinities and femininities and a critique of the dominance of hegemonic heterosexual tough masculinity which had remained unquestioned by the role theorists. Connell builds on this earlier work in his books *Gender and Power* (1987) and *Masculinities* (1995), which have become definitive texts in the area.

In an eclectic attempt to marry aspects of Marxism and socialist feminism, psychoanalysis, gay liberation literature and poststructuralist deconstruction and subjectivity, Connell (1987) provides us with a determinedly masculinist approach to gender differences in a context of the power relationships of capitalist patriarchy. His aim is to deconstruct gender and reconstruct it on the foundations of the three structures: power, the division of labour and cathexis. He suggests greater flexibility in gender relations beyond heterosexual nuclear family relationships. He argues for the common humanity of both male and female people such that intra-gender differences may be as great as inter-gender differences. The strength of his theory of praxis lies in his critique of unquestioned reinforcement of the gender power relationships inherent in sex-role theory and socialization as explanations for gender differences. The underlying assumption of an invariant biological base and a malleable social superstructure in these accounts Connell rightly dismisses as unproductive in challenging the asymmetry of power relationships between men and women:

> The potential effect is to highlight the pressures that create an artificially rigid distinction between women and men, and to play down the economic, domestic and political power that men exercise over women . . . the female role and the male role are tacitly treated as equal and are constructed around ideas of a normative, standard case, rather than the lived experiences of a variety of males and females. (1987: 50–1)

Emerging from this critique of sex-role theory Connell goes on to critique categoricalism. Most authors assume wrongly, he claims, that reproductive biology divides humans neatly into two distinct categories. As a first approximation this may be all right, but when the categories 'woman' and 'man' are taken as absolutes in no need of further examination or finer differentiation, the complexity of lived experience is obscured. The turbulence and contradictoriness within the social process of gender are underplayed, struggle in existing relationships appears as pointless, since the structure and categories are universal.

Connell's view of power, his plea for deconstruction of the categories male and female, and his insistence on practical politics, choice, doubt, strategy, planning, error and transformation for an understanding of gender differences, place his work in the poststructuralist mode. However he strives to maintain a balance between structure and agency by making the structures which govern gender relationships a condition of the various practices which defy categoricalism. He focuses directly on the structure of power.

Power, for Connell, is a set of social relations with some scope and permanence which advantages men in capitalist society. It is multiple in character, including force and violence, inequality of resources in the workplace, household or larger institutions and the ideologies and cultural hegemony which gain assent from the powerless. This structure of power acts as a constraint on social practice so that women are disadvantaged, for example in monogamous marriage where women even yet constitute a form of property belonging to one man. For Connell (1987: 109) there is a core in the power structure of gender in advanced capitalist countries which enables males to control cultural practices, even as they control the productive processes in their own interests.

The four components of this core are:

1 the hierarchies and workforces of institutionalized violence – military and paramilitary forces, police, prison systems;
2 the hierarchy and labour force of heavy industry (for example, steel and oil companies) and the hierarchy of high technology industry (computers, aerospace);

3 the planning and control machinery of the central state; and
4 working-class milieux that emphasize toughness and men's association with machinery.

In society as a whole, then, women are subordinated to men, although at the local level of particular households, particular workplaces and particular settings there may be local victories for women in the everyday gender power struggles.

In *Masculinities* (1995) the theoretical base of male power and the powerful and exclusionary aspects of hegemonic masculinity remain the same. The construction of a tough and virile heterosexual masculinity which inferiorizes women and gay men and gains power for men, which assumes hegemonic form and is difficult to shake, remains as a core theme throughout the book. The insistence on a variety of masculinities and femininities remains. Added in are Connell's own empirical studies of men who both conform to and resist hegemonic masculinity. In these studies some of the fissures in this hegemony are revealed, as well as the inevitable disadvantages and contradictions that many men face due to their inability to conform to its demands. There is also an inclusion of ideas of men's embodiment and the place that this has in the construction of masculinities focused particularly on men's physical sexuality. It is within the empirical studies that the place of leisure in both the reinforcement of and resistance to hegemonic masculinity is elucidated. Connell's conclusion concerning reconfiguration and transformation of masculinities also has some implications for leisure.

In his empirical application, Connell (1991, 1995) uses life-history interviews with several different groups of men to show how their construction of masculinities both reinforces and challenges the hegemonic mode. For those who resist, there are costs in terms of ridicule, a sense of not belonging to the group and, in some instances, a sense of decentring and a loss of focus. He shows that there are fissures in the hegemonic construction of masculinity, alternatives not available in previous generations and possibilities for multiple masculinities which combine elements from different male trajectories. In each of his studies, leisure forms an available space for trying out different masculine subjectivities.

For the five unemployed young men who are outside the 'respectable' working class, three contrasting masculinities are constructed. The first is a masculine protest trajectory, exemplified by violence, school resistance, minor crime, heavy drug/alcohol use, occasional manual labour, motorbikes or cars and short heterosexual liaisons – in other words, a 'pressured exaggeration of masculine conventions' by the relatively powerless (1991: 160). In this context of youth, poverty and marginality leisure is involved in practice and consciousness towards the directly physical; fucking and fighting are the basis of leisure activities which contribute to a sense of masculinity which is obtained outside the workforce. There is a deliberate attempt to build up an appearance of tough masculinity. Yet there are also disjunctions and contradictions, so that protest masculinity is not simply observance of a stereotyped male role. Connell shows how with different individual men it is also compatible with respect and attention to women, egalitarian views about the sexes, affection for children and a sense of display associated with carefully orchestrated body tattoos in one instance (1995: 112). The second trajectory is a masculinity which is complicit with patriarchy in that these men want the benefits of male supremacy, but they do not care to pay the full price of upholding hegemonic masculinity. They opt out of the physical leisure confrontations, manual labour, the maintenance of peer life through leisure and look down on the first group as naively masculine 'ockers'. In the third trajectory, there is the attempted negation of masculinity and re-jection of patriarchy, exemplified by one respondent who cross-dresses and another one who became involved in the environmental movement and has tried to accept at a personal level feminism's critique of men's misogyny.

In this diversity Connell sees possibilities for change in masculinity and thus in gender relationships. Even the contradictions in the first group between the hyper-masculinity of the road and the party scene and the economic logic of egalitarian households and the interest of some in chil-dren pose alternatives not present in their parents' generation.

In another study, Connell (1990a, 1995) uses life-history interviews with six men to examine their involvement with the environmental movement and how masculinity is reconstructed in a setting where feminism is strong. In this study, green involvement was part of their leisure activity for five of the men. The findings of this study show how difficult it is for individual men to challenge the traditional form of hegemonic masculinity without becom-ing 'passive', 'decentred' and/or 'out of focus' (1990a: 471). He suggests the ultimate result may be to modernize patriarchy rather than abolish it, unless there are interpersonal and collective practices which incorporate 'gen-dered counter-sexist politics for men who reject hegemonic masculinity' (1990a: 476). And these, he says, in Marxian fashion, would need to operate in settings such as workplaces, unions and the state which the counter-sexist men's movement so far has scarcely begun to enter. He does not mention leisure, although it is obvious from his empirical studies that this is a key site for challenge and transformation.

Change is a central theme of the life-stories of eight men from a gay com-munity, and in all of them leisure had a part in their journey in establishing themselves as homosexuals in a homophobic world. For example: 'Dean moved to Sydney and immediately began to have sex with men, to come out as gay, and to "rage" around the bars and nightclubs' (Connell, 1995: 157). For all of the men interviewed there were deliberate attempts to challenge, in sexual as well as in other activities, the characteristics of heterosexual he-gemonic masculinity.

Connell turns from the physical to the rational for his final empirical study reported in *Masculinities*. Based on nine life-histories of men in pro-fessional and technical occupations, he shows how these men constructed masculinities in conventional settings of family where the father was the provider and school where football emphasized tough physical masculinity. Yet there was also some distancing from negative exemplars of hegemonic masculinity such as dim-witted footballers and identification with expertise based in strong-minded rationality. Irrationality and emotionality are deliberately kept at bay, although, as with physical masculinity, there are chinks in the armour of the men and irrationality and emotionality creep in. This is particularly so in their relationships with women inside and outside the workforce. The ambiguity is evident in Hugh Trelawney's attempts to change after a physical and emotional crisis of considerable depth:

> I re-examined the way I related to people, my sort of competitive type status-conscious ethos. I looked in particular at the way I related to women. I realized I had lost the person who hated the automatic consideration of females as inferior and who hated the idea of them not getting equal pay. Deep down I was a fucking chauvinist. I still treated the love/sex thing as basically a game, as a funny game, something comparable to football. (Connell, 1995: 179–80)

Connell concludes that, for these men, rationality is limited or disputable and 'there is no straightforward accommodation between hegemonic masculinity and the rationalized occupational world of advanced capitalism' (1995: 178). This study shows again that hegemonic masculinity is hard to shake, but that the chinks are there with possibilities for change and that leisure provides one space for change.

The overall theme of *Masculinities* is the pervasiveness of hegemonic masculinity which is constructed and constrained by the structures of labour, power and cathexis in patriarchal societies. Individual men who challenge hegemonic masculinity face many difficulties and personal costs, as well as some advantages. Connell shows that the fissures are there, and that young men outside the workforce, gay men and men in the 'new middle-class' technologically oriented occupations are using leisure along with other aspects of their lives to construct masculinities which do not completely conform to the hegemonic mode. The value, as in the above empirical applications, has been to point out possibilities for creating cracks in hegemonic masculinity, in spaces outside the workplace as well as within it, even by those who are relatively powerless. The weakness lies in an implicit move from the gulf between genders in terms of relationships of power to a tendency to pose males who conform to heterosexual hegemonic masculinity as the powerful and all other males as well as females as the relatively powerless. It is possible for hegemonic masculinity to be reproduced and also to confer power within the gay culture (see Blachford, 1981). Connell's insistence on heterosexuality as an essential element in hegemonic masculinity obscures this issue. The emphasis throughout the work on gay males as an alternative to hegemonic masculinity ignores the enormous power yet attributed to male ebodiment through valorization of the phallus and inferiorization of the female body, which extends far beyond the physical sexuality discussed by Connell. This question will be raised in more detail, especially with regard to leisure, in the following chapter.

Nevertheless, Connell's conclusion offers up some hope for transformation of hegemonic masculinity. If recognition of multiple masculinities and degendering can decompose the difference/dominance dichotomy, inroads can be made into gender power relationships which shore up hegemonic masculinity. Masculinities reconstructed from the 'positive culture produced around hegemonic masculinity', together with positive aspects of feminine culture, offer hope for 'reconfiguration and transformation of masculinities' (1995: 233). Difference will remain, but optimistically without its implications for dominance/submission. For this to happen Connell sees that there must be alliances with women and other oppressed groups, rather than men-only therapy or men's movement groups. The hope lies in reconfiguration of the elements of traditonal masculinity and traditional femininity. In an argument similar to Butler's (1990), concerning the reconstruction of feminine subjectivities through repeated performative acts, Connell suggests transformation of hegemonic masculinity is possible through enactments of different forms of masculinity and femininity which bring social reality into being. For us the question remains: 'What part can sport and leisure play in this poststructural reconfiguration of multiple gendered subjectivities?' For the argument I am developing in this book, the more specific question is: 'Can leisure spaces be used by men to move beyond hegemonic masculinity to become men who are mentally and emotionally strong, with a secure sense of self-worth?'

Conclusion

Masculinist responses to the feminisms of the last three decades have illuminated the many contradictions that are present for men in patriarchal societies where men have overall power but struggle at an individual level to meet the demands of hegemonic masculinity. The assumptions of physical and mental toughness, success in sport and paid employment, aggressiveness, competitiveness, independence and rationality pose problems for many men, as does the distancing and downplaying of emotional and nurturing, caring behaviour. The work of masculinist writers such as Messner, Kimmel and Connell has raised issues concerning the subjectivities of men in the current cultural climate of the increasing power of women and the challenges that women and men are making to traditional male and female roles. Although the issues raised cover all aspect of men's lives, leisure has a particular place in the discussion, because of its informal norms, the context of intimacy and relationships in which much leisure occurs and the relative freedom of its parameters.

Studies such as Connell's have shown that there is considerable pressure for individual men to conform to heterosexual hegemonic masculinity. This is especially evident in sport and leisure activities where informal norms abound and ridicule is an effective and socially acceptable way of enforcing the norms. Threats to masculinity in the form of taunts about being like a girl, a sissy and effeminate are effective, both tapping in to perceptions of femininity as inferior to masculinity and in reinforcing such perceptions.

The interests that are served by the cultural hegemony of the dominant form of masculinity are overall power in all the institutions of society. While such hegemony continues to distance, exclude and inferiorize an oppositional femininity, women as a whole will remain subordinated to men at an individual, group and societal level. Hegemonic masculinity is not a natural state for men: it is culturally constructed and varies over time, but in the interests of men in gender power struggles, it retains a central core of toughness, physical and sexual prowess and aggressiveness and the distancing of femininity. For individual men, the historically constructed dominant masculinity of the time is fragile and in need of constant proof in the eyes of other men. Yet its maintenance, especially in times of women's increase in power, is vital to men's societal power. It is in men's interests at a societal level to maintain cultural dominance through hegemonic masculinity.

Considering the overall advantages to men of hegemonic masculinity, it is difficult to shake, yet very few real men are able to conform to its ideological attributes. For individual men there is a fragility and vulnerability about their sense of masculinity which requires all sorts of face-saving mechanisms. and a sense of masculinity is a vital part of men's sense of self and self-esteem. At times of social change when traditional sources of male prestige such as provider capacity falter and when women are gaining social power, men turn to sport and leisure activities for reinforcement of hegemonic masculinity. Nevertheless leisure can also be a space for men to challenge, resist and possibly loosen the grip of tough, aggressive, exclusionary masculinity.

There is the possibility through leisure as a personal space to deconstruct and recombine aspects of traditional masculinity and femininity to form masculinities and femininities which are different from one another without dominance and submission. Here again the term hybridity seems appropriate to connote a mixing of the elements of different cultures, in this case male and female cultures. Through repeated performative acts in leisure activities which combine individual capacities and achievement with caring, support, emotional expression, relationality and sharing, in enjoyable circumstances, it may be possible to shift the cultural construction of masculinity beyond its foundation on an opposite and inferiorized femininity. It may also allow men to enlarge their sense of self to include emotions and to allow them a vulnerability that previously has needed to be covered up and protected by men and defended in many indirect ways by women.

I think that women have always known intuitively, or have been taught, that men's egos are very fragile and that part of the feminine role has been to protect and endorse a strong sense of hegemonic masculinity in the men they have relationships with. In this way they have been encouraged to collude with hegemonic masculinity and have helped perpetuate it. Kimmel's analysis certainly resonates with some of my own ways of inter- acting with boys and men during my formative years. However it has needed feminism and responses such as Kimmel's to reveal the wider cul- tural impact of such collusion and to show how individual men can retain a sense of superiority over women while protecting their own vulnerability. Men as a whole gain cultural hegemony which engenders power. When women no longer collude, a very real threat to men's sense of masculinity is posed. Yet, as both Connell and Kimmel suggest, there is the possibility of reformulation of masculinities which draw on the inner strength and honour of men, rather than on outward physical and rational projections. As some of the men in a study of anti-sexist men by Christian (1994) demonstrate, a strong sense of self and a valuing for oneself of the sensitive and caring aspects of men's natures can outweigh the opinions of others. These men are strong in the moral sense suggested by Kimmel. They go beyond the 'poor boy' syndrome to develop masculinities based on inner strength which they yet perceive as different from being a woman. For example, Arnold, who says: 'I don't have to prove I'm a man. I'm not ef- feminate. I'm a man anyway so everything I do is manly, whatever other people think.' Or Martin, who feels he doesn't fit either a macho or a gay model:

> I obviously don't fit the macho image, nor do I fit any gay model, I just see myself as being sensitive. I value my sensitive side. I never doubt it, or see it as a bad value. It's a benefit, not an unmanly attribute . . . It's part of my person- ality as a human being . . . I can't be a surrogate woman. It would be wrong for me to try to be that. (Christian, 1994: 40)

Women's rationality and emotionality may well be different from men's and vice versa, as this man suggests. There remains the possibility of differ- ence without the hierachical valorization of hegemonic masculinity over femininities and other masculinities. Men may nurture and care for children in a very different way from women and express their emotions and moral- ity in different ways from women as Gilligan suggested. What women want perhaps is to be different from men and not to be punished for it by indi- vidual men or by the power relationships of patriarchal society. In contra- diction to both Gilligan's and Chodorow's ideas that men's sense of masculinity is formed for all men in the break away from exclusive moth- ering and consequent distancing of intimacy and emotionality, some of the anti-sexist men in Christian's study had identified with a strong female figure in the form of their mother or another adult woman at a later stage in their lives. What needs to change are the traditional ways for men and women to go about the practices of their everyday lives in family and other relationships, and more generally in leisure spaces, as well as in the labour force. Gendered subjectivities can then be constructed which go beyond protected hegemonic masculinity and inferiorized femininity, but which do not turn men into women, women into men or everyone into androgynous clones.

For this to happen there remains much to be done in challenging and transforming traditional power bases, rigid definitions of masculinity and femininity and, as we shall see in the next chapter, a concerted attack upon phallocentric definitions of male and female bodies and ways of expressing emotions.

6

Embodiment, Emotions and Leisure

Socio-economic, political and ethical changes in the post-industrial, post-modern era have created a shift in Western industrial societies from the pre-eminence of heavy industrial production and scientific rationality, shored up with Christian puritanical orthodoxy, to an emphasis on the service industries, mass consumerism and leisure, pleasure, desire, difference, playfulness and the whole world outside the workplace (Turner, 1996: 2). In this context both the body and emotions have come to the fore as legitimate foci for sociological analysis. 'Given the emphasis on leisure, individual expression and consumption,' claims Turner, 'the body emerges as a field of hedonistic practices and desire in a culture that recognizes the body as a project' (1996: 4). The shift in social relations from the sphere of material industrial production to that of consumption and leisure, in which the body and emotions play a predominant part, has been recognized in social theory by a corresponding shift in emphasis. This shift, together with feminist and masculinist critiques of the male domination of social theory in which rationality and the mind were polarized and prioritized over emotions and the body (see Grosz, 1987; Seidler, 1994), has made possible a new sociology of the body and emotions. In this chapter I explore the implications for an understanding of leisure spaces which these insights have produced. This is done, not only to recognize gender differences, but also to point to the need for leisure research now to investigate ways in which leisure spaces may be used by both men and women to expand their own potentialities and improve relationships between them.

For the sake of conceptual clarity the body and emotions are dealt with separately. Initially there is a brief outline of the sociology of the body pointing to the way that feminists and masculinists have reconceptualized male and female bodies to dismantle essentialist notions of biological masculinity and femininity. Thus they have opened the way for alternative social constructions. Applications to sport and leisure are then made, showing both the remaining dominance of myths concerning the male body which shore up hegemonic masculinity, but also some ambiguities which presage changes which may benefit both men and women.

The second section of the chapter addresses the sociology of emotions, with a focus on Simmel's concept of 'neurasthenia' and city leisure, Elias's concept of 'mimetic experience' in leisure, Lyng's 'edge work' and Hochschild's 'deep acting' and 'feeling rules'. Here again I point to gender differences and, in particular, to the potential for the use of leisure spaces for the legitimation of male pleasure and male violence. As a balance, I also suggest that these spaces may be used in a positive way for emotional release.

Sociology of the Body

In contemporary society there has been a resurgence of interest in the body. We are bombarded constantly through the media with images of the young, healthy, sexy body as essential to social success. The body is commodified to sell diet and health products, fashion, the gym, sport and sporting gear, leisure and travel. Health and fitness focus on the body, sport emphasizes the body beautiful, and the postponement of ageing and AIDS and cancer bring attention to unwell bodies. In sociology the body is the interface between social structures, institutions, culture, ideologies, discourses and individual subjectivity. Yet its introduction as focus for sociological analysis has been relatively recent.

In contrast to anthropology which focused on the human body (albeit a male body) as the constant across cultures and with some control over nature, classical sociology ignored the body in favour of economics, politics and the law. Thus sociology reified Western cultural opposition between culture and nature. For example, Marx was concerned with the material production of goods rather than the reproduction of bodies. Parsons took economics and law as models for the formulation of the basic motives of actor, action, choice and goals. In Weber the body was subsumed beneath the *actor* who appeared as a decision-making agent. The Frankfurt School argued that 'Christianity and capitalism have joined forces to declare that work is virtuous, but the body is flesh and the source of all evil. The love–hate relationship with the body dominates modern culture' (Turner, 1991: 17). Mead privileged the mind over the body – what if his major work had been entitled *The Body, Self and Society* instead of *The Mind, Self and Society*?

One exception is Goffman. The body is the foundation of his theories of stigma, face-work, embarrassment and the social self (e.g. see his *The Presentation of Self in Everyday Life* (1969)). He also recognizes the way that the male body is consistently represented, at least in gender advertisements, as more powerful than the female body (1976). The legacy in modern symbolic interactionist theory has been an awareness of the symbolic significance of the body and gestures to the interactional order.

It is in the postmodern, post-industrial era that poststructuralist sociological theories have resurrected the body as 'a seat of desire and irrationality, emotionality and sexual passion . . . a symbol of protest against capitalist rationality and bureaucratic regulation' (Turner, 1991: 17). There has been a shift from labour to hedonism as a driving force in contemporary society: 'Images of the body beautiful openly associated with hedonism, leisure and display emphasize the importance of appearance and the "look"' (Featherstone, 1982: 18).

Sociologists have looked to the work of Foucault for concepts of power and resistance, bodily discipline, surveillance and self-surveillance to position the body in its social context. Foucault, commenting on materialism in Marx, wonders whether before posing the question of ideology, 'wouldn't it be more materialist to study first the question of the body and the effects of power on it?' (quoted in Gordon, 1980: 58). He was particularly interested in the construction of a micro-politics of regulation of the body and self-surveillance and a macro-politics of surveillance of populations. He saw these as the two places around which the organization of power over life is deployed.

The morphology of the prison 'panopticon', with its central viewing tower and circular, open-faced cells, was the epitome of the public control and surveillance of individual bodies. Its corollary was self-surveillance, through which the individual watched his own bodily behaviour to make sure it conformed to the prescribed norms. The school, the military and the church were institutions which focused on detailed instruction in bodily control and self-surveillance to produce 'docile bodies'. The 'sciences' of psychology, medicine and criminology with their claims to objective 'truth' regulated the internal and external body (see Foucault's *Discipline and Punish*, 1979c, for a detailed discussion). Discourses on sexuality controlled the use of the body in sexual activity making homosexual activity, promiscuity, sex outside marriage, and so on, illegitimate (see Foucault, *The History of Sexuality, Vol. 1*, 1978). The body could also be used to resist such control, although Foucault himself doesn't elaborate on such resistance and the body he speaks of is a male body. Yet Foucault's ideas have laid a foundation for feminist and masculinist poststructuralist explorations of the body in postmodern society with implications for the use of the body in leisure spaces.

Feminist Theory and the Body

Poststructural feminists have applied Foucault's ideas to the control of the female body and developed the idea of the body as a means of resistance to such control with possibilities for re-visioning the female body beyond its inferiorization to its male equivalent. They have also attempted to deconstruct the mind/body hierarchical dichotomy to revalue the part that the body plays in everyday life and experience.

Susan Bordo critiques the 'old feminism' for constructing 'an insufficiently textured, undiscerning dualistic, overly pessimistic (if not paranoid) view of the politics of the body' where power is top-down and repressive: males are always powerful and females always powerless, males dominate and females are subordinate (1995: 23). She draws rather on Foucault's concept of power as a network of non-centralized forces which configure to regulate the most minute elements of the construction of space, time, desire and embodiment. Such power operating 'from below' works through individual self-surveillance and self-correction to norms. These ideas she applies to the politics of women's appearance and to the contemporary disciplines of diet and exercise and the concomitant eating disorders. At the same time such power is also unstable: 'resistance is perpetual and hegemony precarious' (Bordo, 1995: 28). In her view men are not the enemy – they also can feel tyrannized by the forces of power, in spite of the fact that they often have a higher stake in maintaining institutions within which they have historically occupied positions of domination over women. Her work presents a detailed critique of current textual representations of women's bodies and the so-called 'pleasure and power' that they can attain through exercise and diet, used to bring the body closer to the ideal presented in the texts. Yet she sees that women's resistance cannot remain in the textual world but must embrace their lives in the everyday world. She is encouraging women to resist their individualized self-surveillance and the cultural insistence that what they see in the mirror is wrong, defective and a caricature of the idealized norm. She acknowledges that the personal risks of doing this at an individual level are great – as the many women who have been sexually rejected for being 'too fat' and fired from their jobs for looking 'too old' know all too well (1995: 298). She argues the need for women to come together and explore what the culture continually presents to them as their individual choices (or – as in the case of anorexia and bulimia – their 'pathology'). She wishes them to discover, instead, that perceptions of the body are culturally situated and culturally shared. This she sees as the feminist politics of the body (1995: 300). I suggest that leisure spaces may be one place where these things can happen.

In a similar vein, Smith (1988: 41) applies Foucault's concept of discourse to links between dominant discourses on the body and women's subjectivities concerning their bodies. She claims that, in our time, to come to grips with femininity is to address a 'textual discourse' which is incorporated in women's magazines and television, advertisements, the appearance of cosmetic counters, fashion displays and to some extent books. This discourse constructs femininity as different from masculinity and in many ways as the object of male observation and desire. It is different from masculinity in that the female body is presented as never perfect; clothing, colours, make-up, diet and exercise are all needed in order to bring it more nearly into line with the textual image. But women are not the passive recipients of the discourse – it is women themselves who practise this discipline on and against their own bodies, so in a sense the choice is theirs. This self-surveillance is a form of obedience to patriarchy. Throughout life women are constantly creating and recreating themselves in an attempt to bring their bodies and the appearance of their bodies in line with the dominant textual discourse. That they are never totally successful in this endeavour engenders a sense of inferiority and incompleteness, and many women do not like their own bodies or, at least, some aspects of them.

Analyses such as Bordo's and Smith's allow us to see how representations of women's bodies through 'textual discourses' constrain women to surveille their own bodies in order to normalize them. In extreme cases women become anorexic or take recourse to plastic surgery to enlarge breasts, reduce breasts or change the shape of a nose in an attempt to fit the image. Even women who resist by becoming fat in order to avoid entering relations with men in the workplace are acting on assumptions predicated on the doctrines of femininity. For the majority of women the discourse has the effect over their lifetime of a pervasive sense of bodily deficiency. Nor do they gain much in terms of status or material rewards for their trouble; rather to spend such time on 'vanity' is defined as trivial and a sign of the inferiority of women's intellect. So that discourses on the body have, for women, the effect of gaining their collusion to the objectification and inferiorization of women's bodies. Much leisure time is spent in regimes which attempt to improve bodily appearance.

Nevertheless a number of resistances have appeared in recent years. Women who 'pump iron', such as the Australian weight-lifter turned body-builder, Bev Francis, defy the current canons of femininity. Lesbian women have redefined the signs of age such as grey hair and 'character' lines as beautiful. And a popular literature of resistance is growing, such as Orbach's (1979) *Fat is a Feminist Issue*. Women who become conscious of the cultural messages incorporated into their subjectivity through discourses can begin to 're-vision' their own bodies and resist the self-imposed disciplines of femininity (Bartky, 1988: 83). Feminist women who have had access to alternative discourses are able, at least, to question the use of the term 'feminine' in current usage. For example, two feminist women in my study of mothers had this to say about being 'feminine'.

> 'Feminine' is a word dreamed up by men to keep women out of responsible positions.
>   I think it's such a value laden word, it's not difficult to use. I think what 'feminine' implies is that the woman fits the female role very well or tries to fit it and succeeds. I mean there are small and petite women who need a lot of help because they're not very strong, but I don't think that all the attrib·tes of femininity would be confined in one woman because in a society where ·vomen were encouraged to develop the aspects of themselves that they wanted to, that women wouldn't feel the need to fit the feminine role so exactly. (Wearing, 1984: 114)

There is also some evidence amongst younger women of a move away from the ideal of the small, petite, fine-boned woman to a tall, wide-shouldered, well-muscled body, as exemplified by the Australian model Elle MacPherson (see Craik, 1994; Van Gyn et al., 1989).

The French feminists add another dimension to theorizing the relationship between women's bodies and social relationships. They make strong links between women's oppression through language and discourse, and women's bodies and sexuality and the possibilities for resistance. The fact that women have a vagina which sheaths the male penis, lips of the vulva which constantly embrace, plural sites of erotic pleasure and multiple orgasms has been used by some (see Irigaray, 1986) to argue both that women's libido and sexual pleasure is different from men's and that it has been subordinated to phallocentric libido and pleasure and male constructions of sexuality, language and discourse. But these French feminists also attack such phallocentrism. They make fun of the male erection, the male preoccupation with getting it up and keeping it up, and the ways in which the life and death of the penis are projected into other aspects of the culture (Marks and de Courtivron, 1986). They urge women to assert their right to sexual pleasure which is more diffuse and prolonged than men's, to regard the vagina as an active, grasping organ rather than a passive, receptive one and to use their bodies in active pleasurable ways. The word 'jouissance' (sexual pleasure, bliss, rapture) is frequently used by them in connection with women's sexuality. It carries with it the notions of fluidity, diffusion, duration, flow, expansiveness, giving, expending and excessive escape, which have no cultural counterpart in patriarchal societies. These bodily metaphors represent the 'feminine', women's specificity, not an extension of the 'same', that is male culture.

Australian feminist philosophers such as Gatens (1996), Grosz (1987, 1994, 1995a, 1995b) and Lloyd (1989) attempt to deconstruct 'male' dichotomies such as mind/body, culture/nature, reason/desire and male/ female, where the former have been valorized and the latter inferiorized. Grosz argues for a consideration of the body as *the* primary object of social production and inscription and against it being tied to a fixed essence. She insists that the body is lived or experienced by the subject and thus is open to a diversity of interpretations. She says:

> Women's specificities, their corporeality and subjectivities are not inherently resistant to representation or depiction. They may be unrepresentable in a culture in which the masculine can represent others only as versions of itself, where the masculine relies on the subordination of the feminine. But this is not logically or biologically fixed. It can be contested and changed and it can be redefined, reconceived, reinscribed in ways entirely different from those that mark it today. (Grosz, 1987: 15)

In *Volatile Bodies*, Grosz explores this idea further, suggesting that if the body is not a natural fact, as has been suggested, but is itself volatile, then 'gender' can no longer be conceived as a malleable overlay on a static category 'sex'. Both sex and gender are then open to reinterpretation in the current socio-political and historical context, to give more value to women's embodiment. Other feminists such as Butler (1993), Gatens (1996) and Nicholson (1995a, 1995b) provide similar arguments. According to them sex is not a pre-given object, but an ideal construct reified through cultural discourses. Thus over time it becomes a regulatory power governing bodies and is implicit in the very formulation of the subject from birth onwards. In their view gender subsumes sex allowing for the reformulation of what it actually means to have male or female genitals. Thus they hope to transcend the interpretation of female bodies as inferior to male bodies due to lack of a penis and to rewrite the definition of female bodies as strong, capable, active, enduring and sexually powerful.

Masculism and the Body

Feminists aren't the only sociologists who have applied poststructuralist ideas to the body. Masculinist literature, such as that by Connell (1987, 1995), Craig (1992), Messner (1992a, 1992b), Morgan (1993) and Turner (1984, 1996), has turned attention to male bodies and the constraints placed on the male body in contemporary society. Connell argues that there is a hierarchy of masculinities with hegemonic, heterosexual, macho masculinity having the most power and prestige in Australian society. The plight of homosexual, sensitive, non-athletic men, men who do not fit the bronzed Aussie image, is posed and their inferiorization deplored. Similarly Messner looks at the place of sport in the construction of an acceptable male body and a 'winning' male subjectivity, and the impossibility of this achievement for all males and for any males at later stages of the life-course. Morgan points out that what has been conceived as men's preoccupation with the penis and its size representing virility and sexuality may, in fact, be a myth and that adolescent embarrassment at unexpected erections is closer to the truth. Whether this is so or not, he does succeed in pointing to the fragility of the male organ and the huge defences that men and male-dominated society have had to institute to construct the male body and the male organ as all-powerful.

This literature suggests that in the social construction of male bodies, the majority of men are also disadvantaged. Yet the myth that Morgan seeks to explode is the very basis of the power of phallocentrism in language, culture and representation which poststructuralist feminists are seeking to subvert. Whereas masculinists point to the sense of powerlessness that many men feel when they compare their bodies with the masculine ideal, feminists point out that it is this very myth that gives men power and constructs women's bodies as different and inferior. Other masculinists such as Kimmel (1996) demonstrate the many and various ways that men in the American culture, over a century and a half, have used sport and leisure as a means of proving a muscular manhood that distances and excludes womanhood. It seems to me it must be in men's overall interests to preserve the myth of male bodily power, otherwise why bother?

While there may be differences in the feminist and masculinist poststructural perspectives of the body, in terms of who is disadvantaged and where the power lies, both perspectives point to the social construction of the body and therefore to the malleability of its meanings and the diversity of individual subjectivities that can be constructed around embodiment. Some of this diversity will require, however, considerable resistance to dominant discourses on male and female bodies. In the following section I examine some of the ambiguities that arise in leisure and sport due to male and female embodiment (i.e. how we live in and interpret our bodies) and suggest that these ambiguities may create space for change.

The Body, Leisure and Sport

In an application of poststructuralist feminist ideas to the way that women use their bodies in space, Iris Young (1990) shows how women's actions are confined and they do not use their full potential in sports and in other leisure activities such as dancing. Young points out that even though there is no eternal feminine essence, there is a common basis underlying individual female existence under present social and cultural circumstances which influences the ways that women use their bodies in space and which helps to define women as subjects. In this I agree with her especially as she does not see this commonality amongst women as essentialist, but open to redefinition.

Young points out that even relatively untrained men engage in sport with more free motion and open reach than do their female counterparts. In throwing, running, climbing, swinging and hitting, girls and women do not use the whole of their bodies in the way that men do, nor do they reach, extend, lean, stretch and follow through.

> Thus, for example, in softball or volleyball women tend to remain in one place more often than men do, neither jumping to reach nor running to approach the ball. Men more often move out toward a ball in flight and confront it with their own countermotion. Women tend to wait for and then *react* to its approach, rather than going forth to meet it. We frequently respond to the motion of a ball coming toward us as though it were coming at us, and our immediate bodily impulse is to flee, duck, or otherwise protect ourselves from its flight. (Young, 1990: 146)

The consequences for women, she argues, are that they most often do not realize their full potential in sport, and experience a greater or lesser feeling of incapacity, frustration and self-consciousness. Young recognizes that this is not true for *all* women. Women can be trained in sport to overcome the cultural obstacles placed in their way from a young age. Constraints begin to appear as soon as they are told not to get hurt, not to get dirty, not to tear clothes and not to attempt dangerous challenges. In order to transcend such prescriptions a conscious effort is needed. Boys have been encouraged to use space quite differently from an early age – they see it as their natural right to throw their bodies into the available space, to get dirty and to attempt challenging bodily tasks.

When women do make the effort to refuse what they have been told they are and to reach towards their potential in the area of bodily movement and the use of space, there is some evidence from the leisure literature of a corresponding increase in self-confidence and a new and exciting awareness of bodily power. For example, women who participate in outdoor adventures such as rock climbing, canoeing, camping, bush walking, scuba diving, body-building and weight-lifting report emotional, physical and psychological benefits (see Beale, 1988; Brace-Govan, 1997; Burden and Kiewa, 1992; Mason-Cox, 1992; Miranda and Yerks, 1985; Scherl, 1988). The empowerment of the physical and emotional element when women venture beyond previously prescribed constraints is spelt out by Burden and Kiewa:

> Outdoor adventure is high on emotion, but also on self-control. The element of uncertainty, which often translates into an element of physical danger, means that fear is frequently a component of outdoor adventure. Other components include exhaustion, wild elation and deep relaxation. Emotions are heightened to an extent not often experienced in the mediocrity of the workaday world. At the same time we learn to recognize our emotional mood, make allowances for it if possible and when necessary, but control dysfunctional emotions (such as paralytic fear or hopeless pessimism) through focusing and attention to task. This element of self-control unlocks physical and mental barriers and extends our capabilities into previously unguessed realms. It is a process of empowerment. (Burden and Kiewa, 1992: 30)

Feminist writers such as Bryson (1987) and Hargreaves (1994) rightly question women's entry into male sport on male terms and the desirability of women's acquisition of male aggressiveness and violence. Nevertheless, they also suggest that it provides women with opportunities for self-expression and an increase in confidence and self-esteem. It is an arena for subjectivities for women which are not passive, acquiescent, self-effacing and based on cultural prescriptions for female bodies and those aspects of them which are associated with reproduction. It is also a source of a sense of physical liberation, as the following incident illustrates.

> I told them I was having a baby in July. Consternation! Most of the club were on the cliff (including several doctors) and messages were relayed from climb to climb, and up and down the ropes, to the effect that Moffat was having a baby and what was the quickest way to get her off the cliff? One would have thought I was about to be confined on the Great Terrace.
> I refused to be stampeded. I had come to the meet to join the club if possible and I was going to lead my climb to qualify. Besides, since we were on the Great Terrace, I pointed out that the easiest way off was to climb. So I led Red Wall and Longland's Continuation – barefooted of course – while a frieze of Pinnaclers sat on the top and watched critically. I felt like a cripple who rediscovers his body while swimming. Here on the airy slabs of those two delightful climbs, where the holds are one-toe holds in places and the run-outs are long, I could forget for a while my pear-shape and feel the old elegance. And, not illogically, there flashed through my mind the hope that the baby would be a girl. (Moffat, 1961: 120–1, quoted in Talbot, 1988a: 110–11)

Women who do engage in physical sporting activity in a non-submissive way appear able to integrate worthwhile aspects of male and female subjectivities, namely, confidence with appreciativeness and firmness with gentleness

(Heaven and Rowe, 1990). This remains so in spite of the fact that at the top level of elite, competitive women's sport, when women are pushed beyond what their own bodies signal is enough, they pay a heavy physical price (Zakus, 1995). The contradictions in sport for women will remain. However it is a leisure arena where women can both challenge and resist dominant male definitions and control of the female use of the body, not only by participating and seeking change but also by promoting 'counter-hegemonic' sporting activities which involve neither aggression, violence and excessive individual competition nor overuse of the body's physical capacity.

There is also some evidence that leisure, in areas other than sport and outdoor adventure, can be a means of freeing the body from social constraint for women. For example, in her study of young women and dance, Griffiths (1988) found that women dancing with and for each other could be an open celebration of the sensuality of the female body. One of her respondents, Deborah, expresses it this way: 'The most enjoyable thing I found in dancing was the "free" feeling. You just hear the music and it completely takes over. It's very relaxing as you use every part of your body and move freely' (Griffiths, 1988: 118).

The feminist literature shows, then, that going beyond previously defined boundaries for women's use of their bodies in leisure space, results in an increased sense of confidence and control, a femininity that is expansive rather than constrictive and an increase in personal power. On the other hand, masculinist studies of men who go outside the norms of masculine use of leisure space, show considerable ambiguity in self-definition and the threat of a loss of power. For example, Burt's (1994) examination of men in ballet brings out the contradictions for men when they are in a position where they are the objects instead of the subjects of gaze, where they are really a chivalrous support for the main female dancer instead of being the central figure themselves and where the use of the male body for ballet has been constructed as effeminate and/or gay. In order to compensate and to defend a masculine identity there are always opportunities for the male dancer to be seen as active not passive, to dominate and to appear to be in control of the ballerina, as well as to demonstrate his own strength. There have also been attempts to show that modern dance is tough or that it is not soft like ballet. Burt uses the example of ballet to demonstrate, once more, that 'the construction of modern masculine identity is actually conflictual and contradictory, and requires the help of complex and deeply rooted structures which surround and defend images of men in cultural forms' (1994: 54). The advantages for men of going outside recognized male leisure spaces are not as obvious as those for women – the risk is ridicule and diminution of a sense of masculinity, as it has been culturally defined. The possibilities that these ventures have for rewriting the script of masculinity have yet to be explored.

At the other end of the spectrum Tomkins (1994) shows that even within such a so-called male preserve as football (i.e. soccer), the image of masculinity does not match the real men that play. The societal view that soccer is the sacred preserve of men and that women do not, should not and indeed cannot play has no real substance in the rules, coaching manuals and indeed in the physical characteristics of the men who play. The necessity of a large, heavily muscled, athletic man, whose movements are co-ordinated and controlled by a rational and composed mind, unaffected by any emotions, is not borne out by closer examination of the men who play. Tomkins claims that 'the physical aspects of the ideal type seem inappropriate to the bodily abilities that are required: the game gives no rewards for sheer physical size or strength' (1994: 286). Nor is the large, muscled man necessarily the type needed in order to play the game successfully. Men like George Best, for instance, who weighed ten and a half stones when he first played professional football, are diminutive when compared with the ideal presented in the media. The media images, especially of professional football players in the tabloid press, rely on evocative language and dramatic pictures to perpetuate the myth. For real men there remains the conflict of not measuring up to the ideal typical mythical masculine body. Then again, the game is changing, becoming more 'feminized', more women are playing and emotions on the field, especially after a goal is scored, are not debarred. There is the possibility therefore of unwrapping some of the masculine myth to uncover some of the real men who play and of opening up this sporting space for women and for mixed teams, where interactions between real men and women are possible, on the basis of their abilities rather than their gendered stereotypes.

The move of women into leisure areas which have formerly been considered masculine preserves and kept sacred in order to shore up hegemonic masculinity indicates a possible change in subjectivities for women away from that predicated on the fragility of the female body. This would seem to advantage women in terms of self-definition and power. On the other hand, the ambiguity experienced by males concerning their masculinity when they venture into areas which are considered spaces for female bodies indicates a threat to traditional masculinity and a loss of status and power. Nevertheless, there is also the possibility of destabilizing rigid masculine stereotypes with possibilities for positive changes for men. The recognition of the real sporting abilities of men who do not conform to the idealized masculine image should benefit men. The 'feminization' of sports which previously have been masculine enclaves to include women, and the legitimacy for men in these sports to express emotions other than anger and aggression, should also open up possibilities for men to move beyond rigid cultural prescriptions associated with male embodiment.

The question, then, that remains unanswered for me is: 'Where are the studies of the real men and the real women who use their bodies in leisure space in a way that increases the humanity of the contact for the benefit of both, instead of reinforcing stereotypes of difference and maintaining the myths which shore up hegemonic masculinity and male power?' In interactions between men and women, aren't there some men and some women who do not hide behind the stereotypes and who actually accept each for their respective abilities and interact on this basis? To date, in the leisure literature, where interactions have been observed and analysed it has been generally on the basis of difference and male domination or male defence of masculinity (for example, see Broom et al., 1992). Where the effects of men's and women's interactions on gender differences in a challenging leisure environment have been studied, both men and women have been able to expand subjectivities beyond conventional body images (for example, see Mason-Cox, 1992). However, these studies have still focused on difference and looked at the effects on men and women separately and individually. A change of focus to the investigation of relationships and interactions which enhance both men and women (and there are some) seems timely. How is the body used in these relationships to minimize the culturally constructed, gendered hierarchy, to equalize power, to communicate effectively and to co-operate and share experiences? In the present context, the more specific questions are: 'How are leisure spaces used to this end?', or 'How could leisure spaces be used to this end?'

Poststructural feminist theory concerning the body has provided some conceptual tools for such a project. The body that one lives in day-to-day must influence one's subjectivity in some way. These feminists claim, however, that it is the cultural construction of the meaning of such bodies that impacts on the actor's own individual construction of subjectivity, not the body per se. In addition, they point to the many subjectivities that can be constructed for males and females and to the possibility of multiple subjectivities for individual men and women. Thus, this theoretical perspective opens the way for challenging and transforming the binary opposition of male and female bodies so that the male body is always imbued with power and the female body inferiorized, due to its lack of a phallus. It is now possible, theoretically, to move beyond subjectivities for both men and women which are rigidly based on bodily sex difference. It is time for these theories to be put to the test empirically. The sphere of leisure seems an obvious space for this to be done, especially in terms of interactions between men and women.

Leisure as Excitement and Release of Emotions

With the postmodern shift in emphasis in sociological analyses from production to consumption, from the discipline of the work sphere to the relative freedoms of the leisure sphere, from the public to the private, from exclusive focus on the mind to inclusion of the body, has come a corresponding shift in emphasis from the rational to the emotional. For example, in a special issue of the *International Journal of Sociology and Social Policy* (1996), the editor claims that:

> No social relations are carried out in the absence of either thought or emotion.
> It immediately follows that the sociology of emotions is not so much a nascent,

exotic sub-discipline of sociology as it is a level of analysis that must be carried out if meaning is to be found in any system, any social process, or in any social relationship of the everyday world. (Tenhouten, 1996: 1)

If this is so, then meaning to be found in the sphere of leisure must, at one level, be dependent upon analyses which incorporate the sociology of emotions.

In classical sociology, Georg Simmel considered the impact of the move to the city on the emotional life of people following the Industrial Revolution and the need for excitement through leisure. In the twentieth century, sociologists such as Norbert Elias, Stephen Lyng and Arlie Hochschild have considered the part that emotions play in the complexity of modern living, including emotional outlets through leisure. For the male theorists leisure remains an outlet which acts as a safety valve to compensate for the control imposed in the city, in the workplace and in civilized society. Hochschild presents a more 'feminized' version of the sociology of emotions. It is not surprising, then, that the sociology of the emotions has something to contribute to our understanding of leisure in today's society, for both men and women. In this section I consider the contributions of Simmel, Elias, Lyng and Hochschild, and speculate on future directions for the study of leisure and emotions.

Simmel: Leisure in the Metropolis

The metropolis for Simmel (1978) is the epitome of industrialized society with its personality type, division of labour in production and consumption and its money economy. Here, human beings are subjected to increase in nervous life and develop psychological defence mechanisms to distance the shock experience of urban existence. For example, the encounters with many different people on a daily basis cannot be dealt without psychic overload, unless many of these encounters are distanced and made impersonal. The continual bombardment of the senses by light, sound, technology and encounters with innumerable persons in the course of the day, according to Simmel, produces a tendency towards the 'blasé attitude' and 'neurasthenia'. 'Neurasthenia' refers to a condition in which the individual becomes desensitized to existing stimuli: all things are experienced as being of an equally dull and grey hue, not worth getting excited about. Yet there is still a thirst for more amusement and greater excitement which has not been satisfied by the fleeting, intense stimulations of the city. New and ever-more stimulating experiences are needed to produce excitement.

Against this background Simmel is critical of those 'fillings-in of time and consciousness' that lie outside the sphere of work and constitute leisure. Individuals in the city still wish to assert their individuality and differentiation through leisure pursuits, while seeking to belong to their own social group and its life (Simmel, 1978, quoted in Frisby, 1989: 80). For example, in the field of fashion, the individual seeks differentiation but also imitation.

New fashions for old distractions and stimulations constitute an essential part of leisure-time consumption and there is an increase in the rapidity of the turnover time of fashions themselves. Places of entertainment and theatres (and today I feel sure he would include films and television) are increasingly devoted to 'the titillation of the senses and intoxication of the nerves by colourful glamour, light, music and above all the excitement of sexual feelings' (Simmel, 1978, quoted in Frisby, 1989: 83). The never-ending search for such excitement and its inability to give the searcher lasting satisfaction forms an ideal basis for commodification – the customer must keep coming back. Simmel's crucial instance of the commodification of this aspect of metropolitan life is prostitution, where money is exchanged for a 'fleetingly intensified and just as fleetingly extinguished sexual appetite'. World exhibitions and trade exhibitions come under his critical eye, as would our large shopping malls. The effect of the concentration of a world of commodities in a confined space is to overpower, disorientate and hypnotize the individual whilst the wealth and colourfulness of the display is 'appropriate to over-excited and exhausted nerves' need for stimulation' (Simmel, 1978, quoted in Frisby, 1989: 84).

Simmel provides a framework which posits leisure as a space in contemporary society for excitement and release of emotions. Most of these spaces are commodified and provide only temporary and unsatisfying heightened emotional excitement. He does suggest, however, two leisure spaces which are outside the commodification process and which may provide some emotional satisfaction, that is, sociability and adventure. Sociability depends on sociation which is the form, realized in innumerable ways, in which individuals grow together into units that satisfy their interests (1950: 41). Sociability is the pure play form of sociation where individuals meet together purely for the sake of meeting with others, with no serious motive or goal in mind – 'sociability has no objective purpose, no content, no extrinsic results, it entirely depends upon the personalities among whom it occurs. Its aim is nothing but the success of the sociable moment and, at most, a memory of it' (1950: 45). Although it reflects society, it is time out from the seriousness of work, politics, money, and so on. He gives the example of the party. The typical expectation for a party is that people will interact, but their interaction is not limited to practical everyday concerns – in some cases conversations about everyday concerns are actually considered poor taste. The person who insists on bringing the practical workday concerns into the conversation is likely to be considered a bore, just like the recluse who sits in the corner and refuses to mingle. In city life such sociability is a leisure form where individuality and reciprocal interaction can be intermixed: 'the pleasure of the individual is always contingent upon the joy of others and each participant "acts" as though all were equal' (1950: 46). Conversation in which talking is a legitimate end in itself and coquetry or flirting in which there is a play form of erotic drives are variations of sociability which Simmel sees developed to a high degree in city life and (in pure forms) outside of commodification (1950: 50–1).

Adventure also, for Simmel, is a dropping out of the turmoil of everyday existence, in this case to experience the new, 'something alien, untouchable, out of the ordinary ... an island of life which determines its beginning and end according to its own formative powers' (1965: 248). The adventurer sets challenges, the achievement of which brings satisfaction and a sense of personal control. The experience extends beyond the island of the adventure to everyday life through reflection.

Simmel's work is male, in that he is concerned with public leisure spaces where men have predominated and he assumes the male experience generally to be generic. Nevertheless he has alerted us to the vital connection between modern city living and the search for emotional excitement through leisure experiences. Much of his analysis *is* applicable to contemporary leisure experiences and the emotions that are sought through these experiences. The colour and glamour of commodified city leisure spaces provides a heightened excitement which temporarily assuages 'neurasthenia' and the dull grey hue of the desensitized emotional state. Contemporary advertising for leisure experiences as diverse as harbour cruises, film-going, watching football, gambling on horse racing or at the casino, drinking Coco-Cola, dining out and dancing visualizes light, colour and glamour and promotes excitement as a selling point for these commodified forms of city leisure. Not only is emotion a crucial factor in leisure, it also sells leisure.

Norbert Elias: *Leisure as 'Mimetic Experience' in a Civilized World*

Elias (1986a) also posits the individual in modern society as one whose emotions are generally held in check and who finds emotional release through leisure experiences. Elias traces the historical process of the development of behaviour which is understood as 'civilized' from the thirteenth century to modern times. In 1280, for example, people ate with hands from a common dish, blew their noses in hands or on the tablecloth and defecated in public. Two centuries later, a favourite leisure activity was to burn two dozen cats.

He shows how profound redefinitions of 'normal' and 'proper' behaviour occurred through powerful psychological and institutional barriers to the old indiscriminate enactment of feelings, both enthusiastic and aggressive. Well-policed social distinctions were put in place between 'civilized' and 'uncivilized' sections of society, for example between the manners of court society and peasant society in the Middle Ages.

The civilizing process, then, through social structure and individual construction, produces a new kind of typical individual whose emotional life is more closely bounded and controlled by feelings of revulsion and shame, delicacy and propriety, the separation of public and private spheres of existence and the banishing of excesses of self-castigation as well as self-indulgence.

Elias claims that:

In the comparatively advanced societies of our age, many occupational, many private relationships and activities give satisfaction only if all the people concerned are able to maintain a fairly even and stable control over their more spontaneous libidinal, affective and emotional impulses as well as over their fluctuating moods. Social survival and success in these societies depend, in other words, to some extent on a reliable armour, not too strong and not too weak, of individual self-restraint. In such societies, there is only a comparatively little scope for the show of strong feelings, of strong antipathies towards and dislike of people, let alone of hot anger, wild hatred or the urge to hit someone over the head. People strongly agitated, in the grip of feelings they cannot control, are cases for hospital or prison. Conditions of high excitement are regarded as abnormal in a person, as a dangerous prelude to violence in a crowd. However, to contain strong feelings, to preserve an even control of drives, affects and emotions, steadily throughout one's life is likely to raise tensions in a person. (1986a: 41)

Elias and Dunning (1986) argue that such societies develop some counter-measures against the stress-tensions thus generated. Leisure and sport provide play events, they say, where intense emotions are unleashed in a controlled form – deep-rooted emotions are discharged and accumulated in a relatively pleasurable way. In advanced industrial societies leisure activities such as sport, film, TV, musical events and combat games such as poker and chess, as well as theatre and opera, form an enclave for the socially approved arousal of moderate excitement behaviour in public. They provide a 'mimetic experience' where danger, excitement and possible mock physical aggression are played out in a safe context. The term 'mimetic experience' in Elias's work means experiences which allow one to express emotions which under everyday circumstances would be kept under control. They occur in sites which have been constructed with rules and safeguards, so that the expression of these, sometimes violent, emotions will harm neither the individual nor others who are involved. In this sense they imitate or are at least one remove from the everyday world.

The peculiar emotional stimulation and refreshment provided by the mimetic class of leisure activities, culminating in pleasurable tension and excitement, represents a more or less highly institutionalized counterpart to the strength and evenness of emotional restraints required by all classes of purposeful activities of people in more differentiated and civilized societies. The pleasurable play-excitement which people seek in their leisure hours thus represents at the same time the complement and the antithesis to the periodic tendency towards staleness of emotional valences in the purposeful 'rational' routines of life. (Elias and Dunning, 1986: 73)

Elias examines in detail the place of sports such as football for the release of physical aggression and violence, anger and hostility. For those who play and for those who spectate this is an arena for the arousal of increasing tension and excitement, together with a climax, in the final minutes in a good game, and a denouement (Elias, 1986b). The parallels with male sexual experience don't need to be drawn. The emotions discussed are *legitimate* emotions for men whose day-to-day occupational involvement inhibits such expression. So the pleasure they experience in these leisure pastimes has a gender focus.

Dunning (1986b) makes the links between the spectator violence that can erupt into hooliganism, as well as the contained violence of aggressive sports such as football, and the norms of culturally constructed masculinity. Dunning hypothesizes that the violent behaviour of football hooligans is centrally connected with the norms of masculinity that 'place an extreme stress on toughness and ability to fight' and 'are, in that respect, different in degree – though not in kind – from the masculinity norms that are currently dominant in society at large' (1986b: 241).

In a similar vein, Lyng's (1990) analysis of 'edgework' in leisure suggests the need in alienating, bureaucratized society for personal challenge and mastery. He claims that leisure pastimes such as skydiving, hang-gliding, scuba diving, rock climbing, motorcycle racing/car racing and downhill ski racing involve the thrill and excitement of pushing oneself to the edge of life, sanity, consciousness or order. Lyng hypothesizes that due to alienation in labour and excessive beauracratization in the modern world there is a need for self-realization and self-mastery through risk-taking activities. Failure to master the situation generally results in death, or at least debilitating injury. The reward for employing the necessary skills, 'mental toughness' and 'survival capacity' is a sense of control and mastery, a catharsis of a sense of powerlessness. In a passing phrase he comments that 'edgework is more common among males than among females' (1990: 872). His explanation is that men, due to their socialization, 'have a distorted sense of their ability to control fateful circumstances' (1990: 873). Hence he limits his explanation to the situation of males.

These three authors all suggest that society today acts like a pressure cooker for the compression and containment of emotional expression. Leisure, then, becomes the safety valve for emotional outbursts in safe and legitimate environments, where rules presumably prevent damage to the self and others. Once again the self is enhanced through leisure which links pleasure and emotion in a beneficent way, for men at least.

On the other hand, this work opens the way for an examination of the pleasure and excitement of violence in leisure, which to date has been little explored in the leisure literature. The assumptions, for example, underlying most of the approaches adopted in this book up to this point have been that leisure offers a relatively free space in contemporary society for positive, self-enhancing experiences, which are for the good of all. The possibilities of leisure providing free space for emotions and actions which are potentially destructive to the self, as well as to others, have rarely been attempted (for exceptions, see Cuneen et al., 1989; O'Malley and Mugford, 1991; Rojek, 1996). Simmel's idea, for example, that leisure provides excitement for jaded nerves in the metropolis, but that this is an excitement that tantalizes, rather than fulfils, leading us on to seek ever-more thrilling and perhaps dangerous experiences, could be applied to the fleeting pleasures of power over others which, at the extreme, could even underlie serial murder (see Rojek, 1996). Along the way, it opens up many possibilities for critical examination of the flip or downside of leisure which future leisure research needs to explore in order to round out conceptualization and understanding of leisure in the postmodern era.

Elias and Dunning's work, when taken up with a feminist lens, can also make links to the legitimation of violence for men in circumstances other than that contained by sport. For example, Gagnon's (1996) study of the links between the sport culture of Canadian ice-hockey and domestic violence against women shows how violence, legitimated by the game, can spill over into expressions of emotion through violence in the home.

For most of us, however, Elias claims, outbursts of intense physical aggression which result in serious injury or death are only experienced or witnessed second hand through newspapers, television and spectator sport (1986b). There is some evidence that the demand for spectator violence is increasing. In Australia, the popularity of television programmes such as the Saturday-night spectacle of muscled men and women challenging and overpowering their equally muscled opponents, in *The Gladiators*, attests to this. In the USA 'extreme fighting' takes the violence one step further for the few combatants, but also for the many thousands who watch:

> The combatants go on to a field enclosed by many thousand spectators and hammer each other before a huge, live national and international TV audience. Almost anything short of eye-gouging and biting is permitted. Only a few holds are barred. Combatants wear special equipment which turn their bodies into offensive weapons. Bleeding often occurs, serious injuries are common. Contests end only when time runs out. (Attwood, 1997: 32)

The difference here from the violence allowed in American football and boxing, claims the journalist, is only one of degree. According to the Elias thesis 'extreme fighting' is an indication that the civilizing process must be becoming tighter and the demand for 'mimetic experience' through leisure stronger. Do such 'mimetic experiences' provide only temporary and tantalizing refreshment for jaded spirits, so that more and more extreme emotional situations are necessary to reach the excitement threshold, as suggested by Simmel? If so, leisure itself can be dangerous.

So what about women? Where are the leisure pastimes that allow the release of similar emotions for them – or are they absent because these emotions are not legitimate for them? Some sports also act for women as a legitimate release of feelings. For example, as one woman badminton player says: 'It's got my adrenalin flowing now, you see [laughs]. You really look forward to it, thrashing that shuttlecock, I think that's it, getting rid of that emotion' (Talbot, 1988a: 11). And more and more women are becoming involved in aggressive contact sports such as rugby union, as well as in the spectatorship of potentially violent sports on the field and as represented on television.

This could be due to women's increasing involvement in the civilizing process of the workplace and public sphere. Nevertheless, for most women the 'mimetic' experience is gendered. It is an outlet through films, soap operas, novels, magazines, music, for expressions of the need for love and understanding which cannot normally be explored in family situations. In women's experience the 'ethic of care' for others ensures that the needs of others in the family take precedence over one's own (Bella, 1989; Freysinger and Flannery, 1992; Henderson et al., 1996). Anger, hostility, physical aggression, mastery and violence remain illegitimate emotions for women and, for the most part, their leisure activities, spaces and experiences reflect this inhibition. In my own experience, it was surprising to hear two dozen women talk about the deep feelings of anger which rose to the surface in a self-defence class where they were encouraged to express physical aggression.

Arlie Hochschild: 'Feeling Rules' and 'Deep Acting'

When a woman enters the relatively new arena of the sociology of the emotions, her perception reflects her gendered understanding. Hochschild goes beyond the outward constraint, the outward look and the outward appearance to the self-reflective, inward look of emotional contemplation and emotional management. Hochschild draws on the work of Goffman (1961, 1969), who suggests that social rules govern how people try or try not to feel in ways appropriate to the situation. Thus, people try to pay tribute to the official definitions of situations with their feelings, in situations such as weddings, funerals, and so on. Hochschild terms these social norms or social rules, 'feeling rules'. She, however, goes further than Goffman, by showing how people not only try to conform outwardly, but do so inwardly as well. Whereas Goffman claimed that 'When they issue uniforms, they issue skins' (1974), she adds 'and two inches of flesh' (Hochschild, 1979: 556). 'The very topic, sociology of emotions,' she says, 'presupposes a human capacity for, if not the actual habit of, reflecting on and shaping inner feelings, a habit itself distributed variously across time, age, class, and locale' (1979: 557). Goffman, she says, has blurred the distinction between 'surface acting' which focuses on outward demeanour and 'deep acting' which draws on emotional depth. She examines how people manage the feelings they are supposed to have through emotion work, which refers to the act of evoking or shaping, as well as suppressing feeling in oneself. This work seeks to make feeling and situation consistent. It is guided by 'feeling rules' and frequently accomplished by 'deep acting'.

Hochschild's feminized version of the sociology of emotions draws our attention to gender differences in 'feeling rules' with possibilities for change: 'Indeed, a good place to study change in feeling rules would be the strata of persons for whom the *right* of men to cry, or feel fearful, is extended over a greater range of situations, and for whom the *right* of women to open anger is extended over a larger, sanction free zone' (1979: 572). In addition she notes the commodification of feelings, especially for women in the service industries, where cheery feelings are sold for profit, perhaps at the expense of inner well-being.

In a study of flight attendants, Hochschild shows how in a predominantly female occupation emotions which were 'once idiosyncratic and escapable are now standardized and unavoidable' (1983: 185). The 'sincere smile' becomes linked to advertising and corporate profit. Workers are trained to produce such a smile. Human emotional and caring labour, which is assumed to come naturally to women, is commercialized. In her study, the men who were employed as flight attendants were less constrained by these feeling rules and were perceived by passengers to occupy more instrumental than expressive roles. For women, the result is 'deep acting', where true feelings are hidden and the smile covers all. In addition, those with lower status, usually women, do not have the protection of 'status shields'. Status shields are the resources actors have for protecting their sense of self. Those with higher status have more of these resources, for example the protection of assault on a supervisor's feelings and the assigning of lesser value to a subordinate's feelings.

Hochschild does not take her analysis into the leisure sphere. The logical extension for us is that when the uniform of the occupation is removed, provided it has not penetrated too many layers of flesh, a space in leisure is created where there is a need to express both hidden and sincere emotions. The assumption has been that the family provides the space for such leisure, for both women and men. But in another study, Hochschild (1989) looks at the home situations of men and women partnerships where both are equally involved in the workplace. Here she also finds that gendered 'feeling rules' allocate to women the general responsibility for emotion work, both for themselves and for the family. So we come again to the question: 'Where do women find the emotional outlets through leisure that each of the theorists discussed here indicate are necessary for emotional well-being in today's society?' The assumption that women find it in the family does not quite fit the reality.

In a later article, Hochschild suggests that women's movement into the workforce has constituted a revolution, but that this revolution is stalled due to the slow compensatory changes in men's sharing in work in the home and the rigidity of workplace schedules. 'Instead of humanizing men, we are "capitalizing women"', she claims (1994: 19), so that women are now putting on the tough emotional armour that Elias has suggested is necessary to cope with the exigencies of the public sphere in civilized society.

If, in addition, women are more likely than men in the workforce to be required to employ 'deep acting' to sell their emotional moods, the need for alternative leisure spaces, apart from the family, for emotional expression for women becomes imperative.

In many ways Hochschild's empirical work validates the ideas of Simmel, Elias and Lyng concerning the constraints imposed on individual expressions of emotion in contemporary society and the consequent need for leisure spaces where these emotions can be expressed in a safe environment. Where her work differs is in the recognition of power differentials, especially those of gender.

Simmel, Elias, Lyng and Hochschild have alerted us to sociological constraints on our emotions in contemporary society. They have attempted to show that the ways we express our emotions are not simply the result of our individual psychosexual development as psychologists would have us believe. Simmel points out the need for emotional self-protection in metropolitan society and the consequent need for exciting outlets, most of which are commodified and give fleeting satisfaction. Elias sees that the ways we both constrain and express our emotions are historically and culturally constructed. There is a need in modern society for an emotional 'armour', not too thin and not too thick, to protect ourselves from that society and to protect society from our emotional outbursts. There is also a need for safety valves through 'mimetic experience'. Hochschild says we put on emotional 'skins' when we put on occupational uniforms. We are governed by 'feeling rules' and 'deep acting' which place a layer beneath the rational and logical in our lives. We need places where the skins can be removed and the feeling rules and deep acting challenged.

In many ways these theorists perpetuate the concept of leisure as compensation for the disciplinary practices of the workplace, which Marx characterized as alienation. They, however, go further than the simple binary opposition between work and leisure to tap in to the structuration of emotions in a civilizing, city-centred culture in which individual emotions are employed in the interests of capital as well as, on occasions, in the interests of individual well-being. The sociology of emotions has alerted us to the potential for leisure spaces to contribute to the expression of emotions in a positive way under the emotionally constrained circumstances of contemporary society. In so doing it has added another layer beneath the material and the rational to account for patterns of leisure behaviour and culturally constructed subjectivities. It has reminded us of the emotional investment that we have in leisure.

Recognition of the commodification of emotions and of leisure, however, puts some qualifications on the potentiality of leisure spaces to fulfil the need for emotional release for all people. Leisure as excitement and 'mimetic experience' validates many current leisure practices, but also warns of the ephemeral nature of the satisfaction of much leisure experience and of the possibility of leisure's insatiability. As with other perspectives on leisure, a feminist approach to the sociology of emotions adds another dimension to an understanding of gendered leisure and the potential for change. In addition, the sociology of emotions has opened the way for an investigation of the downside of leisure, which is needed to balance previous emphases in theory and research on the 'sweetness and light' of leisure, that is, the purely positive, self-enhancing effects of leisure spaces. The space that leisure can offer for emotional release that is destructive to others and/or to the self has yet to be researched and strategies for change suggested.

Conclusion

In the sporting sections of the popular press we are used to seeing representations of muscular male bodies in aggressive poses vanquishing opponents using physical power. When the less frequent images of women in sport appear, they are generally less aggressive and more graceful, with some attempt to portray feminine attractiveness along with sporting ability. Bodies in sport assume definitive gendered characteristics which shore up hegemonic masculinity and downgrade female bodily power. Feminist poststructural analyses and concomitant masculinist analyses have alerted us to both the power and the vulnerability of these images of male and female bodies. Their power is to present to us cultural ideals which we come to accept as normal and against which we measure our own bodies and bodily performance. So we attempt to normalize our own bodies, to make them conform. The result is 'docile bodies', that is, bodies that obey the dictates of cultural discourses and reinforce and reify sex differences. Self-surveillance and body work through various sporting and leisure activities shore up the myth of the all-powerful male body and the less powerful, graceful female body.

However, poststructural feminist theory does not end there. The theorists discussed in this chapter who have applied their ideas to the sociology of the body have pointed also to the fragility of the images presented, to the excessive body work necessary to conform to the mythical male or female ideal and to the possibilities for using our bodies in ways that challenge and go beyond culturally constructed and prescribed masculine and feminine bodies. Butler, Gatens, Grosz and Irigaray have each challenged the limitations and lacks allocated to female bodies in societies in which males are dominant and have urged women to break out of cultural constraints. The warning at the individual level, given by Bordo, is that there will be costs for women who do so in societies where it is in male interests to continue to valorize the male body and male strength and to inferiorize female bodies. There will also be costs for individual males who step out of leisure spaces which have hitherto reinforced hegemonic masculinity and into traditionally female spaces, in terms of loss of power.

One answer has been to suggest the use of leisure spaces in a collective way to destabilize the myths and move on to a more open society for both genders. To date this collective action has been confined to single-sex groups. It remains to be seen whether men and women working together can break down some of the bodily stereotypes and transcend the narrow focus of the use of gendered bodies in sporting and leisure spaces. For this to work, however, according to the analyses presented in this chapter, men will need consciously to use their bodies in ways that do not threaten or dominate women and that allow women to expand, rather than contract, their bodily use of space. And women will need to make full use of this space. There has been some indication that this may already be happening in some outdoor adventure areas, but leisure research has, as yet, not investigated men's and women's co-operative attempts to transcend cultural prescriptions for male and female bodies. Poststructural feminist theory has had much to contribute to the sociology of the body in shifting the thinking beyond reified sexual attributes – research now needs to put some of this thinking to the test.

In the same way that poststructural feminist theory has challenged the mind/body dichotomy of male theory which valorized the mind and relegated the body to the sphere of the natural, it has also attempted to deconstruct the rational/emotional dichotomy. In this dichotomy 'male' rationality has been all and 'female' emotionality to be avoided at all costs, especially in intellectual activity such as theory building. Such challenges have allowed the emergence in recent years of a sociology of emotions which acknowledges the part that emotions play in every sphere of social and private life. Seidler claims that, 'Feminism has been crucially important in questioning the terms of modernity through challenging the abiding distinction between reason and emotion' (1994: x). He goes on to point out that men have had the power since the Enlightenment to shape reason in their own image and to identify it with the dominant forms of masculinity. In the everyday interchanges between men and women this gets translated into men's ability to silence the challenges of women by refusing to listen to their 'emotional outbursts' until they calm down and learn to 'talk rationally' (1994: 28). In theory building the consequences have been similarly to valorize rationality at the expense of the body and emotions. For Seidler, male dominance of theory, along with the masculine presence in the public sphere, has served to deny men's existence as bodily, emotional and spiritual selves: 'These aspects of our experience are silenced or denied as we enter the ground of public life, which is traditionally a masculine world of the rational self, in which our social and political theories have traditionally grounded themselves' (1994: 68).

It is not surprising, then, that when male sociologists do turn their attention to conceptual analyses of emotional life their theories are grounded in the constraints on the expression of emotions experienced in the public spheres of the city, employment and sporting arenas (Elias, Dunning, Lyng) and outward appearances (Goffman). These theorists have shown that contemporary living in public spheres requires an emotional armour which protects the individual from bombardment of the psyche with the overstimulations of light, sound, colour and constant contact with innumerable other human beings in the course of the day. As well the armour is a means of survival in impersonal and bureaucratized workplaces, where expressions of emotion would be construed as weakness, sickness or, at least, insubordination. The assumption, then, is that sporting, leisure and private family spaces will provide arenas for the necessary release of controlled emotions in a safe environment.

When a feminist theorist such as Hochschild ventures into the sociology of emotions, she directs our thoughts to the internal and private aspects of the emotional work needed to bring our feelings into line with social and public demands. In the workplace she emphasizes the commodification of women's supposedly natural talent for cheerful, smiling, happy and nurturing emotions and the 'deep acting' that is, in fact, required for these emotions to be consistently displayed. Nor are the family, family leisure spaces or sporting arenas necessarily the places where women can have the 'mimetic experiences' available to men. Too often it is here that women are also required to support others and to be the objects of their emotional release. In some cases they are even the recipients of the emotional release of violence. Hochschild does not specifically examine the place of leisure as a release for women's emotions, but her work points us in the direction of the need for alternative emotional spaces for women where 'deep acting' is not required. In the best of all worlds, one would hope that there may also be leisure spaces where men and women can support each other in the enjoyment of 'mimetic experiences' which benefit both and not one at the expense of the other.

At the end of this chapter on leisure and the sociology of the body and emotions, it is clear that these two aspects of human experience are not separate entities, but linked to one another in very many aspects of everyday living, including leisure. Freund points out that our feelings are constantly in process and are not only expressed through mental activities but through the mind and body acting as a unity, so that emotions are always in some way embodied (1990: 458). This means that increased and perpetual control over emotions, without the opportunity for emotional release through 'mimetic experiences' as suggested by Elias, can result in emotional–somatic responses which are problematic for health. Feminist and post-structural theories are helpful here in suggesting that both men and women can and should refuse what they are told by society they should be and feel and reach towards their potential. This applies especially in the use of one's body and in the positive expression of emotions. In Foucault's terms the essence of the power relationship is not to *discover* what we are, but to *refuse* what we have been told by dominant discourses that we are and to imagine and build up what we could be (1983: 16). Leisure spaces may be used to this end, perhaps in different ways by men and women, but also hopefully in co-operation. The object is to go beyond the use of the body in rigidly defined gender practices and to expand emotional agendas beyond those tied to 'feeling rules' which are gender specific and socially sanctioned. Leisure may be one space where this can happen. At the very least it has the potential to provide spaces for repeated performative actions which contribute to selves which are becoming more than 'docile bodies' which house crippled emotions.

7

Public Leisure Places and Spaces: Urban Sociology

Urban sociology, like sociology generally, has moved from the functionalism of the 1940s and 1950s, through Marxist and neo-Marxist power and class analysis, to poststructuralist analysis. Women have largely remained invisible, or have been added in, never part of theory construction or the research agenda which has remained 'rational', 'scientific' and 'technological'. Some notable feminist exceptions introduce a woman's eye view and ask us to imagine how a 'feminine' city might look. In so doing they are asking planners to open up city spaces to many uses so that they might be accessible and pleasurable for women and other marginalized people. In this chapter I examine the conceptualization of public places in the city as leisure venues for the male gaze of the *flâneur*. Drawing on feminist theorization of such *places*, I suggest instead the concept of 'chora' as a safe *space* for social interaction which women as well as men may enjoy and which may enhance rather than diminish a sense of self or identity. Such public spaces may be arenas for resistance to domination, rather than places of surveillance and control. Further, they may be spaces for alternative subjectivities, spaces for leisure experience through interaction which becomes part of the self and is lasting rather than fleeting. In this chapter I draw the majority of my examples from the city of Sydney, the city of my birth, the city of my own life and leisure experiences as a woman.

Urban Sociology

The ideas of the Chicago School (1920s–1940s) were for many years the chief basis of theory and research in urban sociology. Predominant ideas included the *ecological approach*, that is, environmental advantage, equilibrium, invasion, succession, competition and survival of the fittest. Use of city spaces depended on the natural terrain in a functional manner (Park, 1952). In Sydney, for example, industry grew up around the waterfront for easy access to overseas shipping. The CBD for business and administration was also close to the water and road and railway transport systems. These systems radiated from it to the separate, suitable residential areas for workers and bosses; bosses in the pleasant, leafy North Shore and workers initially close to the city, then in the flatter, hotter western suburbs. *Urbanism as a way of life*, with its impersonality, anonymity and 'world of strangers', suited the money economy and developing business and industry values (Wirth, 1938).

Those influenced by Marx, such as Harvey (1985) and Castells (1977), emphasized the *created environment* and its continual *restructuring* due to the social and economic power struggles of industrial capitalism. Postmodern urban theorists, on the other hand, include: a new radical scepticism about the role of scientific knowledge; a new concern with aesthetics rather than morality; enhanced reflexivity on the part of individuals about their identity and the grounds for their conduct; a magnified importance for the mass media in the framing of everyday life; an intensification of consumerism, the demise of socialist politics and its replacement by the local and personal politics of new social movements (Savage and Warde, 1993: 138). As such, their analysis has made room for a diversity of interests, cultures, needs and subjectivities in urban planning. Nevertheless, on the whole, they too project male images as the keys to city development. 'For urban elites,' say Savage and Warde (1993: 46), 'the management of image has become a vital aspect of economic policy and political focus.'

In fact, the concept of the image of the city has been an underlying construct for urban planning since the seminal work of Lynch (1960). Lynch moved the thinking about the city beyond its 'stationary physical parts', 'the city as a thing in itself', to the city as it is perceived by its inhabitants (1960: 2–3). To this extent he did include people and their perceptions in his analysis of the city. His fieldwork involved both men and women in interviews concerning the structure and identity of their own cities, in this instance Boston, New Jersey and Los Angeles. As people walked through their city they recorded their impressions of its paths, edges, districts, nodes and landmarks. He coined the term 'imageability' to denote 'physical qualities which relate to the attributes of identity and structure in the mental image' (1960: 9). This image was based on 'physical, perceptible objects' (1960: 46). The viewer saw the object as he passed by and it was incorporated into his overall image of that city. Lynch's analysis relied on the common themes which arose from the repeated references to certain general physical characteristics. The viewer was undifferentiated by gender, class, race, ethnicity, age or disability and the conceptualization relied on a rational subject looking for order in his city and his view of objective forms. The images of Boston, New Jersey and Los Angeles which Lynch presents include commercial, industrial, administrative and residential areas as well as thoroughfares, landmark buildings and natural attributes such as the Charles River in Boston. I would contend that while Lynch does include people in his city and their subjective perceptions, it is a view which presents the interests of employed males as the interests of all.

These theorists, then, in their so-called 'gender neutrality', have treated male interests and world-views as universal. Where women have been included, their place has been seen as in the home and their spaces confined to the suburbs. Feminist planners such as Saegert (1980) show how, in the post-Second World War era, space in cities was planned on the assumption that men travelled to work in the central business district and women stayed in the suburbs to care for the family. This dichotomy is culturally based and forms a symbolic system of ideas which informs and guides our thinking of the city and our personal lives in terms of polar opposites. Saegert contrasts the fictional nature of this dualism with contemporary reality in which the lives of women, occupational structures and the demographic composition of urban areas are all undergoing change and hence are making these dichotomous categories inappropriate. The assumption that women stay at home while men go out to work is no longer valid, yet, as Harman, working from a socialist feminist position, points out:

> To the degree that women carry dual work loads and function in cities that do not accommodate their (oftentimes) fragmented and disparate activity patterns then terrible assaults are made on their share of time. The result is guilt-ridden women trying desperately to give lie to the old adage 'you can't be in two places at once' . . .
>
> We face infinite difficulties in untying the straitjackets imposed on women by the nexus now forged between urbanisation, capitalism and patriarchy. (Harman, 1983: 125, 129)

The plans for the city of Sydney for the twenty-first century (see Department of Planning, 1995; Sydney City Council, 1995), for example, do not appear to include the possibility that women and children as well as men may wish to enjoy the public leisure spaces being provided. 'The artists' impressions look pretty on paper but are often not desirable living or working places' (Sydney Morning Herald, 1995: 10). The place for women and children remains in the suburbs, out of sight and out of mind. Factors such as distances to activities outside the home, lack of transport, lack of family-friendly facilities in public spaces and time schedules imposed by household duties and childcare make involvements in pursuits outside the home difficult, if not impossible for many women (Palm and Pred in Saegert, 1980: 100). These factors act as constraints on women's participation in leisure pursuits/activities in the city and so they do not become a part of the social value of the city unless they are specifically addressed in planning. Yet there is increasing evidence that women play a large part in the decision-making processes concerning family leisure choices (Labone and Wearing, 1994).

If women do not see the city as a viable venue for their leisure, then they will not venture into the spaces from which they feel alienated and so they will not participate in the process of making the place a valued community resource. There are, however, areas such as Leichhardt in Sydney and Lygon and Brunswick Streets in Melbourne where other cultural influences have included the family, so that resident usage of the many culturally diverse restaurants and coffee shops includes families. The family then becomes part of the public use of the space for leisure, women and children are included in the space and it contributes to their leisure experience.

In a radical attempt to rethink public space in the interests of women, Hayden suggests strategies for reclaiming public spaces for parents, children, older citizens and all women. These include:

1   'childspaces' in shopping centres, banks and department stores, baby-changing areas in men's and women's rest rooms, lower windows in public transport, child-sized furniture in restaurants, etc.;
2   green lights and safehouses for the elderly, women and children;
3   better public transport and safe zones and better street lighting;
4   an attack on the use of public space for sexist advertisements and pornography.

On the last point, Hayden comments:

> ... many twentieth-century urban men behave as if good women are at home while bad ones adorn the billboards and travel on their own in urban space; at the same time, many urban women are encouraged to think of emotionless, war-mongering, and sexual inexhaustibility as natural to the Marlboro cowboy, war heroes' statues, and every other male adult ... By presenting gender stereotypes in the form of non-verbal body language, fifty feet long and thirty feet high, billboards turn the public space of the city into a stage set for drama starring enticing women and stern men. (1984: 214–24)

As an example of women's right to public space, she cites the 1975 general strike – involving housewives, nurses, secretaries, architects and cabinet ministers – in Iceland. Family life stopped, offices stopped and factories stopped as 25,000 women, old and young, flooded into the main square of the capital city to demonstrate for equal rights. These women held their citizen right to the city for 24 hours. It was the first nationally organized strike of women citizens anywhere in the world. On a smaller scale the Australian 'Reclaim the Night' is also a claim by women to public spaces.

Melbourne architect Dimity Reed, one of Australia's few high-profile female architects, says:

> That's the really damaging thing, because our cities are built with male values. And they're the dominant values. The effect of this male dominance is that we've gone through decades of what I consider very careless building, because its been largely to do with investment building ... Building has lost that view that it's a cultural contribution ... What architecture really is, is the background to our lives. It's a stage set against which we act out everything. (Sydney Morning Herald, 1994)

Feminists such as Sandercock and Forsyth (1992) and Watson and Gibson (1995) are now turning their attention to phallocentrism in planning theory. Phallocentrism refers to a general process of cultural representation where

the phallus and the male body are valorized and male world-views are privileged to the exclusion of, or at least the inferiorization of, the female body
and female ways of thinking and being in the world. Sandercock and
Forsyth claim that 'in the developed countries of all the subfields within
planning, theory remains the most male dominated and the least influenced
by any awareness of gender' (1992: 49). They critique male theory for its
bias in defining planning as the linking of scientific and technical knowledge
to action in the public domain. They see greater hope for feminist theory in
an expansion of a hermeneutical approach which embraces subjective
knowledge as the foundation of a radical planning approach, if women's
views are included. In poststructuralist feminist fashion they turn attention
away from women as the objects of theory and research and posit women
as the initiators of both. They also insist on the diversity of women, so that
single women, poor women, battered wives, black women, non-English
speaking background (NESB) and lesbian women are included in feminist
planning theory and research. At the same time they recognize that the vulnerability of all women 'who continue to undertake the bulk of unpaid domestic work and are engaged in low-wage work and unorganized informal
markets' must be taken into consideration in any planning theory. In a more
articulated postmodern framework, Watson and Gibson (1995: 260) argue
for a postmodern politics of planning that recognizes a textured and
complex understanding of power and difference which includes gender,
race, class, ethnicity and sexual orientation.

Deconstructing Urban Theory: the Flâneur and the Choraster

Poststructural feminist writers, such as Irigaray (1986), Lloyd (1989) and
Grosz (1986), urge feminists in the social sciences to go one step further and
subvert male domination of the very concepts on which phallocentric
theory depends. Grosz, for example, argues for the utilization of strategies
for the development of women-centred knowledges. Theories which begin
from women's views and experience of the world, instead of the assumption
that the male experience covers all humanity, she claims, may more adequately include women. Strategies she suggests for subverting male domination of knowledge include serious questioning of: phallocentric
adherence to universal concepts of truth and methods of verifying truth; objectivity; a disembodied rational sexually indifferent subject; and the explanation of women's specificity in terms that continue to valorize and
privilege the masculine. Instead she advocates the development of alternative ideas based on women's embodied experiences of the world. Grosz
herself enters the sphere of urban theory to question and subvert male theorization of space and to suggest an alternative which presents a feminized
version of space (1995a). In this section I examine the idea of the *flâneur* as
a fundamental concept underpinning much of male urban planning and
suggest instead Grosz's concept of urban space as 'chora'. This concept

opens the way for public leisure places to become 'spaces' which incorporate 'social value' instead of passing 'image'. Possibilities for these spaces to contribute to women's 'becoming' or expansion of the self then open up.

Feminist writers, such as Pollock (1988), Ryan (1994), Wilson (1995) and Wolff (1985), drawing on poststructuralist and postmodern perspectives concerning women and the city, attempt to deconstruct the fundamentally male conceptualization of the city dweller in modernity as the *flâneur*. The concept of the *flâneur* arose along with the proliferation of public places of pleasure in the developing cities of the nineteenth century (see Benjamin, 1973). The *flâneur* is 'a new kind of public person with the leisure to wander, watch and browse' (Wilson, 1995: 61). The *flâneur* spends most of his day simply looking at the urban spectacle; he observes new inventions and passes the hours by shopping or window-shopping, looking at books, new fashions, hats combs, jewellery and novelties of all kinds. He is a gentleman, has some private wealth and stands wholly outside the productive process (Wilson, 1995: 61–2). As Wolff (1985: 45) points out: 'There is no question of inventing the *flaneuse*: the essential point is that such a character was rendered impossible by the sexual divisions of the nineteenth century.' Although Pollock, Wolff, Ryan and Wilson acknowledge the increasing, if limited, involvement of middle-class women in the commodified areas of departmental shops and cafes, they yet perceive the predominant perception of the inhabitant of public leisure spaces as the male *flâneur*.

> It is this *Flâneur*, the *Flâneur* as a man of pleasure, as a man who takes visual possession of the city, who has emerged in postmodern feminism discourse as the embodiment of the 'male gaze'. He represents men's visual and voyeuristic mastery over women. According to this view, the *Flâneur*'s freedom to wander at will through the city is essentially a masculine freedom. Thus, the very idea of the *Flâneur* reveals it to be a masculine concept. (Wilson, 1995: 65)

Yet Wilson goes on to point out the deep ambivalence towards urban life inherent in Benjamin's meditation on the *flâneur*. It is, she claims,'a sorrowful engagement with the melancholy of cities', arising partly from 'the enormous unfulfilled promise of the urban spectacle, the consumption, the lure of pleasure and joy which somehow seemed destined to be disappointed' (1995: 73). Ultimately, however, *flâneuring* is a passive, noninteractive pastime and the *flâneur* becomes a figure of solitude and anonymity in the city labyrinth, so that Wilson claims 'The *Flâneur* represented not the triumph of masculine power but its attenuation' (1995: 74). It appears, then, that neither men nor women will ultimately benefit from city planning which perceives the inhabitants as *flâneurs* and the places as objects of the male gaze rather than spaces for interaction.

Grosz (1995a: 55) is critical of male perceptions of public space: 'The ways in which space has been historically conceived have always functioned either to contain women or to obliterate them.' She provides a more 'feminine' conceptualization through the term 'chora' (1995a). Grosz argues that 'chora', Plato's space between being and becoming or the 'space in which place is made possible', contains many of the characteristics which masculinist knowledge has expelled. Rather than being the object of the stroller's gaze, the concept of 'chora' suggests a space to be occupied and given meaning by the people who make use of the space. The space gives birth to the living experiences of human beings – it is open to many possibilities.

> *Chora* then is the space in which place is made possible . . . It is the space that engenders without possessing, that nurtures without requirements of its own, that receives without giving, and that gives without receiving, a space that evades all characterization including the disconcerting logic of identity, of hierachy of being, the regulation of order . . . While *chora* cannot be directly identified with the womb – to do so would be to pin it down naively to something specific – none the less it does seem to borrow many of the pardoxical attributes of pregnancy and maternity. (Grosz,1995a: 51)

By reappropriating the implied maternal dimensions of space Grosz suggests that we might reorient ways in which spatiality is conceived, lived and used and thus make way for women to reoccupy places from which they have been re/displaced or expelled and also expose men's appropriation of the whole of space.

Her articulation of spaces in the city as 'chora' or 'the horizon of becoming' (1995a: 56) highlights previous male perceptions of leisure areas in the city as places, objects of the gaze, rather than as spaces for interaction. In the former view, the users of such public places become *flâneurs* involved in fleeting observations rather than interacting people with possibilities for expansion of the self through leisure experience. The latter view suggests instead the term 'choraster' as a feminized conceptualization of those who interact in a constructive or creative way with others in city leisure spaces.

Following de Certeau (1988), I would distinguish between the more objective (male?) concept of 'place' and that of 'space'. Place has a distinct location which it defines, place is fixed and implies stability. Space, in contrast, is composed of intersections of mobile elements with shifting often indeterminate borders. 'Space is practiced place,' says de Certeau, 'the street defined by urban planning is the place which becomes transformed into space by the people who use it' (1988: 117). 'Chora', in this sense, is a space whose meaning can be constantly redefined by its inhabitants. Space allows for people to construct their own meanings in relation to the self, identity and subjectivity in a leisure process (see Rojek, 1989) which is ongoing and changing. The self that goes away from the space is rarely the same as the self that enters. As Bella (1989) has observed in relation to leisure, for women it is the interaction with other people, the opportunity for relationality in leisure that is important. So an emphasis on space and interactions in city spaces offers a feminization of this concept. 'Chora', like the womb, which takes on its meaning when it becomes inhabited by the developing foetus, takes on its meaning from its inhabitants.

The geographers Mowl and Towner (1995) use the term 'place' in much the same way that I am using 'space', and claim that 'Leisure places are not simply physical areas on a map, they are individual human creations, which are in themselves the products of social, cultural, and political processes' (1995: 114). They give an example from their own study of the leisure of women in South Gosforth (Newcastle) and Wallsend (North Tyneside) in the UK.

> Some of the women involved in our study described how they had created their own private leisure places; their own centres of meaning. One such woman, 'Alice' from South Gosforth, described how the secluded row of terraced houses on which she lived had been an important leisure venue for herself and other women when they all had young children and consequently their spatial mobility was most restricted. All the houses on the terrace had very open front gardens with no hedges and the children on the terrace, who were all of a similar age, regularly played in each other's gardens. Through the children the mothers became friends and would get together in one of the houses each day for a coffee and a chat while the children played together ... The women on this terrace had effectively created their own leisure place. (Mowl and Towner, 1995: 112–13)

The interactive dimension of the use of public leisure space or 'chora' suggests that the concept of 'social value' in this space may be of greater value in future planning and present need than that of 'image' associated with the gaze of the *flâneur*. It is a concept more attuned to the feminine emphasis on social relationships in leisure (Bella, 1989). When the term is applied to a physical place with which people interact and to which they attach cultural meaning, it represents a social process where a place acts as a material resource which over time has social significance for a group of people. Social value, then, refers to the meanings attached to places by groups of people. The place becomes a space, taking on the sense of social value: 'Social value is about collective attachment to places that embody meanings important to a community. These places are usually community owned or publicly accessible or in some other ways "appropriated" into people's daily lives' (Australian Heritage Commission, 1992: 10).

The experiential worth derived from the history of the place and its representation sets the scene for its social worth. Its maintenance and the continual interaction of people with it ensure the persistence of its social value. As social value is a process dependent on its dynamic relationship with those who use it, the meaning may change and develop over time. The people who give social value to the 'chora' the 'chorasters' are those who 'practise' the place, who use it, experience it, give it social meaning.

One such space for me is the harbourside salt-water swimming pool at Manly in Sydney. To this space my mother, father, brother and myself walked every morning before my father went to work. Here we were greeted by other families whom we knew, also out for their morning swim. Here I learned to swim and by the age of three could competently swim out to the pontoon, about 25 metres from the sand. The pontoon itself was an exciting place – a large and a small slippery dip, a running wheel and diving boards offered challenges which I mastered as I grew. The meaning of this public leisure space for me was a special family time, a sociable time, a space which offered pleasure (I still love the water and swimming) and challenge in a safe context. When I revisit this space now, the memories return, but the space has changed. It remains a scenic spot, but the pool area has been reduced, the pontoons are gone and the people picnicking on the grass and sand are mainly spectators, with few swimming. Serious swimmers now use the Olympic Pool nearby which is the standard 50 metres long, has regulating lanes, is heated in winter and costs $2.00 a visit! Small children are confined to the babies' pool. The beautiful city of Sydney abounds in such scenic spots around the harbour. In their development for the Olympics in the year 2000, the danger is that they will be promoted as images, along with the Opera House and the Harbour Bridge as part of the 'tourist gaze', objects to be looked at and admired perhaps, but in which there is little social value in the sense that I am using the term here.

I would suggest that the conceptualization and promotion of public leisure spaces in terms of 'image' incorporates the fleeting, ephemeral and voyeuristic elements of the gaze of the *flâneur* as well as suggesting a commodified pre-determined mass experience. As Lefebvre observes:

> Leisure spaces are the object of a massive speculation that is not tightly controlled and is often assisted by the state (which builds highways and communications, and which directly or indirectly guarantees the financial operations, etc). This space is sold, at high prices, to citizens who have been harried out of the town by the boredom and the rat-race. It is reduced to visual attributes, 'holidays', 'exile', 'retreat' and soon loses even these. (Lefebvre, 1974: 84)

Social value, on the other hand, can incorporate the historical associations which have, over time, been given to the space by the variety of people who have inhabited it. And, for the present people, it allows for individual experience. Where the 'image' of the place has been all in urban planning, I suggest instead a space for 'social value' where the interests and needs of local residents and local communities, including women and children, are involved both in the process of planning and in an interactive experience which will extend for the visitor beyond that of his/her visit.

We can learn something of such social value from children's play and urban parks perspectives. Children do not make very good *flâneurs*. They are not content with just 'looking at' the beautiful scenery – they want some activity and interaction. They are better 'chorasters' than adults. And not all adults have forgotten the enjoyment of play. Elements from children's play environments that need consideration in making public leisure spaces user friendly for women and children and other adults, and which add social value, include:

Safe challenge: a play area should have a challenging environment to allow for physical development without being exposed to unnecessary hazards (Moor et al., 1987: 10).

Diversity and clarity: just as children's needs are dynamic, so too must play
   areas provide a diversity of challenges/activities. Opportunities for
   sensory stimulation are vital.
Graduated challenges: play environments should cater for a wide range of
   challenges (Moor et al., 1987: 11).
Flexibility: there must be 'physical elements' that are capable of manipulation so that, as children learn and develop, the area can continue to
   function as an appropriate learning arena.

In a similar vein recent planners in the area of urban parks are suggesting
that these parks should be 'user friendly' and 'family friendly' if they are to
meet the needs of the families who are expected to use the parks. The views
of families are important, rather than top-down male management decisions. For example, Roberts (1986: 266) looks at the 'implications of
visitor use information for park management planning'. He uses Centennial
Park in Sydney as a case study to highlight the part visitor-use information
can play in park management. In relation to Centennial Park, Roberts
(1986: 268–9) found that 'the results of the . . . user survey have challenged
management to justify many traditional management policies'. The user
survey proved useful in many areas including forthcoming events, traffic
management, staff changeover, financial and staff resources, promotion of
the park, interpretive material, re-allocation of use and future management
planning (Roberts, 1986: 269–70). Through utilizing visitor-use information,
park management planning can help ensure that parks are 'people parks'
and not 'park managers' parks' (Roberts, 1986: 272).

Van de Water suggests some necessary qualities if parks are to be 'family
friendly': 'provision of family activities (that) includes an awareness of user
needs and appropriate design. As well as providing basic amenities, "family
friendly" urban design must include the qualities of sociability, convenience, attraction and safety' (1993: 26). And other park planners (e.g. see
Deary, 1985) make specific suggestions such as safety, access and consideration of the needs of the local residents, in order that parks may provide
families with access to recreational/leisure experiences.

The city of Sydney has some notable urban parks which provide welcome
green space in a busy business and commercial environment. Areas such as
Hyde Park, the Botanic Gardens, the Domain and Centennial Park provide
images for the tourist and locals alike of restfulness and leisure in a dynamic
metropolis. No doubt they will be used during the Olympic Games in the
year 2000 for these purposes. Yet the question of their use by all remains
unclear. Sitting next to an elderly lady on a bus one day, shortly after a day-
light rape at the gates of the Botanic Gardens, she told me how she lived
within walking distance of the Gardens but seldom used them now. Previously one of the highlights of her everyday experiences had been a stroll
through the Gardens on a sunny afternoon, the harbour glinting in the
background. But now she was afraid to do so alone. There is a need, at this
time of intensive allocation of resources to the refurbishment of the city of

Sydney prior to its dramatic presentation to the rest of the world for the Olympic Games in September 2000, for an emphasis on the social value of such places to locals as well as visitors. For women, creating a safe and friendly chora where they can experience leisure becomes a priority.

That such planning is possible is exemplified by a space created for the 1988 Calgary Winter Olympics. Prior to the Olympics, few 'people places' were located in the city because of the emphasis on commercial construction during the boom. However, during the Olympics, the downtown core became a magnet for informal interaction such as pin trading, pancake breakfasts and people-watching, partly due to the construction of a permanent Olympic Plaza adjacent to the new city hall on land desired by developers for a shopping mall. During the Olympics it was the site of the nightly medal ceremonies and it provided a unique, multi-purpose 'people place' in the downtown core. A variety of forms of entertainment – free as well as paid – was provided in the new Performing Arts Centre adjacent to the Plaza. In the words of one Calgarian: 'While we were waiting for the free breakfast, we started talking to the people around us ... people from Germany, California and Chicago. That was great' (Hiller, 1990: 128). Having defined the location as safe and friendly, people began to talk to one another and on occasion visitors found themselves invited home for a drink. Inter-subjective bonds among friends and kin became extended to strangers also. The place became a space for interaction between visitors and hosts and has remained so since the Games.

The Self in Public Leisure Space

The use of public leisure spaces in the city for resistance to dominant discourses on womanhood is now being recognized by feminist writers (Wilson, 1989, 1991; Johnson, 1994; Huxley, 1994; Ryan, 1994). I, however, would like to suggest that such spaces offer a further opportunity for the development of the self which goes beyond incremental resistance to male power.

Space in the sense that I am developing it here involves interaction with others and, as I see it, becomes integrated into one's sense of self. It contains the possibility of stretching towards the future, of becoming, of the development of self. The feminist geographer Massey (1994) critiques the male view of space as physically bounded, passive and static and suggests instead a dynamic interactive construct which is inextricably implicated in social relations and identity. The question could then be asked: 'Why would women want to enter the public spaces of the city, if they are alien to their way of viewing the world in general and leisure in particular and if they are unsafe places for them?' Apart from issues of equity of access to publicly funded resources, there is the important issue of the opportunity that such spaces present for experiences and interactions which enlarge the self. For women whose leisure time and leisure space are generally constrained by family responsibilities and the ethic of care (Deem, 1986; Henderson, 1990), there is a corresponding narrowing of sense of self. The self is predominantly defined in terms of the space of home. The links between leisure and identity (Kelly, 1987a) and space (as I have defined it) and identity (see Godkin, 1980; Massey, 1994) suggest that if women have access to public leisure spaces in the city, it can provide interactions and experiences which extend their horizons beyond the constraints on individual identity imposed by their relegation to the home.

Other writers, concerned with a social psychological analysis of tourism, have posited the connection between space and generally male identity through tourism (see Cohen and Taylor, 1976; Godkin, 1980; Colton, 1987; Haywood, 1988; Pearce, 1990; Brown, 1992). Brown, for example, claims that tourism is an encounter, an interaction with the environment in a state of heightened consciousness. The places of tourism thus provide individuals with profound centres of meanings and symbols endowed with cultural significance which are in some ways different from their own environments (Brown, 1992: 64). Pearce (1990: 32) observes: 'Meeting new people, making friends and expanding one's view of the world through these contacts is a little publicized but important social impact.' Incorporating feminized concepts of tourism, Wearing and Wearing (1996) argue that tourist spaces allow for interaction with people from a diversity of cultures in leisure experiences which offer the possibility of self-reflection and self-enhancement. City spaces may have a similar impact.

Simmel's analysis of the fleeting over-excitements of leisure in the 'metropolis' as a counter-balance to the protective emotional coating of neurasthnia are very much in line with the concept of the male *flâneur* (Simmel, 1978). Nevertheless, he also provides us with some insights into individual identity in such a complex environment which can include women. In complex industrial society, Simmel (1936) argued that the very variety of groups to which one may belong produces a unique pattern of group affiliations for each person, thus contributing to individuality. In simpler societies, one's web of group affiliations tended to be concentric reinforcing the values and assigned statuses of that society. In contemporary society, however, they do not necessarily overlap, providing opportunity for individual identity construction. Presumably contact with spaces which are different or other to the private sphere of the home can also add to the variety open to one in terms of identity construction. In terms of Mead's self (1972), the 'me' which is socially constructed through contact with 'significant others', 'significant reference groups' and the 'generalized other' is open through such contact to both growth and constraint. In addition, for Mead, the self is an 'I' which selectively synthesizes the societal input into the 'me'. Presumably this cumulative 'I' can be enlarged by interaction in alternative space. The 'me' and the 'I' which make up the self must be changed in some way by the interactions and symbols experienced in this space. And this self is taken home. The 'chora' of public, city, leisure space provides a venue for the 'choraster' to rethink identity and to enlarge the 'I'.

Poststructural feminist writers such as Butler (1990) deny the essential, rational 'I' constructed by male theorists and the binary opposition of the objective and subjective concepts of the self. For her, the self is a political construct and there are many subjectivities, many 'I's. She maintains subjectivity is a process of 'becoming' through repeated performative acts. She argues that gender is not a cultural inscription written on sexed bodies but a process through repeated performative acts which are culturally discursively constructed. She thus opens up possibilities for the self to grow and enlarge. This self may or may not conform to one's socially prescribed identity. Identity, or rather subjectivity, is not, in Butler's terms, a unified concept. Subjectivities are politically constructed and possibilities exist for the subversion of the sex/gender dichotomy through the proliferation of cultural/discursive gender behaviours. In poststructuralist thought the subject is not a rational whole but a changing contradictory site, thus making possible a new politics of identity that can encompass gender, race, class and sexuality without a hierarchy of causation or political action. As McRobbie points out:

> Feminist postmodernism does not eliminate the subject or the self but finds it in operation as a series of bit parts in the concrete field of social relations. Politics must therefore imply subjectivities in process, interacting and debating
> . . .
> This might mean living with fragmentation, with the reality of inventing the self rather than endlessly searching for the self. (1993a: 138 and 140)

Focus on public leisure space may enable a 'becoming' beyond categories assigned at home: the performative acts of this space may allow a 'becoming' beyond that possible at home. In Grosz's terms, they may expand 'the horizon of becoming' (1995a: 56). They may, on the other hand, reduce this horizon by male definition and control of public space. Nevertheless the possibilities for alternative and or multiple subjectivities through access to city spaces remain. The project ahead, says Grosz,

> . . . is to return women to those places from which they have been dis- or re-placed or expelled, to occupy those positions – especially those which are not acknowledged as positions – partly in order to show men's invasion and occupancy of the whole of space, of space as their own and thus the construction of spaces available to women, and partly in order to be able to experiment with and produce the possibility of occupying, dwelling or living in new spaces, which in their turn generate new perspectives, new bodies, new ways of thinking. (1995a: 57)

Both possibilities are suggested by the following city tale written about Sydney.

> A mother and daughter come to Sydney for a holiday. The women are not complete strangers to the big city, but it is not home. They view their home town as friendlier, safer and, although not without glamour, less multicultural,

less sophisticated, far less exciting. Being in Sydney reinforces their sense of themselves, as belonging to and coming from another place. Both women continually constitute 'the city' as experience, as location, as concept. Such imaginings of space shape contexts in which mother/daughter relations are constituted, negotiated, reinforced and possibly transformed.

For the mother and daughter Sydney is romanticized and 'othered' as a place of fascination, of danger, of pleasure, of increased possibilities for consumption and most importantly increased opportunities for sociability. They stay with friends in an inner-city suburb, close to transport and the city centre. Both women enjoy the visit, shopping, visiting museums, art galleries and Darling Harbour – sometimes together, sometimes singularly, sometimes with friends. The daughter goes to nightclubs noted for their great dance music and sexual harassment free environments. Sydney is experienced as pleasurable, exciting and liberating for women, liberating for mothers and daughters. They feel 'good' there.

Another view of the city, however is generated by the daughter's intended visit to friends living in a distant suburb. The ground of the women's interaction shifts, in relation to each other and in relation to 'the city'. The proposed visit generates tension between mother and daughter. The mother becomes afraid for her daughter, fearful of this city. To reach her friends the daughter must walk to the railway station – an inner-city station, a site sensationalized/sexualized/exoticized by sections of the media as a place of deviancy, of violence, a place frequented by would-be rapists, bag snatchers, muggers, misfits in general – people not like us. More alien residents? (Larbalestier, 1994: 189)

Is it possible to reduce the latter and enlarge the former for women? When specific inroads are made into male domination of public leisure space, it is not surprising that there is a tangible reaction to any erosion of male power and control.

In the city of Sydney there is, and has been, a space specifically set aside for women's bathing since 1914. This space has been of special value to women as a safe public leisure space in which they can be hassle-free and transcend some of the normalizing aspects of the male gaze. Comments such as the following concerning their experiences of using the baths, collected in recent qualitative interviews (see Woodberry, 1995: 26), indicate the value of this space to women.

> It's a little piece of heaven here . . . You can sunbake in the semi nude if you want to and nobody is bothering you. You just please yourself. (Dot)
>
> This is one place they can come without being embarrassed in a swimming costume. All those lumps and bumps. I mean who cares, no one cares . . . And you don't have to swim in skimpy costumes, you can swim in your clothes if you want to. Muslim women swim in their . . . they don't swim in western swimming costumes, I've seen them swim around in something like nighties. (Liz)

These baths, commonly referred to as Coogee Women's Pool, are located on the southern rock platform of Coogee Beach, Sydney. They are managed jointly by the Randwick City Council and Coogee Ladies Swimming Club.

In 1992 Mr Lion Wolk, a resident of Coogee, lodged a complaint with the New South Wales Anti-Discrimination Board, alleging that the council had breached the Anti-Discrimination Act by allocating the baths for the sole use of women. After much debate and lobbying and at least two tribunal hearings, in March 1995 the Minister for Energy and Local Government announced that the council was granted exemption under section 126A of the Anti-Discrimination Act, to continue to operate the baths for the sole use of women and children under 13 years of age. This does not prevent the occasional male from trying to intrude on this women-only space. Woodberry concludes:

> Women need safe outdoor leisure and recreation settings for the spaces within to be inhabitable. It is in relation to the exterior that the individual shatters, carves up and landscapes – or seascapes – the self. It is in relation to others that the individual cuts through the boundaries of personal identity and recreates the interior. (1995: 35)

It is spaces like these in the city which enable women to be 'chorasters' rather than objects for the gaze and control of male *flâneurs*.

Conclusion

In this chapter I have looked at feminist critiques of the male bias in urban sociology and the consequent male colonization of public spaces. Male urban theorizing has conceptualized the frequenters of city leisure spaces as *flâneurs*, strollers at large in a city spread out for their gaze, providing distinct images to be enjoyed but quickly passed over. Instead I have posited Grosz's concept of 'chora' to denote city spaces inhabited by 'chorasters', men, women and children whose interactions and leisure experiences in such spaces enable a 'becoming' beyond that of home, school and/or work.

Space, in the sense that I have developed it here, is inextricably implicated in social relationships and one's sense of self. It remains no longer feasible, then, to conceptualize city spaces as static entities or bounded places for the voyeuristic gaze of strolling *flâneurs*. In the postmodern era, city spaces, if planned in consultation with the people and with consideration for their social values, can incorporate a multiplicity of meanings and become dynamic areas for interaction and an expansion of the self. For this to be so, however, urban planners must make these spaces safe, yet challenging, for women, children and older citizens, as well as for those whose ethnicity or disability may previously have debarred them from the use of such space. It will be interesting to observe the use of the city spaces being massively redeveloped in Sydney for the Olympics in the year 2000. Will visitors and locals be merely *flâneurs*, or will they be chorasters who take away with them a self that has been challenged and enlarged by their use of these leisure spaces?

In this chapter it has been demonstrated that feminist theory and feminist theorizing can add another dimension to the conceptualization of leisure experience. The instance has been the conceptualization of public leisure spaces in the city, but the perspective presented has wider ramifications for tourism, as well as for other aspects of leisure. If we fail to draw on insights provided by feminist theorizing in future developments of leisure, we limit the possibilities that leisure spaces may provide for expansion of the varieties of selves who desire leisure experiences in the millennium.

In the following chapter, I turn to the personal spaces that women make for leisure experiences which provide possibilities to resist male domination and contribute to subjectivities beyond those 'feminine' ones which keep them subordinated to and serving males.

8

Personal Leisure Spaces: Poststructuralist Theories

In the previous chapter, I examined the potential of public leisure places to provide spaces where women as well as men could interact in a safe and meaningful way so that the self of home and work is expanded and enlarged. In so doing I incorporated the poststructuralist feminist challenge for women to subvert male colonization of knowledge and theory. This I did with reference to the conceptualization of public space and its relevance for leisure use. In this chapter, initially I examine the implications of poststructuralist feminist theories for the construction of personal leisure spaces by postmodern women. This leads me to rewrite the concept of leisure to incorporate women's experiences of the world, previously neglected in male-dominated leisure theory. The concept of leisure as 'personal space' or 'my space' is suggested. This conceptualization is not dependent on the paid work/leisure dichotomy redolent of much male theory and incorporates the ideas of resistance, relative autonomy and the enlargement of the 'I' which have been suggested in earlier chapters of the book. Thus, I suggest a feminist postmodern interactionist perspective which enables leisure theory to open its doors to insights from poststructuralist theory and to throw some light on leisure spaces and the self. Then I examine ways in which a diversity of women have made spaces in their lives for themselves, 'true' leisure in my own feminized version of the concept. For working-class women and women of colour, this has often been in very oppressive circumstances. Finally, the potential of leisure as 'personal space' for men as well as women is explored. In the ideal world, there would also be possibilities for leisure as 'our space', for men and women together. There remains, however, much work to be done at a structural level before it may be possible for both men and women to have equal access to personal leisure space.

Women in the Postmodern World

The term postmodern is a multi-layered concept that directs our attention to a variety of major social and cultural changes taking place at the end of the twentieth century. Whereas the Enlightenment heralded modernity, that is, an historical period when industrial production, rationality, positivistic science, objectivity and belief in absolute truths, order and stability prevailed, postmodernity is the current period in which all of these certainties are being challenged in some way. The changes taking place include those in the modes of production and consumption, telecommunications and computer power, technology and dissemination of information, as well as in modes of thinking, theorization, artistic endeavour and cultural practices (see Featherstone, 1991; Lyon, 1994, for more details concerning these concepts of postmodernism).

One mark of the postmodern period has been the challenge to established gender, ethnic, racial and environmental regimes through social movements. Counter-cultural movements of the late 1960s, such as the women's movement, have led to significant changes in social structure and cultural attitudes which have enabled women of the postmodern era to begin to challenge the very foundations of language, subjectivity, representation, theory and cultural analyses in patriarchal societies. As Huyssen points out:

> Directly and indirectly, the women's movement has nourished the emergence of women as a self-confident and creative force in the arts, in literature, film and criticism. The ways in which we now raise questions of gender and sexuality, reading and writing, subjectivity and enunciation, voice and performance are unthinkable without the impact of feminism, even though many of these activities may take place on the margin or even outside the movement proper. Feminist critics have also contributed substantially to revisions of the history of modernism ... This is also true of the 'new French feminists' and their theorisation of the feminine in modernist writing. (1990: 270)

The postmodern critique of modernism has provoked two responses: a conservative one, which tries to recover the fragments of a unity shattered by modernity; and a more radical one, which rejoices in a plurality of languages and modes of thought and denies the imposition of 'totalizing' concepts upon the variousness of reality (Grace, 1994: 7). In this chapter, I adopt the latter view denying the totalizing impact of a unitary view of 'woman' which has been largely defined by and inferiorized by male language and discourses. Rather, there is a celebration of difference and its potentiality for breaking out of passive and inferiorized femininity. The potential for confusion and distress for women in the postmodern era due to the marketing of women's bodies in sport and leisure and the various attempts to normalize them into the 'Barbie doll' image or the muscular athlete is recognized. Nevertheless my emphasis is on the more constructive use of contradictory discourses for resistance, subversion and the rewriting of feminine subjectivities.

In this chapter, then, women in the postmodern world means a diverse range of women of the 1990s who have a new self-confidence to challenge the givens of their existence, to resist what they have been told they are and to reach towards what they could be. I have used some of the ideas of post-structuralist theory to suggest ways in which this may be done and to resignify the concept of leisure so that it is appropriate for women in a diversity of situations. I argue that leisure spaces can provide possibilities for women of colour, as well as working-class and middle-class white women, to rewrite or resignify women's subjectivities so that they are no longer inferiorized. In the latter part of the chapter I go on to ask whether leisure as personal space may be used constructively by men as well.

In order to do this, I draw on poststructuralist theories such as those of Foucault and the French feminists which have provided some conceptual challenges to the more macro-analyses of the power struggles of class and gender provided by structuralist feminists in the early stages of the women's movement of the late 1960s.

Foucault, resistance, power and heterotopias

One of the most influential thinkers in poststructuralist thinking, Michel Foucault, a French philosopher, challenged the top-down, repressive ideas concerning power which pervaded meta-theories such as those of Marx. Power for Foucault (1980, 1983) is evident in a multiplicity of sites such as the body, discourse, knowledge, subjectivity and sexuality, where there is the possibility of struggle and resistance. He identifies three types of struggle:

> either against forms of domination (ethnic, social and religious); against forms of exploitation which separates individuals from what they produce; or against that which ties the individual to himself [sic] and submits him to others in this way; struggles against subjection, against forms of subjectivity and submission. (Foucault, 1983: 212)

It is the third type of struggle, that is, the struggle for feminine subjectivities that are not inferiorized to masculine subjectivities which leisure as space can help to achieve.

In Foucault people are never just victims. Although they are constrained by subjectivities, normative sexuality and 'docile bodies' constituted through powerful, normalizing discourses and self-surveillance, they are 'free' in the sense that they can choose to resist. Women in structuralist feminist theory have been presented as universally oppressed, although the form of oppression may vary trans-historically, trans-culturally and across class and race divisions. Foucault's idea of resistance allows for a more flexible and optimistic situation grounded in the everyday experiences of individual, real-life women. By resistance he means the struggle against the form of power which pervades everyday life and constitutes individuals as subjects in the sense of being subject to somebody by control and dependence and subject to their own identity by a conscience or self-knowledge (Foucault, 1983). Gender in this notion can take many forms within the individual, within her life-cycle and between women. Contradictory discourses and subjectivities and oppositional positions of the relatively powerless in society allow space for resistance to dominant ways of thinking and speaking, surveillance and normalization. Resistance is a strategy where deployment of power is the aim rather than revolution and the false promise of liberation. For Foucault,

> there is a plurality of resistances, each of them a special case: resistances that are possible, necessary, improbable; others that are spontaneous, savage, solitary, concerted, rampant, or violent; still others that are quick to compromise, interested or sacrificial ... the points, knots, or focuses of resistance are spread over time and space at varying densities, at times mobilising groups or individuals in a definitive way, inflaming certain points of the body, certain moments in life, certain types of behaviour ... (1980: 96)

In applying these ideas of power and resistance to the concept of space Foucault argues for the necessity in contemporary urban society for spaces for resistance. 'Space,' he says, is 'fundamental in any form of communal life; space is fundamental in any exercise of power' (where he means resistance). In particular he suggests the need for 'heterotopias', that is, 'those singular spaces to be found in some given social spaces whose functions are different or even opposite of others' (Foucault, 1984: 252). In contrast to 'utopias' which are fictional critiques of society, without any actual locality, 'heterotopias' for Foucault can be 'real' existing places of difference which act as counter-sites or compensatory sites to those of everyday activity. He gives examples of brothels, churches, hotel rooms, museums, libraries, prisons, asylums, Roman baths and the Scandinavian sauna which provided specific alternative spaces for men in the public arena. But they are also powerful sites of the imaginary, and offer 'a realization that makes me come back towards myself, to reconstitute myself where I am (heterotopia)' (Foucault, 1986: 24). So I am suggesting that both physical and metaphorical leisure spaces can act as heterotopias for struggle against and resistance to domination of the self and inferiorized subjectivities. They also provide a space for reconstituting the self and rewriting the script of identity. There is room here for subjectivities other than those that are ordinarily prescribed for one. Unlike Foucault, however, my concern here is the construction of such spaces for and by women in the practice of their everyday lives, not necessarily in the public sphere where men remain dominant.

In this sense, for women, leisure is a 'heterotopia', a personal space for resistance to domination, a space where there is room for the self to expand beyond what it is told it should be. It is a space where the 'I' can resist and move beyond the societal input which constructs the 'me' of the self (for discussion of these terms and interactionist theory, see Chapter 3). Of course leisure conceptualized as 'my space' can also include other people, relationships and group resistance – it is personal space in the sense that the person chooses to use the space for themselves in some way.

Poststructuralist feminist subjectivities

Leisure spaces (heterotopias) for women provide spaces for rewriting the script of what it is to be a woman, beyond definitions provided by powerful males and the discourses propagated as truth in contemporary societies.

Gender power relations in present society continue to construct the feminine as lacking in phallic terms, 'other' and inferior to the masculine. However, by deconstructing the term 'woman', by recognizing its political construction and the diversity of femininities, poststructuralist feminists such as Butler see the possibility for new configurations of the term. Butler argues that it is by repeated performative acts that womanhood is established and so can be re-established beyond male-dominated cultural definitions (1990, 1992). She says:

> In a sense what women signify has been taken for granted for too long, and what has been fixed as the 'referent' of the term has been 'fixed', normalized, immobilized, paralysed in positions of subordination ... to safeguard the category of women as a site of possible resignifications is to expand the possibilities of what it means to be a woman and in this sense to condition and enable an enhanced sense of agency. (Butler, 1992: 16)

Braidotti's (1993) claim that poststructuralism has a great relevance for feminism because its redefinition of thinking enables new visions of subjectivity, incorporating living transformations, has some basis in arguments such as Butler's. Butler's exegesis is but one of the various poststructuralist attempts to deconstruct a fixed notion of identity. In feminist poststructuralist thought 'the essence of femininity is seen as a historical construct that needs to be worked' (Braidotti, 1993: 9). 'Woman' then becomes a problematic category. In the Italian connection, 'woman' is a concept to be analysed and challenged. The feminist task is a new exploration of an autonomous *differenza sessuale*, one which is not based on a term that has been used to keep women in their inferior place (Bock and James, 1992: 6). In this tradition, de Lauretis (1990) argues that 'woman' is a female-embodied social subject that is based on its specific, emergent, conflictual history which can include sex and gender, but also race, class and other significant socio-cultural divisions. The starting point, then, for feminist redefinitions of female subjectivity is paradoxical: 'In feminist theory one speaks as a woman, although the subject "woman" is not a monolithic essence defined once and for all, but rather the site of multiple, complex and potentially contradictory sets of experience, defined by overlapping variables' (Braidotti, 1993: 7). Poststructuralist feminism has moved from the deconstruction of the notion of 'woman' as presented in traditional thinking, where female subjectivity is a given based on natural biology, through an analysis of the fragments of woman existing in differential positions in society, to an umbrella notion of 'woman', which recognizes both commonality and diversity between women and men, between women and other women and within each woman. 'Can there be fragments if there is no whole?', asks Braidotti (1993: 11). As Poovey points out:

> All women may currently occupy the position 'woman' . . . but they do not occupy it in the same way. Women of color in a white ruled society face different obstacles than do white women, and they may share more important problems with men of color than with their white 'sisters'. By deconstructing the term 'woman' into a set of independent variables, this strategy can show how consolidating all women into a falsely unified 'woman' has helped mask the operations of power that actually divide women's interests as much as unite them. (1988: 59)

In my view 'woman' is indeed an unstable, historically produced category, which has been socially constructed in male-dominated societies on an inferiorization of traditional femininity. For example, the delegation of nurturing/caring tasks to women as their 'natural' duty and the consequent societal devaluation of these tasks has systematically sterotyped, constrained and devalued women's subjectivities as mothers, wives and grandmothers, together with their caring roles in the community and their extensions of these roles in the workforce. If, however, the concept 'woman' is open to diversity, to change, and to redefinition, there is the possibility of rewriting the script for women so that these tasks are re-valued and other avenues for a sense of self-worth are opened up. Nevertheless, 'woman' is also the subject of feminist politics where to speak as a woman recognizes some commonalities as well as diversity.

This leads us to the question: 'How can postmodern women, that is those who are challenging the definition of women as "other" to and inferior to men, use leisure to rewrite femininities which are not in the shadow of masculinities?' I have suggested that the concept of leisure as 'personal space' or 'heterotopia' allows us to listen to the voices of a diversity of women who tell us how they use this space to enlarge what it is for them to be women.

Leisure as 'Personal Space'

In the 1970s feminists asked, 'Is leisure an appropriate concept for women with its male connotations of non-paid-work time and freely chosen activity?' (Anderson, 1975). In the 1990s as a feminist, I wish to retain the concept 'leisure' but in poststructuralist fashion reserve also the right to re-signify its meaning incorporating women's perspectives.

Poststructuralist feminists such as Lloyd (1989) and Grosz (1989), have challenged and deconstructed many of the binary oppositions beloved of male post-Enlightenment rationality. They have sought, for example, to eliminate the feminization and inferiorization of terms such as feminine when set in opposition to masculine, body in opposition to mind, nature to culture, intuition to rationality. While some male writers on leisure have begun to apply poststructuralist theory to leisure in a questioning of the work/leisure and production/consumption dichotomies where the former are prioritized and the latter inferiorized (e.g. Rojek, 1993a: 143), it has been left to poststructuralist feminists to suggest ways in which the deconstruction of these dichotomies may be specifically applied to women's experiences of leisure. For example, in my own study of mothers of first babies (Wearing, 1990a and 1990b), it was very hard for women to define motherhood indistinguishably as work or leisure and for most the creation of a space for themselves (physical or metaphorical) during the day became a safety valve for sanity. In this chapter, in poststructuralist fashion, I want to resignify the concept of leisure in a way that recognizes the daily experiences of women's lives, where the work/leisure dichotomy is substantially diffused.

So leisure here does not signify non-work time, activity or experience or space – it is resignified to mean personal spaces, physical and metaphorical, where women can explore their own desires and pleasures and perform acts which allow them to become women in their own right, to constitute diverse subjectivities and femininities which go beyond what women have been told they should be.

In terms of poststructuralist theory the concept of leisure as 'personal space' draws on Foucault's ideas of power and resistance and, in reference to space, to 'heterotopias'. In terms of poststructuralist feminist theory ideas of subjectivity and of rewriting the script of what it is to be a woman are incorporated.

The expansion of the concept of leisure that I am suggesting, then, is that of space, one's own space, that is, space physical or metaphorical over which one has control to fill with whatever persons, objects, activities or thoughts that one chooses. There are many possibilities here. These could include: a mental space in the midst of routine household tasks; a time space when obligatory tasks are done; a money space created by money, however little, kept aside from necessities; an activity space where no activity, familiar and loved activities or new and challenging activities are pursued; or a pleasure space for experience of pure pleasure suggested by the French feminist's concept of 'jouissance'. As well the space could conceivably be ideas, writings, poetry, art, sculpture, crafts, an emotional space for emotions in a safe environment, a physical space such as dance, sport or rock climbing, or a space away such as a holiday or a supportive space.

In the writings of the black American bell hooks, we find some excellent examples of these spaces, created by women under the oppressive conditions of African-American women in the USA. hooks (1993), writing of these women's resistance to their continued devaluation and oppression by the dominant culture, discusses ways that they have refused to be the 'mules of the world'. She focuses on self-recovery, self actualization, self-help, healing and reconciliation. She urges self-actualization as part of black women's political efforts to resist white supremacy and sexist oppression, thus linking the personal and the political in a practical way: 'Desiring to create a context where we as black females could both work on our individual efforts for self-actualisation and remain connected to a larger world of collective struggle led me to consider writing a self-help book that would especially address our concerns' (hooks, 1993: 5).

The strategies hooks suggests to address these concerns include creating spaces for spirituality, literature, support groups, story-telling, controlling financial and workplace stress, imaginative spaces and spaces for mental and physical pleasure. I use her own words to describe these spaces as I understand them.

Spirituality

... in the traditional world of black folk experience there was (and remains in some places and certainly many hearts) a profound unshaken belief in the spiritual power of black people to transform our world and live with integrity and oneness despite oppressive social realities. In that world, black folks collectively believed in 'higher powers', knew that forces stronger than the will and intellect of humankind shaped and determined our existence, the way we lived ... They knew joy, that feeling that comes from using one's powers to the fullest. (hooks, 1993: 10)

Literature

Our literature has helped healing. Much of the celebrated fiction by black women writers is concerned with identifying our pain and imaginatively constructing maps for healing. (hooks, 1993: 10)

Support Groups and Story-Telling

Of a support group she held for black women students, she says:

Our collective hope for the group was that it would be a space where black women could name their pain and find ways of healing. The power of the group to transform one another's lives seemed to be determined by the intensity of each individual's desire to recover, to find a space within and without, where she could sustain the will to be well and create affirming habits of being ... Conversation and story-telling were important locations for sharing information about the self, for healing. (hooks, 1993: 13–14)

Financial and Workplace Stress

Freeing my life of financial stress gave me yet another space to feel inner peace. And I have tried to share with other black women the strategies I used. (hooks, 1993: 59)

These strategies included living within one's means, keeping records and budgeting for necessities.

Imaginative Spaces

> ... in the midst of racism we had places where we could undo much of the psychological madness and havoc wreaked by white supremacy ... Clearly if black women want to be about the business of collective self-healing, we have to be about the business of inventing all manner of images and representation that show us the way we want to be and are. (hooks, 1993: 80–3)

Mental and Physical Pleasure

> Some of us are unable to imagine and create spaces of pleasure in our lives. When we are always busy meeting the needs of others, or when we are 'used to pain', we lose sight of the way in which the ability to experience and know pleasure is an essential ingredient of wellness. Erotic pleasure requires of us engagement with the realm of the senses, a willingness to pause in our daily life transactions and enjoy the world around us ... Singing, dancing, walking, or sitting meditation can all be used as a practice to bring us back in touch with our bodies. (hooks, 1993: 116, 126)

In my terms, all of these strategies are leisure spaces for women to rewrite a sense of self-worth and subjectivity which honours, rather than devalues, their femininity. hooks also discusses the use of alcohol and drugs as spaces for pleasure and escape in a painful world. She sees these spaces as counter-productive to 'a constructive "healthy" process of recovery' (hooks, 1993: 71, 73).

It is not inevitable, then, that women will use the 'freedom' of leisure spaces in a constructive and self-enhancing way. The destructive side of leisure spaces needs far more investigation in feminist leisure research than has been the case to date. Leisure as personal space may indeed provide time out for women, but here, as in other aspects of their lives, ambiguities and contradictions remain.

All women may not have similar very strong cultural traditions or the experiences of pain that many black women have, but these discourses, at least, open up the possibilities through leisure spaces for postmodern women to rewrite a strong and valued womanhood.

Spaces to Be: Women in Leisure Research

In leisure research we also find examples of women's use of such spaces for themselves. The support and sharing that comes from meeting with other women in similar situations has been well documented. For the working-class adolescent girls of McRobbie's (1978) study, their bedrooms provided a space for support and some resistance. For young mothers, meeting in play groups or in informal neighbourhood groups or to exchange childcare or to go on a picnic provides women with a space to share friendship and information as well as enjoyment (Wimbush, 1988; Wearing, 1990a and

1990b). One working-class mother in my study, for example, valued the space that a picnic with other mothers and children provided:

> We've got a reservoir up here at Prospect. We went about 3 or 4 weeks ago, we loved it. Actually we were saying 'gosh look at us here – our husbands are working away and we're enjoying it'. We probably felt a bit guilty, but I mean women are the ones that have to bring up their children, I suppose, more than the husband does. That just crossed our minds, but then we just got on and enjoyed it.
>   We just ended up taking Kentucky Fried.
>   We couldn't be bothered making anything and just stayed on our blankets and enjoyed it. (Wearing, 1990a: 54)

For the middle-aged women in Freysinger and Flannery's study, leisure is also a space for themselves where they resist the 'ethic of care': '. . . you need to have some time to yourself, you know, leisure time. You need to get away, you have to get out. I need all that different kinds of, of life to keep me sane' (1992: 314). Older women whose husbands had retired, in Cronin's (1995) study, made space for themselves by going out with friends, having friends at home, doing courses and sometimes simply marking out their own space at home:

> That is another thing I can do even if my husband is home, and a lot of women couldn't do . . . I will sit here with my legs up and read in the middle of the day and I will do it regardless of him. I used to do that when he was working so why should I give that up because my husband is retired? You have got to keep doing the things that you used to do before your husband is at home. Okay maybe you will hear [him say] 'oh well nice book?', and as he walks off I will say 'Yes I haven't finished it yet'. In the end that stops because he will hear you saying that and get used to it so in the end you have no problems. Tanya – Western Suburbs (Cronin, 1995: 106)

For older working-class women, Dixey found that bingo provided a space for sociability and support: 'Many of the elderly women would arrive up to two hours before the afternoon session started, to eat, talk, knit, read or play cards' (1988: 96). Spaces of the mind or 'minute vacations' were found in Henderson and Rannells's study of farm women, allowing women brief escapes in the midst of a busy day:

> . . . and one afternoon, it was really a hot muggy day and the sun was shining. Maybe it was around 4.30 pm and I came out of the (hay) mow and sat on the elevator . . . In looking west . . . beside our house, there was a row of maple trees that my dad planted, many years ago, beautiful great big trees, and I said that to me the way the sun filtered through they must have seen something like that to get an idea for their church chapels and the like. To me it was a really moving experience, just extremely. I've never had anything like that. (1988: 12)

In another study of older women, Heycox (1997) found that women who participated in a theatre group with the political purpose of making older women visible to the community in general and to politicians in particular also found this to be a personally liberating experience. They said it was extremely enjoyable, 'lots of fun', enabled them to share experiences of being older and built self-confidence. For some women the process occurred the other way. They joined the group for personal reasons and found themselves involved in political actions such as those staged by the theatre group. Thus community spaces became a part of an enlarging sense of self.

Dance, sport and exercise have provided spaces for women who participate to get in touch with and enjoy their control of their own bodily involvement (Griffiths, 1988; Hargreaves, 1989, 1994; Currie, 1996).

Hargreaves claims that, in the writing of her book on the history and sociology of women's sports, 'I have spoken to hundreds of women who participate in sports – for recreation, to escape from home, for social reasons, to lose weight, to get fit, to compete – and most of them talk about a sense of well-being and enrichment that comes into their lives as a result' (1994: 289).

For the mothers in Currie's study of the effect of exercise classes on their stress levels, this space was important for their sense of self beyond that at home and at work. Penny is 27 years old with a young child and many family stresses in her life. She says:

> I have a brother who I don't see or hear from due to a feud. Another brother with a life threatening disease. My husband's brother has cancer, another one with medically acquired AIDS. My grandmother has suffered a stroke and is angry and resentful, apart from other problems such as home, income, Christmas etcetera. I am suffering a lot from stress and I was getting a lot of severe headaches.
> . . . the class does help to a degree, I can come here and forget who I really am and escape to another being, another person.
> . . . Feeling like I'm doing something for myself instead of staying home like a home bound mother. I am feeling my age and feel young again, feeling my body react to exercise and feeling good about myself and my body again. (1996: 210–11)

Another mother said: 'Well once the music starts, and I get into the exercise, I just find that I am in a totally different, you know [pause] space . . . rather than at work, which you know is really good' (1996: 276).

In a study of the leisure of mothers of children with intellectual disabilities, time and space away from their care was a rare commodity. When it was achieved, the impact on the woman's sense of self was remarkable. Adele, whose 18-year-old intellectually impaired son remains primarily her responsibility, says of herself and her leisure spaces:

> The other thing that I've probably gained most benefit from was when I started running on my own and that to me was very indulgent at the time. I felt originally, quite selfish but the benefits were enormous. I always bite my nails and

I found that after three weeks that I'd stopped biting my nails because it was obviously just a stress thing. There was this huge stress release and again, the important thing about that, once I started doing it, and I also lost a bit of weight at the time. People started asking me if they could come with me and I started to think about it and realized that one of the most important things about it was that I was on my own. I always used to think that was odd to want to be on your own because I'm basically a person who likes to be with people, but I'm starting to see the value in having real times just for yourself and no one else . . . I think women see themselves in particular roles rather than as particular people and that's why I liked my ski weekend, where I wasn't anybody's mother or anyone's spouse. I was just me. (Bathurst, 1995: 70)

Davidson's study of women's holidays also reinforces the sense of space that is an essential element in women's own constructions of their leisure. She found that simply 'going away' is not a holiday if a sense of 'space' is not achieved:

. . . simply getting away from the home, the place where the normal work is done, does not necessarily result in a holiday experience. A holiday is achieved when and where the women are able to negotiate the roles and relationships that will occupy the holiday space, consequently there are many situations which women did not describe as a holiday, even though these were 'getting away'. On the other hand, women would identify experiences that were located in the home environment as a holiday if roles and relationships had been negotiated to culminate in a sense of space. The site of the holiday is just one of the negotiable components, and where roles and relationships have been successfully negotiated it is possible to find a holiday space in the normal work environment, that is, the home. (Davidson, 1996: 86)

One of her respondents tells of a weekend away with her women friends which enabled her to explore other aspects of her identity than that of wife and mother.

Probably about once a year I go away with the girls you know for a long weekend or four days . . . Last year we went to M. for *Phantom of the Opera* for three days. It was very nice and in a couple of weeks we're going to S. When I'm with the girls we go out at night, and sleep-in in the morning, and go shopping and the movies. When we went to M. we saw about five movies in one weekend, it was great. We just had a really good time. Then we went to *Phantom of the Opera*, then we went out that night to the club and you know night clubs and, yeah, it was just totally relaxed and easy. (Davidson, 1996: 76)

Spirituality, literature and other imaginative spaces such as art, music, theatre, story-telling and humour are areas for future investigation in leisure research. How can women use these spaces to include repeated performative acts which enable them to become women beyond their male-dominated socialization and stereotypes? How can women develop these personal spaces to rewrite the script of their subjectivities so that they are beyond inferiorization to predominant aggressive, controlling, competitive masculinities?

Leisure as 'Personal Space' for Males

We need now to ask the question: 'Does the feminization of the concept of leisure as "my space" also enhance our understanding of men's leisure?' And the corollary is: 'Has feminist theory contributed to an understanding of leisure in general?' I will leave the latter question to the concluding chapter of the book – here I address the former.

In the traditional male view of leisure and the family, the family itself has been constructed as a heterotopia, a sphere for relaxation and recuperation from the paid workforce, a leisure space of relative freedom in contrast to the demands and restrictions of the workforce. In the nuclear family, at least, family time for men means meal times, playing with the children, getting out into the garden, games of cricket and football played in back-yards and safe streets, and perhaps cups of tea and a listening ear, provided by the wife, as well as a space for sexual release. The family is also the place for picnics, barbecues and entertaining which provide sociable outlets with family and friends. For many men, the family is leisure. For example, in Williams's study of working-class men and women in a Queensland mining town, leisure is perceived by the men as a compensation for the stringencies of work and a release into freedom to enjoy family life or pursue hobbies and sport. These men made comments such as: 'Home is a haven, I can potter about, have a beer, watch TV'; 'It's always good to get home – time off for the garden – what I really like doing'; and 'Much rather be at home than out at work. Much better to be loafin' around at home' (Williams, 1981: 174).

In one of my own studies (Wearing, 1984), a young truck driver who enjoyed and was proud of his involvement in the care of his one-year-old daughter, bathing her, feeding her, changing her nappy and putting her to bed, when asked, described these activities as his wife's responsibility but his pleasure or leisure. As Shaw (1985) found in her study, the choice men had concerning their involvement in childcare and household tasks enabled them to construct some of these activities as leisure for them.

On the other hand, men also cherish their own space at home, but apart from the family. This is a place where they can indulge their own fantasies, hobbies and interests. In Australia it is symbolized by 'blokes' sheds'.

It would be a mistake to underestimate the importance of sheds in men's lives. Many men clearly do feel a sense of powerlessness with their lot in life, and a small space of their own does not seem too much to ask. It affords them a sense of independence and autonomy while at the same time maintaining the family close at hand. The shed can be a refuge from turbulent times, a constant when all around is changing. (Thomson, 1995: 39)

In these sheds men make their own rules of chaos or order, store precious paraphernalia, make things, collect things, think and sometimes socialize with other males. It is place of their own, away from the demands and order of the female domestic domain. As one retired man said: 'You put down a cup of coffee on a table in the house, and a moment later the wife swoops down with a dishcloth, lifts the cups up and wipes away a possible coffee ring stain' (Thomson, 1995: 38). American men also have their own spaces in the den or the basement.

There is, then, an ambivalence here for men. On the one hand, the family symbolizes a leisure sphere in opposition to the rigours of paid work, yet, in some senses, it also restricts men so that the conceptualization of leisure as 'personal space' also applies to men. Time with wife and children can be leisure, but there is a need also for time out for themselves. The expectation that men in the family will take responsibility for childcare for any length of time is not a reality, even in countries such as Sweden where public policies for many years have attempted to equalize sex roles (see Scott, 1982). This means that men can take time, if they wish, away from wife and children. In Australia, the 1991 National Recreation Participation survey (quoted in Veal, 1993: 38) showed that men participated significantly more than women in away-from-home activities such as competitive sport, socializing at the pub or hotel and visiting clubs, and in electronic games at home. These are activities which generally exclude the presence of children. Generally men have the choice to include women and children in their leisure activities or not. The power differentials between men and women even in this postmodern era allow most men greater choice than their female counterparts and greater access to personal space.

For men, then, there is often greater choice concerning personal space for leisure than for women in the family situation. Nevertheless, the family can also be a place of pressure for men, can be seen as women's territory and can form the background pressure to work harder in the paid workforce, often including overtime and/or an extra job in order to provide for family needs. Some recent research (Labone and Wearing, 1994) also indicates that women are the family members who choose family leisure activities. For some men the family is also an extension of their work roles, where home entertainment of business colleagues or potential clients assists in their upward promotion. A so-called 'leisure' activity under these circumstances represents work and leisure for both the husband and the wife. The work/leisure dichotomy, then, does not always work for men either. The two often overlap, as in the case of middle-class management men who use the business lunch or dinner and the golf course or squash court to network and close deals. Drinks at the pub may provide a similar opportunity for working-class men. Men who construct their leisure as their own personal space may, as with women, be coming closer to a form of leisure which recognizes enlargement of the self as a core element of the leisure experience. Men as well as women can use personal leisure spaces or heterotopias to enlarge the sense of self beyond those of the dominant gender discourses.

For example, meditation, writing, reading, music, art and gardening may provide reflexive spaces for men to resist what they have been told they should be and to become something greater.

This argument, however, must not overlook the reality of the continuing power differentials between men and women in all the institutions of industrialized societies, including the workforce, education, religion, the media and the family which have enabled men more often to have access to personal leisure space than women. Yet it seems reasonable also, under the increasing pressures of the postmodern era, to conceptualize leisure for both men and women, old and young, those with power and the relatively powerless, as 'personal space' where subjectivities may be reviewed and some resisted while others are revitalized or reconstructed. Personal leisure space may provide one arena where men and women can move beyond the strictures of cultural gender stereotypes. It may be a space where hegemonic masculinity and inferiorized femininity are resisted, challenged and subverted.

Conclusion

In this chapter I have argued that in the postmodern era of the last decade of the twentieth century women are challenging the construction of their subjectivities as 'other' to and inferior to dominant forms of masculinity. Some postmodern theorists have claimed that 'a fragmented, disjointed, and discontinuous mode of experience is a fundamental characteristic of postmodern culture, of both its subjective experience and in its texts' (see Kellner, 1992: 144, for a discussion of this position). I have argued, however, that such a deconstruction of the subject and identity in postmodern conditions need not result in fragmentation, but rather in an expansion of the self beyond the rigid stereotypes and certainties of modernity, especially as far as gender is concerned. Rather than dissolving into so many droplets like oil on water, I have maintained that there is the possibility of recombining the fragments into a new and enlarged self which goes beyond previous social constraints. I do not see the postmodern deconstruction of self as necessarily irreversible and destructive, but with the possibilities to be forward looking, constructive and liberating for the self. Further, I have endeavoured in this chapter to show that in the relative freedom of personal leisure spaces there is opportunity for such an expansion of the self. In so doing I have suggested the possibility of rewriting the script of 'woman' beyond its phallocentric definition and also the possibility of rewriting the script of masculinity beyond its phallocentricity. I have also drawn on poststructuralist theory to rewrite the concept of leisure so that it reflects spaces that women make for their own sense of self-worth and pleasure – spaces of negotiation, resistance and possible transformation.

My arguments in this chapter have shifted the terms of discussion beyond notions of gender socialization that presume a given or fixed concept of the adult self which is functional for the individual and for industrial society, which is implicit in functionalist theory (see Chapter 1). Nor is the self that I suggest overly determined by its relationship to the means of production, as in the Marxian problematic (see Chapter 2). Rather, I argue that by repeated performative acts which allow for self-recovery, self-actualization, self-help and healing, women can resist forces of power which constrain and confine them. The roles of wife and mother can be incorporated, but there is also the opportunity to move beyond these subjectivities to those which may be idiosyncratic to the private but cumulative 'I' of the self, to break out of the socially prescribed 'me's' which include gender specification. In this sense I have extended the argument of Chapter 3 on interactionist theories of leisure as a social space for 'freedom to be', to incorporate post-structuralist ideas on rewriting the script, multiple subjectivities, resistance and individual agency which allow for personal as well as social leisure spaces as areas for enlargement of the self. The self that I am envisioning here is not the unified and consistent 'I' of modernity, but a synthesis of many subjectivities, past and present, a cumulative self which has some power to act as well as to react to social and cultural prescriptions.

Feminist leisure research has provided us with many examples of ways that women, even in very oppressive circumstances, have been able to create personal leisure spaces for their own sense of an expanding self, in some instances, they say, to maintain a sense of sanity. Areas as diverse as minute vacations in a busy day, reading, exercise classes, friendship groups, jogging time, theatre, story-telling, writing, bingo, dance, music, outdoor adventure, sport and holidays have been shown to be such personal spaces for women. Some of these, such as dance, sport and outdoor adventure, extend knowledge and feelings concerning the female body and its links to concepts of the self, as was suggested in the section on the sociology of the body in Chapter 6. Others, such as friendship groups and street theatre, allow for expression of emotions in a safe environment, as shown in the section on the sociology of emotions in Chapter 6. And many, by claiming women's right to occupy leisure space both physically and metaphorically, challenge male cultural hegemony and hegemonic masculinity, as discussed in Chapters 4 and 5.

This chapter has thus extended the ideas presented in earlier chapters in the book to challenge the traditional work/non-work dichotomy which reinforced the binary opposition between paid work and leisure so that paid work remained the central category and leisure its complement. For women, this opposition, even with the increase of women in the workforce, remains inappropriate and does not reflect the meanings that leisure has for them. Leisure as personal space, on the other hand, is able to encompass many experiences where the boundaries between work, both paid and unpaid, and leisure are more diffuse. This concept of leisure makes strong links to the self, allowing for special spaces where there is room for a sense of personal expansion beyond the everyday activities of life. There is room for repeated performative acts which move the self beyond normative cultural constraints. Leisure, then, produces spaces for becoming and can expand the horizons of such becoming.

I have also argued that the concept of leisure as personal space gives similar opportunities for men, some of whom may already be privileged in this regard, to move beyond cultural prescriptions of hegemonic masculinity and an over-investment in the workplace, the provider role and aggressive competition with other males. It also allows for particular personal spaces to explore alternative aspects of masculinity, free from the ridicule and censure of other males which masculinist studies have suggested act as strong incentives for males to pursue hegemonic masculinity. In so doing, such a concept of leisure may enable men to move beyond the 'poor boy' syndrome to experience those aspects of self, such as free expressions of emotions, other than anger, which have been stifled under patriarchy (see Chapter 5 for this discussion). If repeated performative acts are necessary for men to shore up the fragile subjectivity of hegemonic masculinity, then repeated performative acts in personal leisure spaces could conceivably enable men to move beyond such a vulnerable sense of masculinity to a stronger and more liberated sense of self.

To date, although there have been numerous studies of men's public leisure in areas such as sport where the values of hegemonic masculinity are reinforced, there has been little leisure research which addresses men's personal leisure spaces. This is in line with the visibility in research generally of men's public selves while their private selves, have been almost invisible (Christian, 1994: 187). Do men, in fact, allow other subjectivities to come to the fore when they are fishing on their own, meditating, reading, listening to music, cooking, rocking the baby, writing creatively and when they are interacting with their partners in mutual leisure activities? For example, the author of a qualitative study of anti-sexist men claims for himself a subjectivity other than that of domination and control in the sexual act. He says:

> My view about much recent writing on masculinity is that often I cannot relate it to my own experience . . . There was much discussion of domination and control rather than shared physical enjoyment and it made me wonder how many other men feel as I do, that sexuality and domination are not inherently connected. In the context of hegemonic masculinity male sexuality seems to be socially constructed in terms of domination, but for me sex is about shared pleasure, not about dominating. Am I peculiar as a man in feeling that way? Or are there other unresearched non-predatory heterosexual men who feel as I do? (Christian, 1994: 188)

If hegemonic masculinity can be challenged by men in the personal leisure space of heterosexual intercourse, surely it can be challenged and transcended in other personal leisure spaces for men, for those who are homosexual as well as for those who are heterosexual? There may even be the possibility of 'our space' where men and women interact with each other with mutual respect and liking in shared enjoyable activities or non-activities. The following quote from a young mother who was able to share a weekend away from her children with her husband suggests that such an experience is possible.

> We went down to *Phantom of the Opera* and we stayed overnight and came back the next day, the kids stayed here. I had a ball. That was the first time in six years that I never had the children to be responsible [for]. It was just wonderful and you could lie in bed until seven o'clock and they're not going to come and jump all over you. It was just nice. I enjoyed it, it was nice for my husband and I to be on our own, and not have to sort out the arguments in the back seat of the car on the way down and the way back. Oh definitely [it was a holiday] it was only for 24 hours, maybe a bit longer. We left on the Saturday, we had dinner in M. in Chinatown, and then we went on to the *Phantom of the Opera*. We went out to my brother's place, stayed the night. We went to the market on the Sunday morning and we were home about 4 o'clock I think in the afternoon, picked up the kids and came home. (Davidson, 1996: 76)

I am not suggesting here that we should ignore the structural inequalities that continue in our society to constrain women's access to personal leisure space when compared to the access that is available to their male counterparts. Much work remains to be done at political, policy, institutional and group levels before equal access is achieved. For example, in the two crucial areas of childcare and women's sport, there remains a need for strong policy support and an increase in government expenditure. Nevertheless, in the postmodern era, when social movements such as the women's movement have achieved some shifts in the balance of gender power, women are in a better position to challenge gender inequities in the leisure area as in other social spheres. By making spaces in their everyday lives for the expansion of the definition of self, individual women can take a step in the right direction. Such action also holds out possibilities for communal action for change. Shifts in gender power relations since the inauguration of the women's movement in the late 1960s have allowed women initially to question and document male domination. Further shifts in women's power base in the postmodern era have enabled women to question the very foundations of knowledge which privilege male constructions of the social world and to deconstruct monolithic notions of male domination. In the area of leisure, feminists need to move beyond the continued documentation of women's oppression to see the many and varied ways that women and men can challenge and change male domination and also to suggest ways that both genders may work together to bring about change.

As we enter the twenty-first century, social changes and the thinking of the postmodern era challenge us to critique fixed immutable notions of masculinity and femininity, along with other totalizing concepts, so that women and men can resist what they are told they should be and reach towards what they want to become. Personal leisure space as a resource to assist in this 'becoming' has been minimally tapped as yet. Now is the time to explore and exploit its full potential for women and men from a diversity of social situations, and to break out of confining, inferiorizing constructions of femininity and dominating forms of masculinity into liberating, self-expanding ones. The following chapter looks at the possibilities that post-colonial theory has for extending these ideas to women in colonized situations in developing countries as well as in Western industrialized ones.

9

The View from the 'Other', from Margin to Centre: Postcolonial Theory

In the previous chapter, poststructuralist theory as applied in a feminist context enabled the deconstruction of the binary opposition of paid work and leisure, where leisure in traditional male theory had been posited as dependent upon and complementary to paid work which was assumed to be universal and dominant. Instead, my own feminized concept of leisure as 'personal space' was suggested, thus providing a more flexible approach to the everyday leisure experiences of both women and men. In this chapter, in similar fashion, postcolonial criticism enables us to destabilize and deconstruct Eurocentric homogenizing notions of the colonizer and the colonized. In Eurocentric theory, the former was assumed to be superior and the colonizer's knowledge and formulation of history was assumed to be universal, correct and rightfully dominant. One effect of postcolonial criticism has been to 'force a radical rethinking of forms of knowledge and social identities authored and authorized by colonialism and Western domination' (Prakash, 1994: 87). Feminist postcolonial criticism has been particularly concerned with the lived experiences of women who cannot be fitted into Eurocentric, Western middle-class white theorization, as formulated by male theorists and their feminist counterparts. In view of the long history of women's work, 'not only outside of wage-work, but *in one way or another*, "outside" of the definitive modes of of production' (Spivak, 1988b: 84; original emphasis), we may assume that this criticism applies as much to leisure theory as to any other.

In this chapter, initially I outline the origins and concepts of postcolonial theory and its feminist application. Feminist postcolonialists such as Spivak have argued that the voices of colonized women have been silenced and that it is necessary to fill in the fissures apparent in colonial histories and archives in order to construct the perspectives of these women. I argue, instead, that the strength of postcolonialism is its insistence on the view from the 'other', to give insight into the subjectivities of colonized women, especially with regard to leisure. So, I go on to present the voices of women who have been constructed as 'other', so that their perspectives can be grasped as they tell us of their everyday experiences of leisure and the ways that they make time and space for themselves. Today there are many voices of marginalized women, from those of women of colour in the UK, Australia, the USA and Africa, to those of immigrant, ethnic and refugee women in cultures not their own. I cannot do justice to all in one chapter. I have chosen two rather extreme examples: Australian Aboriginal women and Bosnian refugee women in Slovenia. One is an instance of extreme marginalization, with some possibility of moving from margin to centre, through spaces made and voices raised. The other is the opposite, a sudden enforced move from centre to margin, with the corresponding change in consciousness and action. The question is then raised: 'Can a concept of leisure as "personal space" enable a diversity of women to take personal and political action which will benefit them?'

Postcolonial Theory

A collection of historians writing from India, Britain and Australia in 1981 formed the group who produced the writings entitled *Subaltern Studies* (see Guha, 1981–9). The term 'subaltern' is taken from Gramsci's work on 'the subaltern classes' where he extends the class-position/class-consciousness argument of the Marxian problematic to the cultural and political position of powerless groups who are, for the most part, outside the dominant mode of production. He is critical of the Leninist intellectual's role in absorbing these groups into the dominant hegemony of the time in Italy, thus ignoring their insurgencies, rebellions and struggles (Gramsci, 1978). The *Subaltern Studies* group use the perspective of the subaltern to combat the persistence of colonialist knowledge in nationalist and mode-of-production narratives. The subaltern, then, is a figure produced by historical discourses of domination; nevertheless, it provides a mode of reading history different from those inscribed in Western elite accounts. Reading colonial and national archives against the grain and focusing on their blind spots, silences and anxieties, these historians uncover the subaltern myths, cults, ideologies and revolts that conventional history overlooked or misrepresented in its presentation of cause and effect. They seek to uncover the peasant from elite interpretation and positivistic historiography. By focusing on the peasant's insurgent consciousness, rumours, mythic visions, religiosity and community bonds, they enable the subaltern to emerge with forms of sociality and political community at odds with nation and class and the models of rationality and social action that conventional history uses. They want to retrieve the will and consciousness of the subaltern, although the terms 'subaltern' and 'sub-alterity' by definition signify the impossibility of autonomy. (See Prakash, 1994: 88–92, for a more detailed discussion of these terms.)

Theoretically, then, *Subaltern Studies* arose as a critique of Western based material accounts of colonized countries such as India, where the colonizer and the colonized were dichotomized and the view given was that of the Western colonizer. This view was assumed to be both universal and correct.

The subaltern in these elite histories, at least in Marxian accounts, were exploited and dominated, with no resources and no agency. Critical *Subaltern Studies*, on the other hand, relying on concepts of power from Foucault and difference and deconstruction from Derrida, sought the fissures in these accounts to construct alternative views of history. In these alternative constructions, both Foucault's and Derrida's critiques of Western thought intersect with postcolonial criticism. Foucault is relevant because his views on power, discourse and subjectivity offer wider application than those of top-down, unrelenting, production based oppression. As well, they posit a powerful critique of the rule of modernity which the colonies experienced in a peculiar form. Derrida's ideas expose how notions of difference and the binary oppositions of Western thought have enabled East/West, traditional/modern, primitive/civilized to be constructed as hierarchized opposites where the latter suppress and marginalize the former as 'other' and inferior.

The concept of 'other', which is also basic in postcolonial theory, was developed in this context by Bhabha (1983). Bhabha claims that colonial discourses propagated by the powerful colonizer produce stereotypes of the colonized as fixed, other to and inferior to the colonizer. Once this stereotype is in place, it becomes a regime of truth which is already known yet anxiously repeated in order to justify conquest, surveillance and control. Yet it is an ambivalent production, for the object of colonial discourse, he says, constitutes 'that "otherness" which is at once an object of desire and derision, an articulation of difference contained within the fantasy of origin and identity' (1983: 19). Due to this very ambivalence which contains both a derogated object and a subjective otherness, it is possible, from the space of that otherness, to identify and transgress the limits or boundaries of colonial discourse. The concept of 'otherness' thus enables postcolonial theorists to attribute subjectivity and a valid view of colonization to the 'other', a view which has the potential to destabilize and transform dominant knowledges concerning 'degenerate types on the basis of racial origin' (1983: 23).

Spivak takes the terms 'subaltern' and 'other', and the methods of examining history used by *Subaltern Studies* historians, to seek to uncover women's position in colonial India. She argues (1988a) that histories constructed by British colonial rulers and elite Indian nationalists have stifled the voices of the heterogeneous array of rural gentry, impoverished landlords, rich peasants and upper-middle-class peasants who formed the subaltern classes. Due both to their heterogeneity and their position, in many instances outside the capitalist mode of production, it was not possible for them to move in Marxian terms from a class-in-itself to a class-for-itself and so to speak with a consciousness of their oppression. For similar reasons (that is, their heterogeneity and their position outside the dominant mode of production), women in India cannot speak with a united voice of their exploitation and oppression. Patriarchal social relations compound this, so that Spivak contends that 'the subject of exploitation cannot know and speak the text of female exploitation, even if the absurdity of the non-representing intellectual making way for her to speak is achieved. The woman is doubly in shadow' (1988a: 288). She goes on to argue that, in the case of Indian suttee, the subjectivity of the Indian woman has been manipulated first by male dominated Hindu beliefs, then by white colonial men 'saving brown women from brown men'. In both instances the Indian woman continues to be construed as 'other' to, and an object to be manipulated by dominant male discourses. Nor do dominant international feminists escape. They too, she claims, continue to see their own perspective as universal and where difference is recognized it is yet constructed as *other to* and *different from* themselves. She concludes that: 'The subaltern cannot speak. There is no virtue in global laundry lists with "woman" as a pious item. Representation has not withered away. The female intellectual as intellectual has a circumscribed task which she must not disown with a flourish' (1988a: 308). Spivak's work, in the postcolonial mode, has had an enormous influence on feminist thinking. Her argument warns feminists to be very careful in our interpretation of the situation of subaltern women who, she claims, in many cases cannot speak for themselves.

bell hooks, a black American feminist who writes in the postcolonial mode, also critiques the imperialism of white, middle-class, American intellectual feminism and urges feminists to listen to the voices of marginalized people such as poor white women and black women. The liberal feminism of the 1960s in works such as Friedan's (1963), she sees as wanting a better deal for the bored leisure class of middle- and upper-class housewives which has little relevance for the need for survival of oppressed working-class and black women and men. Liberal feminism, which has dominated feminist theory in the American context, puts individualism and women's quest to be equal with their male counterparts as centre. In her view it ignores the struggles and experiences of those on the margins. She argues for the voices of marginalized women to be heard and for the validity of their experiences of everyday life, oppression and resistance for programmes for liberation:

> Frequently, white feminists act as if black women did not know sexist oppression existed until they voiced feminist sentiment. They believe they are providing black women with 'the' analysis and 'the' program for liberation. They do not understand, cannot even imagine, that black women, as well as other groups of women who live daily in oppressive situations, often acquire an awareness of patriarchal politics from their lived experience, just as they develop strategies of resistance (even though they may not resist on a sustained or organized basis). (hooks, 1989: 10)

In another article, Spivak (1988b) gives a splendid example of hooks's exhortation to move from margin to centre instead of the reverse in feminist thinking. And, in doing this, she comes close to a common experience of oppression for women from both West and East due to male domination in the social construction of female sexuality. She takes as her starting point physical clitoridectomy in the East and moves from this margin or centre (depending on your own perspective) to the corresponding symbolic suppression of the clitoris in the West. Whether physical or symbolic, clitoridectomy demonstrates the international definition of woman as sex object and legal object, denying her sexual subjectivity and sexual pleasure. She says: 'The pre-comprehended suppression or effacement of the clitoris relates to every move to define woman as sex-object, or as a means or agent of reproduction – with no recourse to a subject-function except in terms of those definitions or as "imitators of men"' (Spivak, 1988b: 151).

She claims that, by excluding the clitoris and defining women in terms of the uterus or reproductive function, capitalism, patriarchy and the family are able to objectify and control women. The economic consequences of such definition varies from the dowry system of traditional societies to the centrality of private home ownership in capitalist societies. In the examples that she gives, the effacement of women's subjective sexual pleasure has had both personal and structural consequences for women's subordination in a variety of societal situations. Here is a theme, she maintains, that both the old washerwoman by the river in India as well as the educated postgraduate student in the Sudan would understand. So she sees the consciousness of oppression arising from the subjective experience of the subaltern, while constructing feminist theory from the physical experience of the margin to the symbolic significance in the centre.

In this chapter, then, I am applying the principles of postcolonial theory to seek to understand the everyday leisure experiences of marginalized women, women who may or may not be involved in capitalist modes of production, women who have been constructed as other *to* and different *from* the dominant modes of femininity previously represented in the discourses of colonial, imperialist, white middle-class intellectual feminists. In order to do this I want to present two examples of views from the 'other'.

The View from the 'Other': Leisure in the Lives of Pacific Island and Aboriginal Women

In the 1970s feminists asked: 'Is leisure an appropriate concept for women with its male connotations of non-paid work time and freely chosen activity?' (Anderson, 1975). In the 1990s feminists retain the concept 'leisure' but in poststructuralist fashion reserve also the right to resignify its meaning incorporating non-exclusionary women's perspectives. These are those which are appropriate for women other than Eurocentric, white, middle-class educated or professional women as well as those that are. Postcolonial feminists insist that the voices of these women be heard in order to develop strategies for dealing with their oppression. Some severe critiques of feminist colonialist assumptions have been voiced by women of colour and women in developing countries. The following example has specific reference to leisure.

Women's Liberation or Women's Lib is a European disease to be cured by Europeans. What we are aiming for is not just women's liberation but a total liberation. A social, political and economic liberation. Our situation is very different to that of the European women. Look around you and see, especially in town. Hundreds of our women slave every day for white women. They cook, clean, sweep, and wash shit for crumbs from European women. European women thought up Women's Liberation because they didn't have enough to do, and they were bored out of their minds. They wanted to be liberated so they could go out and work like men. They were sick of being ornaments in the house. They hate their men for it. That's not our position at all. Our women always have too much to do. Our women never have the leisure to be ornaments. Our societies are people oriented so we care for one another. Our situation also affects men. (Mera Molisa, 1978: 6)

For this Vanuaaku woman, middle-class European women have too much leisure time and not enough to occupy them, but her own people never have this luxury. Jolly (1991: 57) comments that similar sentiments have been expressed by many Aboriginal spokeswomen in Australia and by some women holding high political or bureaucratic positions within other Pacific states, as well as by women of colour in the USA, Britain and in international forums. The concept of leisure as free, non-work time cannot apply to the circumstances of these women, can the concept of leisure as 'personal space'?

Grace Mera Molisa, whose words are quoted above, has, in fact, over her lifetime written some evocative poetry to express the needs of her people and in particular the women of her country. In this way she has made a private space for herself, to express her own thoughts and the experiences of the women of her country. Writing poetry for her is both a space for resistance to male domination and also a space for her own enlargement. For women such as these the spaces that they make in their day for themselves, through activities such as reading, writing, poetry, art, music and dialoguing with other women are a matter of survival, as well as chance to expand the self and relate to others. One of the criticisms that women such as Molisa have made of European feminism is its preoccupation with individual autonomy and personal psychology, rather than values of community and kinship. I return to this issue later in the chapter. My own writing on leisure in the past has had this focus. On the other hand, I would argue that the concept of leisure as 'personal space' can incorporate both individual autonomy and the values of interpersonal and community relationships that are so important to colonized women. It can also incorporate possibilities for political action.

In the Australian situation, Aboriginal women in Australia are asking white Australians to listen to *their* voices, to let them represent themselves in feminist analyses (Huggins, 1994). What do they have to say, then, when it comes to their everyday experiences of leisure? They do not use the term, yet it is woven into their everyday lives as a physical and metaphorical, personal and communal space which has a meaning for them that is different from that of their everyday duties (i.e. a 'heterotopia').

In traditional Aboriginal Australian culture, women do have a physical space of their own, the women's camp or *jilimi*, where women find female support and a safe environment (Bell, 1990). Located behind the *jilimi* is the 'women only' ground where *yawulyu* ceremonies which celebrate their rights to land and their responsibilities for the maintenance of harmonious relations of people to land are performed. Bell (1990: 14) proposes that at stake for both the Aboriginal and non-Aboriginal woman is 'the right to retreat' and to make decisions concerning her life. For Aboriginal women these rights existed by virtue of the sex-segregated nature of the society. Unlike the spaces created for women in white society as a result of the women's movement, such as women's refuges, for Aboriginal women a retreat to the *jilimi* is neither a retreat from heterosexual activity, nor a threat to their economic well-being.

When an Aboriginal woman moves in to the fringes of towns and cities there is considerable disruption of her own cultural mores; nevertheless something of her right to retreat, to a space of her own, to a sense that her sexuality is her own and not owned by a man or men, and her tradition of not being economically dependent on a man or men, persists. For example, in her autobiography, Ruby Langford (1988) tells of her life in a white society alternating between country towns and droving camps and inner city living. There is much pain and suffering here, but through it all she manages to carve out spaces for herself in her everyday life. Sometimes these spaces are debilitating escapes such as drink, at others they are times to think and at others they are supportive such as the inner city sewing and craft circle which saved for a group holiday to the Red Centre. Ultimately she achieves a space for herself to write her book.

In her own words:

> I fished in the river for yellow belly perch, using mulligrubs (like a witchetty grub but smaller) or worms for bait. . . . The perch took the bait quietly and if I was lucky I'd catch two or three, about ten inches long and good eating. Early in the morning there were also plenty of ducks. I had a .22 rifle and when I shot some I waded into the cold water and swam out to get them. It was getting towards winter. Across the river and behind me were herds of piebald and skewbald horses. These were the times I had to myself – the men gone to work, the kids still asleep – and I sat on the bank fishing and thinking about my life. (1988: 83)

> Every Tuesday I went to the sewing and craft classes in Redfern. I had finished the satin lining for my coat. I made pillowslips, mended and patched for the kids, and did machine sewing for the old girls who couldn't see well. We talked about families and grandkids, crafts and politics. We cooked damper and scones and hot meals for the staff at AMS (Aboriginal Medical Service) and we held fêtes to raise money. We were saving up for a holiday in the bush, and we'd decided to go to Ayers Rock. (1988: 211–12)

> At sewing class I'd heard about an Aboriginal hostel in Granville for people who'd raised their families and didn't want to become live-in baby-sitters for the kids. It was the first of its kind.

> I moved in there on 11 August 1987.

> The place was called Allawah, meaning 'sit awhile'. It was a huge house with

rose gardens and stained glass windows and a hallway big enough to swing ten cats. I had a room of my own and a sunroom off that for a study.

I unpacked my books and bought a typewriter (my other one had packed it in), a desk and a filing cabinet. Out side my window a hibiscus opened its buds and the noise now was not traffic but birds. (1988: 267–8)

Historically, in Australia, a large majority of Aboriginal women were devalued, used as unpaid servants for wealthy pastoralists, raped and abused by white men and under constant surveillance by autocratic, bureaucratic government officials or by patriarchal missionaries. Many mothers had their babies removed from them to missions or government run institutions. Girls were here trained to become domestic servants. It was only through getting her grandmother to tell her story for the book that Sally Morgan (1987) was able to uncover a proud Aboriginal heritage, long hidden beneath her grandmother's fear and shame at the hands of white people. Her own language had also been buried. It was not until the end of her life that, to some extent, her grandmother could rewrite her sense of self-worth and pride. Morgan writes her grandmother's words:

Well, I'm hoping things will change one day. At least, we not owned any more. I was owned by the Drake-Brockmans and the government and anyone who wanted to pay five shillings a year to Mr Neville to have me. Not much is it? I know it's hard for you Sal, hard for you to understand. You different to me. I been scared all my life, too scared to speak out. Maybe if you'd have had my life, you'd be scared too.

Aah, I can't really say what will happen. I s'pose it don't concern me no more.

As for my people, some of them are naughty, they drink too much. Grog's a curse, I've seen what it can do. They got to give it up. They got to show the white man what they made of.

Do you think we'll get some respect? I like to think the black man will get treated the same as the white man one day. Be good, wouldn't it? By gee, it'd be good. (Morgan, 1987: 350)

Throughout Langford's and Morgan's stories, the other space that becomes apparent is an unquenchable sense of humour, even in the most difficult of circumstances. The women laugh at themselves, as well as at those who dominate them. The phrase 'taking the mickey out of' someone recurs in both books and refers to incidents where their 'superiors' are made to look foolish, embarrassed or profoundly uncomfortable. For example, in Morgan's book, her grandmother always went to an enormous amount of trouble when the rent man called, taking pride in serving him tea and biscuits on the front verandah. One day, she proudly showed Sally the empty plate after he had left, saying: 'He really enjoyed the biscuits this morning, he ate the whole plateful.' They both enjoyed the joke – the biscuits were dog biscuits! Humour is a leisure space that crosses the work/leisure boundary and we can learn much from its use by women of colour to release stress and tension and assert some autonomy of subjectivity.

Other Aboriginal women writers, such as Edmund (1992), show both the community spirit amongst the women and the mixture of work and leisure in their daily lives, while working outside the dominant mode of production:

> Collecting firewood was a part of the community life. It was a day of fellow-ship with each other, each family of women working side by side cutting wood up in the ridges, the huge scented gum trees with their clean smooth red trunks standing tall and beautiful. We used to take our lunches and boil up the billies for tea, and make the babies' bottles, though most of the babies were breastfed and strong and healthy and fine little specimens. We didn't have to cut down any trees, just cut the dead limbs lying around the place. There would be a lot of laughter and storytelling about what had happened during the week.
> (Edmund, 1992: 36–7)

Edmund went on to make her sense of community with Aboriginal people public when she was appointed as one of five commissioners to the Federal Government's Aboriginal Loans Commission to assist Aboriginal people to buy their own homes and to set themselves up in business. Later still, after the death of her husband, she combined a sense of her own space through her art with a public presentation of the situation of Aboriginal women through her art. She studied art formally for two years and has held exhibitions throughout Australia:

> Four years after Digger's death I was still fretting for him . . . My doctor had a long talk with me, and he came to the conclusion that I was suffering from a broken heart. He said, 'Go away from Rockhampton and do something you have always wanted to do'. . .
> My inspiration to paint came over me when I visited Alice Springs a couple of years after Digger had died. I was impressed by the beauty of the country and I was touched by the hard and tough way of life that the tribal Aboriginal people live. . . .
> When I came home the next week I bought myself some acrylics, brushes and boards and I released all those feelings that I had inside me by painting two big paintings. They looked OK to me, and so I have gone on painting.
> (Edmund, 1992: 93 and 97)

Another Aboriginal Australian has made space for herself and for her sisters through her poetry. Writing poetry is one of her leisure pursuits, along with taking photographs and following her favourite teams in the Australian Football League. It also forms a severe critique of the colonizer's white condescension, especially that of academic feminism:

> Talk to me about the feminist movement
> the gubba middle class
> hetero sexual revolution
> way back in the seventies . . .
> Maybe I didn't think, maybe I thought women in general
> meant Aboriginal women, the Koori women in Victoria.
> (*Women's Liberation*, L. Bellear)

Like Douwe Edberts
Freeze dry coffee
I stand motionless
But full of feelings
Gin, native, abo, coon
An inquisitive academic
Then asks 'are you Aboriginal?' . . .

Eh Professor, big shot
Big Cheese, or whoever
You claim to be
You've really no idea
Love to chat sister,
But there's faxes to send
And protest letters to write

I turn and walk away
Preserving my dignity
Without humiliating hers.
(*Feelings*, L. Bellear)
*Both poems reproduced with the permission of
University of Queensland Press.*

It may seem a big leap from the voices of these Aboriginal women about the individual spaces that they make in their day for expanding their sense of self and their sense of community with their sisters, to national concerns with rights to land, property, housing, health and education. Nevertheless I contend that the personal spaces that these women have made for themselves may be the beginning of communal action. Bellear, for example, has moved from writing poetry as a personal pastime in which to express feelings of loneliness, injustice and discrimination, to giving public readings throughout Australia so that her voice is heard and Aboriginal women are made visible.

From these writers I learn that it is possible to create leisure spaces which restore a sense of self-worth and autonomy in a world where women's subjectivities have been devalued and inferiorized as 'other' to dominant white and male culture. Their experiences show that it is possible, even under circumstances of extreme oppression, to make some personal space for an enlargement of the 'I' and the 'we'. And in some instances this space has been enlarged again to take on a political dimension, both as a venue for making marginalized people visible and their voices heard, and in solidarity or coalition movements with others. In the following section the voices of other women in marginalized situations are heard. In particular one hears the voices of dispossessed women, where the move for the women was from centre to margin, rather than the other way around.

From Centre to Margin: Bosnian Women Refugees

In my wider reading of the experiences of marginalized women, the most extreme occurred in the writings of women refugees from Bosnia, telling of their experiences in Slovenia. Whereas the Aboriginal women quoted in the previous section began with very few material or educational resources and lived in circumstances of privation, these women began with the resources of middle-class educated women and found themselves, quite suddenly, transported into circumstances of severe deprivation. They found that they were stripped of the material privileges of class and placed in a position of no cultural identity, with no place of their own, no food, few clothes and no means of subsistence (McNeill and Coulson, 1994). Leisure, for them, would be a luxury, if defined in terms of their previous existence. No academic would dare ask about leisure in conventional terms. The conventional work/leisure divide has no meaning here. The concern of these women is day-to-day survival. They write about their struggle for subsistence, ways of eking out meagre resources, finding food and living in very cramped, shared accommodation and making meaning out of their new circumstances. Meaning for these middle-class women, who are doctors, lawyers and teachers, comes now from voluntary work, through teaching the children of the refugees, helping women to develop crafts, sometimes for sale, and carrying out legal and social work through the refuges. In a reverse of their former circumstances, some earned money through creating leisure for Slovenian women, by doing their laundry, cleaning, cooking or sewing. These women were quite suddenly thrust from centre to margin, resulting in an enforced change in consciousness. Former discourses were threatened, destabilized and undermined. Their own personal resources had to be drawn on, both for survival and for a new sense of self. Even in these writings of dire circumstances, glimmers of personal space and an expanding sense of self emerge such as the following:

> I've discovered so much about myself during this past eighteen months, most significantly, I have realized that I am a strong woman. When I look at other refugees I see many strong women. My experience here indicates that it's more likely to be men who break down, seemingly unable to find sufficient flexibility or resources within themselves to make the necessary adjustments between life as it was and how it is now. (Marija) (McNeill and Coulson, 1994: 20)

> Before I came a workshop was planned. Many women in the camp attended. A lot of us have experience of knitting and sewing so there was much interest. The Italians brought all the necessary materials; sewing threads, needles, wool, lace, everything ...
>
> We haven't been treated as sweat-shop labourers or anything like that. They even donated lengths of material so that women could make clothes for themselves. Now anyone can come up here, spend a few hours making something or getting involved with one of the knitting or sewing projects. Patterns are supplied and we can sit around and talk, make coffee, and feel we are being useful. (Zorica) (McNeill and Coulson, 1994: 38)

> Who would have thought that after retirement I would end up teaching in Slovenia? I know I'll work for as long as I'm needed, ten or fifteen years more if I have to. When I walk into that classroom I forget my aches and pains, my

worries and fears. Working with the children, being a part of their lives, makes me happy. (Gordona) (McNeill and Coulson, 1994: 52)

There is some relief in telling this story here in this book, just the value of letting it out . . . (Sarajeka) (McNeill and Coulson, 1994: 68)

These women are strong women, making the most of very difficult circumstances, not just accepting their lot, but making space for themselves and for other women which brings some personal satisfaction, sense of meaning and sense of self. Here are middle-class, educated women forced to take the view from the other, to make sense on a daily, personal basis of a newly acquired marginalization. Leisure as personal space here has meaning for survival, self-respect, support and communal activity. Many of these women belong to the Association for Preventative and Voluntary Work, which supports the development of self-help groups, especially for women in refugee camps. It also attempts to influence the decision- and policy-makers, so it incorporates a political agenda.

Conclusion

In this chapter I have considered the view from the 'other', that is, from the perspective of women who have been marginalized in some way. Postcolonial feminist theory is critical of Western, white, middle-class, intellectual feminism which seeks a better deal for educated women and ignores the experiences of women who do not fit into this category. Although postcolonial feminists, who wish to retain a Marxian analysis of class-for-itself as a basis for consciousness of exploitation and oppression, argue that subaltern women cannot speak for themselves, due to their diversity and their place outside the dominant mode of production, I disagree. I argue rather from a poststructuralist perspective which accords the power of resistance and experience based subjectivity to a variety of those who are subordinated. They *can* speak of their everyday experiences and of the strategies they use to counter their subordination. They have been virtually invisible in theories of leisure which are predicated on dominant modes of production and paid work. They also have been excluded from most feminist theory and consequently from feminist leisure theory and research. They do not speak of leisure in the conventional sense of the term as non-work, but rather of their own ways and means of making spaces for themselves and meaning for their lives in oppressive circumstances. From the voices of women who have been marginalized in some way, I have argued that leisure as personal space provides an avenue for self-expansion, which has the possibility of moving from the self to others and to communal action.

The two opposite, and in some ways extreme, positions that I have taken as examples in this chapter of both marginalization and of the ability to construct and use personal space are Australian Aboriginal women and Bosnian refugees in Slovenia. In the one case the women began with very few material resources, lived on the edges of towns in cramped conditions with few facilities and were ostracized by the white community, yet managed to make spaces in their days which increased their own sense of self-worth and enjoyment of life. I have given examples where writing, art and poetry begun in this personal space became political tools to make the voices of Aboriginal women heard in the public arena and their needs heeded. In other contexts, Aboriginal music, such as that by Christine Anu or the group Yothu Yindi, has followed a similar path, as has Aboriginal dance.

In my second example, the women who were refugees from Bosnia in Slovenia had been suddenly bereft of identity, personal space and possessions. They were unceremoniously projected from comfortable middle-class homes and environments into the dispossessed state of the refugee, moved poste haste from centre to margin. There is certainly no denying their consciousness of oppression, both personal and communal. Here, too, these strong women carved out spaces for themselves and their fellow refugees. They began with individual talents and used these to make sense for themselves of an alien environment and to attempt to change things for others. In neither the circumstances of these Bosnian women nor those of the Australian Aboriginal women can leisure be separated from work, paid or otherwise. Its meaning for the women comes rather from its construction as a way of enlarging the sense of self, the 'I' and the 'we'. It is a personal space over which the woman has some choice and control and in which she can do something that she enjoys and has meaning for her. In it she refuses what she has been told she is and reaches towards what she could be, and, in most cases, takes others with her.

There remains, however, the difficulty with my argument, that I may yet have imposed my own framework of leisure as personal space on to the experiences of these women. In some senses, wherever one writes about the experiences of others, some reinterpretation is bound to occur. The most I have been able to do in the limited space of one chapter has been to present some of the experiences of marginalized women in their own words. I have then drawn on these experiences for an exploration of the appropriateness of the concept of 'personal space' to their lives as women and the possibilities that this construction has for the woman's own sense of self and for communal action. The instances taken have, of necessity, been from the words of women who have been published in some way, so they are, in that sense, selective. For these women, it has been possible to show that their actions which began as personal spaces expanded to become public representations of the voices of their people which enable communal action. So I would contend that it is possible for personal space to be of benefit both to the individual and to the collective or the coalition.

Some feminists would see the approach I have taken here as too individualized to make any inroads into the collective oppression of marginalized women. Yet, as already argued, for the women quoted here, the personal has, in most instances, eventually evolved into some kind of communal and/or public activism, sometimes resistant, sometimes subversive. Nor am I alone, in this regard. I draw here on a similar interpretation given by black feminist Patricia Collins (1990) in her thoughtful and thorough analysis, *Black Feminist Thought: Knowledge, Consciousness, and the Politics of Empowerment*. Collins makes central to her text the subjective experiences and ideas of African-American women who reach beyond surviving, fitting in and coping to a place where they feel ownership and accountability. She discusses safe spaces for black women to find a voice, to resist 'objectification as the Other' and to construct independent self-definitions which 'reflect the dialectical nature of oppression and activism' (1990: 95). Such spaces include institutional sites such as extended families, churches and African-American community organizations where black women interact and are able to let their voices be heard in a safe context. They also include art, music and writing, which is both individual and interactive. For example, blues singers such as Bessie Smith, Bessie Jackson, Billie Holiday, Nina Simone and Esther Phillips voiced expressions of a black women's standpoint and helped black women to own their past, present and future. Collins notes that in the black community self is not defined in opposition to others, rather, 'the connectedness among individuals provides black women deeper, more meaningful definitions' (1990: 106). Yet she also places the starting-point clearly with the individual woman:

> Other Black women may assist a Black woman in this journey toward empowerment, but the ultimate responsibility for self-definitions and self-evaluations lies within the individual woman herself. An individual woman may use multiple strategies in her quest for the constructed knowledge and independent voice. (Collins, 1990: 112)

I have argued in this chapter that the personal space of leisure is a safe and congenial place to begin this individual journey. The possibility is also present for the growth and activities which begin there to spill over into the lives of others, into the community and into political activism so that the voice of the 'other' is heard with a view to change.

Collins is very careful throughout her book to present evidence for the matrix of dominations experienced by black women, balanced by the responsiveness of this domination by human agency. She concludes:

> The existence of Afrocentric feminist thought suggests that there is always choice, and power to act, no matter how bleak the situation may appear to be. Viewing the world as one in the making raises the issue of individual responsibility for bringing about change. It also shows that while individual empowerment is the key, only collective action can effectively generate lasting social transformation of political and economic institutions. (Collins, 1990: 237)

By listening to the voices of women who previously have been excluded and/or marginalized in feminist theorizing, and by redefining the concept of leisure as personal space, I have attempted in this chapter to understand and to include the thinking of these women in feminist approaches to leisure. The voices of these women have emphasized that, for many of them, 'personal' cannot mean the extreme individualism of Western thinking. The concept 'I' as a completely separate subjectivity has very little meaning. This is not, however, a negation of subjectivity and agency. Rather a dynamic is established between agency and structure, the personal and political aspects of personal space, so that one flows into the other and back again. Along the way, my own thinking has been challenged and enlarged and my admiration for the strength and centrality of marginalized women's voices, views and actions has escalated. In feminist thought today, with the insistence on diversity, on the many ways of being women in an unequal world, any discussion of leisure must be able to address the cross-cutting constraints of race, class, colour, culture, knowledge, age, disability and sexual orientation, which form a matrix of power contests and struggles. I have argued in this chapter that the concept of leisure as personal space has the potential to address these issues.

Conclusion

In this book I have traced the development of leisure and feminist theory from its inception in the 1970s, as a critique of the universalism of male leisure experience in functionalism, to the recognition of diversities of leisure experience between women as well as between women and men, posited in the poststructuralist and postcolonialist feminisms of the 1990s. In the former, men's leisure as a complement to their paid work was the assumed norm and women's leisure was described as different from this, without any notion of the power differentials between men and women. Leisure as recreation and compensation for one's involvement in paid work was seen to be equally attained by all. In the latter, there is an emphasis on multiple sites and sources and effects of power, both in conceptualizing and experiencing leisure. As different social theories have gained prominence during the last thirty years, so different facets of leisure experience have been illuminated. When seen through the feminist prism, these theories have been able to bring added understanding of women's lives and women's leisure experiences. Inequity in access to leisure is recognized, but so also are the possibilities for the use of leisure to break out of oppressive relationships of power. In the area of relative freedom which constitutes leisure there is the potential for resistance to societal constraint and for expansion of the self and the exercise of capillary power. The possibilities for the destructive use of leisure space for oneself and others are also there. This aspect of leisure has yet to be researched and forms the topic for a whole treatise, outside the scope of this book.

In this concluding chapter, I summarize what I consider to be the important points from the perspectives that I have discussed in the book. I seek to draw together the contributions that the various feminist theoretical perspectives have made to an understanding of leisure. At the same time, I take what I see as productive from each to contribute to my own conceptualization of leisure as personal space for the enlargement of the self – a space or spaces for 'extending the horizon of one's becoming', as Grosz (1995a: 56) has suggested in reference to women's use of public leisure spaces. In addition, I suggest policies and research which may be based on such theory. Finally I summarize the contribution that feminist theory has made to an understanding of the human phenomenon of leisure in the late twentieth century.

From where I am writing in the approach to the millennium, it is easy to point out some of the gaps in the leisure theories of earlier decades of this century. At the same time I have my own poststructuralist, postcolonial view of leisure which takes into account the subjective experiences of women, both those who occupy a central position in white Western societies and those who previously have been marginalized. Throughout the book I have not lost sight of the structural power differentials between men and women across all of the groups that I have discussed. Rather I have left this in tension with my own version of leisure and feminist theory, including poststructural, postcolonial views of power, which acknowledges the capillary possibilities of power, as well as its oppressive effects. The theories that I have discussed in the book traverse the spectrum from the initial macro-Marxist feminist critiques of functionalism through the microanalysis of interactionism and the more diffuse approaches of cultural studies and sociologies of the body and emotions, to the attempts of poststructuralist and postcolonial theorists to deconstruct the impact of totalizing structures on a diversity of individuals. In this concluding chapter I seek to maintain the balance between the power of structures such as class, gender, race and ethnicity and institutions such as the media, to constrain individual leisure experience and the power of the individual and the group to see, resist and move beyond these constraints through leisure.

Feminist theory in its application to leisure arose in the 1970s along with the Marxian critique of functionalism. Marxist feminists were critical of the functionalist notion that leisure is equally accessible by all and universally good for the individual and society. In their view this notion was a class- and/or gender-based ideology which obfuscated and justified materially based inequalities in other spheres of society, as well as in the access to leisure itself. Leisure research from a Marxist feminist perspective focused on perceived structurally based gender inequalities in access to leisure. The research revealed the disadvantages in access to leisure faced by women generally and particularly housewives and mothers due to family ideologies based on the economic resources of male providers and capitalist producers. Working-class women were doubly disadvantaged due to the powerful structure of class and the added economic and social constraints that this imposed. Women's solidarity and political lobbying, based on a common consciousness of oppression with a view to making women's leisure outside the home safer and more accessible, were strategies for change suggested by feminists such as Deem (1986) and Green et al. (1990), who worked from this perspective.

A more flexible approach was being developed out of the American pragmatism of Mead. Applied to leisure, this approach initially ignored gender power differentials (Kelly, 1983), but the theory itself need not exclude gender analysis (Kelly, 1994). The 'I' and 'me' of Mead's symbolic interactionism assumed a rational subject which synthesized societal input into the socialized 'me', and these 'I's' and 'me's' exemplified a male universal experience of the world. Nevertheless the theory itself is flexible enough to incorporate differential experiences of the world, including gender, as demonstrated by Goffman (1976). In addition, I have argued that the cumulative 'I', provided it includes emotional and intuitive responses as well as rational ones, can incorporate women's subjectivities and those of others who cannot be subsumed under the white, rational, male self. While recognizing that in the present circumstances most men still have greater freedom than women, women can, and do, use leisure as personal space to resist what they have been told they are by dominant discourses and to reach towards what they could be.

In conjunction with the feminist social psychological approaches of Chodorow and Gilligan, feminists in the USA used interactionist insights to demonstrate that women's socialization and world-views such as 'the ethic of care' constrained their leisure participation. Leisure research such as that by Henderson et al. (1989, 1996) and Bella (1989) documents the sense of a lack of entitlement to leisure that middle-class white women have and differences in the meanings of leisure for these women than for their male counterparts. Whereas the men in their lives were more task and achievement oriented, women were more focused on the possibilities in leisure for social contact and the development of relationships with others. Strategies for change, in this focus, have a more individual approach than those suggested by the British feminists. By challenging the perceived constraints of women's socialization, women are encouraged to use leisure to gain individual empowerment.

In the tourism literature (Cohen and Taylor, 1976; MacCannell, 1992), Goffman's interactionism has suggested that the leisure space achieved by crossing cultural boundaries may be used to enlarge a sense of self beyond the confines of one's own cultural prescriptions. The concept of hybridity, in which valuable aspects of different cultures are intermixed, may be applied to male and female cultures as well as to racial and ethnic cultures based on geographical location. Leisure then becomes a space for both men and women to move beyond gendered stereotypes. Nevertheless, without some redistribution of power between tourist and host cultures this option remains open only for the privileged tourist with severe costs for host cultures.

As cultural studies approaches to leisure have developed, different theoretical approaches have been incorporated. From the early Marxian approaches to the leisure of male, working-class post-war youth, which was seen as a form of resistance to the domination of middle-class mores (Hall and Jefferson, 1976), cultural studies have themselves moved through feminist and poststructural approaches. A common thread has been the emphasis on Gramsci's concept of cultural hegemony, through which powerful groups in civil society have values and mores which are in their interests, accepted by all without coercion. There is not necessarily an economic base. Other sources of power include statuses such as gender, age, ethnicity, race and sexual orientation, as well as cultural and subcultural capital. Struggle and negotiation are common, resulting in changes in hegemonic control. Subcultures and counter-cultures contest cultural space and hegemony can be destabilized. Feminist studies of leisure oriented cultural spaces, such as gyms, pubs, pool rooms, beaches, dances and shopping malls, have shown male territorial dominance of these physical spaces and the concomitant symbolic dominance. Increasingly, however, women are contesting such spaces, forming their own subcultures in spaces such as body-building, and using the struggles over hegemonic control to enlarge definitions of womanhood beyond cultural prescriptions. Although not explicit, the idea of public and personal leisure space which can be used by women to expand their sense of self is implicit in feminist cultural studies of leisure.

In the masculinist response to the feminisms of the 1970s and 1980s, leisure is presented as a space which men use to prove their masculinity to other men and to themselves. Hegemonic masculinity is the rough, tough, competitive and aggressive masculinity which is based on difference from a weaker femininity. It is the form of masculinity which brings men power and status. Nevertheless, according to masculinist analyses, such as that by Kimmel (1996), it does not come naturally to men – it is always aspired to but never permanently secured, for it must be constantly proved. In times when some women are gaining power in society and this form of masculinity is threatened, men use men-only leisure spaces such as football clubs to shore up a sense of masculinity which excludes and inferiorizes women. Men, then, according to these masculinists, are not entirely individually advantaged by hegemonic masculinity. Other masculinists document the poverty of emotional involvement experienced by men due to this predominant form of masculinity (Seidler, 1994). My argument is that, if leisure space can be used by men to reinforce a powerful sense of masculinity based on difference from and superiority to femininity, cannot it also be used by really strong men to move beyond such a fragile sense of self with all of the disadvantages of this that masculinists have brought to our attention? Leisure reconceptualized as personal space, even one in which there may be a hegemonic struggle over the meaning of masculinity, may be just as applicable to men as to women.

The fundamental weakness in both cultural studies and masculinist approaches to social theory, when viewed through the feminist prism, is their failure to address issues surrounding gendered bodies. Hegemony and especially the concept of hegemonic masculinity is an amorphous term without some grounding in the social construction of male bodies. For all the valuable contribution made by Connell's (1987, 1995) sophisticated masculinist analysis, with its recognition of male power and the loss in power which must accrue to men if hegemonic masculinity is to be eroded, he downplays the power of possession of a male body in societies where this bodily form is valorized and the female body inferiorized. He conflates heterosexual masculinity with hegemonic masculinity and neglects the power possession of a male body gives to the gay males of his research. In his empirical studies, where male bodies are included, it is with a narrow focus on sexual activity. From a poststructuralist feminist perspective, the power attributed to the male body and the possession of the all-powerful penis, and the inferiorization of the female body due to its lack of a penis, means that even heterosexual men who are furthest from masculinity in its macho form, as well as gay men, can exert power over women. Physical and metaphorical space in the workshop, the factory floor, the boardroom and the home, as well as in the sporting arena, is accorded to male bodies.

Recent feminist focus on the sociology of the body has emphasized perceptions of the body as culturally situated and culturally shared, pointing to male domination of the discourses which have defined the female body as lacking a penis, inferring passivity, receptivity and inferiority (Bordo, 1995). This perception of the female body, in contrast to the male body, is enshrined in the texts of women's magazines, television, cosmetic counters, fashion displays, advertising billboards and more generally in the written word. Women's own self-surveillance accedes to the interests of patriarchy in this regard. Such self-surveillance gains women's collusion to the objectification and inferiorization of women's bodies. Leisure is one space where this collusion is achieved through such vehicles as exercise regimes, fashion, shopping, romance reading and presentation of the self as a sex object. In the sporting arena, Young (1990) has shown how even relatively untrained men engage in sport with more freedom and open reach than do their female counterparts. Yet, argue feminists such as Grosz (1995b), if bodies are not natural givens but surfaces upon which social parameters have been inscribed, they become 'volatile bodies' and both sex and gender are open to re-interpretation. In the current socio-political and historical climate, she claims, such re-interpretation can give greater value to women's embodiment. It is possible then to rewrite the definition of female bodies as strong, capable, active and socially powerful. Leisure is one area where this may happen.

Implicit in feminist and masculinist poststructuralist perspectives on the body is its social construction and therefore the malleability of its meanings. There are, then, many individual subjectivities that could be constructed around embodiment, if individuals were to recognize and resist dominant discourses, or if they had access to alternative discourses. I argue that leisure and sport provide spaces for trying out and changing rigid definitions of male and female bodies. Women who stretch societally imposed limits on the use of the female body by engaging in activities such as rock climbing and outdoor adventure report a sense of empowerment. Leisure, and more especially sport, can be a space for moving the body beyond its previous limits. The possibilities are also there for unwrapping masculine myths surrounding the male body and its use in sport in order to uncover some of the real men who play. There is also the possibility for opening up sporting spaces for interactions between real men and real women based on actual abilities, rather than on the cardboard cutouts of gendered stereotypes. Similarly, leisure may offer spaces for expression of emotions which go beyond gendered stereotypes.

From the works of Simmel (1964) and Elias (1986a) leisure emerged as a space for the necessary release of emotional tension under the constraints of modernity and city living. For Simmel, public places in the city offered spaces for excitement which countered the neurasthenia developed to protect the individual from the constant emotional bombardment of city living. Although most of these were commodified and provided fleeting release, some such as sociability and the adventure, he claimed, provided experiences which could be taken back into the everyday world. For Elias, leisure and sport provide mimetic experiences for the release of emotions in a safe space as a counter to the civilizing constraints on emotional expression brought about by living in modern society. Although both of these men saw this release in relationship to male ways of being in the world, the ideas are applicable to females as well. They may not have similar access to such spaces, but leisure as a relatively safe space for emotional expression can give women, as well as men, the opportunity to explore emotions which are kept in check in everyday living for one's own protection and the protection of others. For women this may include anger and for men the more vulnerable aspects of emotional expression such as displays of true affection and caring. Leisure experiences such as sporting contests, theatre, music, films, television, radio, reading, writing and art may provide spaces for exploring and expanding one's emotional self beyond everyday social constraints including those that are gendered. The feminized version of the sociology of emotions presented by Hochschild (1979) suggests that our emotional selves go much deeper than the surface displays required in everyday life, so that the work needed to release the self from 'deep acting' is considerable. If this is the case, fleeting mimetic experiences through leisure may not be enough. Poststructuralist feminists such as Butler (1990) suggest that repeated performative acts are the way out of constrictive definitions of womanhood. I contend, with regard to the emotions, that leisure may provide a space for both women and men in which to engage in repeated performative acts which tap into deeper emotions over a period of time, thus going beyond fleeting excitement and release.

Poststructuralist feminist theory attempts to deconstruct the binary opposition between the mind and the body and the mind and emotions where the former is valued over the latter. Revaluing the body and emotions taps into traditional female ways of thinking and being in the world and validates them, so that leisure as personal space for exploring these aspects of self acts as an enabling space for women. For men it may open up a space for moving beyond previous emotional constraints.

Urban sociology, along with general trends in sociology since the 1970s, has moved from Marxist to poststructuralist analyses. Male world-views have presented physical spaces in cities as spaces open to unencumbered males about their business or pleasure in the city environment. Poststructural feminism has encouraged women to be subversive of male theorizing and to incorporate concepts more aligned with the variety of women's ways of being in the world. In the area of urban sociology these feminists have been critical of the perception of the inhabitant of the city as a *flâneur* who strolls about directing a voyeuristic gaze on the city's spaces, buildings and people. Grosz (1995a) suggests a more feminized concept of city space as 'chora' – a space for becoming – a space which extends the horizon of becoming. It includes interaction with others and possibilities for extension of the self beyond that which is confined by everyday practice. It is open then to both men and women as a leisure space for new experiences of the self. Such a conceptualization also holds out new possibilities for the leisure spaces which are part of the tourist enterprise, as I have argued elsewhere (Wearing and Wearing, 1996b).

From my summary in this chapter it is clear that insights from poststructuralist feminism have contributed significantly to the argument that I have developed throughout the book. In Chapter 9 I set out in more explicit form some of the main concepts of poststructuralist theory as it has been applied in feminist thinking. Poststructuralist feminism presents a view of women that moves beyond that of woman as powerless victim of the oppressive structures of modernity. Incorporating a view of power which is not only top-down and repressive but also capillary, poststructuralist theory presents women as able to resist, struggle, negotiate and sometimes transform, at an individual, communal and political level, aspects of their lives which are oppressive. Nor is the concept 'woman' universally the same but experienced differentially by women within one culture and across cultures. And women themselves construct subjectivities which do not necessarily form a consistent whole. The 'I' of the self is cumulative and able to change with new input and through repeated performative acts which may challenge and transform traditional notions of womanhood. This does not mean, however, that women do not have some aspects of their lives in common. For example, present social constructions of the female body, almost universally present it as lacking a phallus and therefore not as strong, or active as the male body. Similarly, as Spivak (1988b) points out, there is almost universal symbolic, if not physical, elimination of the clitoris as a site of women's sexuality, forcing a focus on women's reproductive capacity rather than subjective aspects of her sexual pleasure. In addition, structural constraints remain. In Western societies state legislation has enabled women to receive educational benefits along with men and has redressed some of the imbalances in the workforce and law, but there remains much to be done at a structural level before women will hold, on their own terms, the positions of power currently held by men. In developing countries women yet experience gender oppression, along with class and race oppression.

Another aspect of poststructuralist feminism is its concern to deconstruct the binary oppositions of malestream post-Enlightenment theory. So there is an attempt to deconstruct the hierarchical dichotomies: mind/body, rational/emotional, culture/nature, public/private, self/other, male/female, work/leisure. This has also led to attempts to rewrite scripts so that the former are no longer prioritized over the latter, but both are valued and interconnected. My own attempt in this book combines an attempt to deconstruct the work/leisure and the male/female dichotomies so that women's experiences can be valued and included in a leisure theory which can address both women's and men's leisure in a liberating way.

Poststructuralist feminism also seeks to incorporate into theory concepts which are more directly aligned with women's experiences of the world, so that male domination of social theory is subverted. Failure to do this with regard to leisure theory perpetuates 'the revolving door' phase of leisure and tourism scholarship. Rather, in this book I have attempted to move on to the 'door ajar' phase where new scholarship challenges the discipline. In this model, 'knowledge is viewed as social power and feminist analysis of the nature and construction of knowledge becomes an essential underpinning critique of gendered power relations' (Atichison, 1996: 38). Hence, I have incorporated into the notion of leisure space the idea of 'chora' or space for becoming, for broadening the horizons of the self. I have then rewritten the script of leisure as personal space, both physical and/or metaphysical, over which the individual has some autonomy both to do something or nothing for her/his own satisfaction and to be alone or to include other people. This is a space where both women and men can resist what they have been told by society they ought to be and reach towards what they could be. It is also a space where, by repeated performative acts, they can expand subjectivities beyond gendered stereotypes.

Postcolonial feminist theorists such as hooks (1989), Spivak (1988a, 1988b) and Collins (1990) are critical of Western, white, middle-class, academic feminists' appropriation of feminist theory in order to get a better deal for women who are already privileged in many ways. Little consideration has been given to the voices and world-views of 'other' women. The continual presentation of the middle-class, white woman's experience as universal has had the effect of silencing the voices of other women. Construction of poor women, black women and ethnic women as 'other to' with implications of lesser importance is severely criticized in this literature. Postcolonial feminism urges that the voices of these 'other' women be heard along with their own experiences of suffering and oppression. When this is done, the family, for example, is not seen as oppressive but rather as a source of support and solidarity for its many female heads. Nor is paid work in conflict with caring for the family, but part of the caring responsibility. The idealized version of femininity is not one of female fragility, but of physical and emotional strength, that of active women who head families and instigate community action. There is a move in this literature to break down the self/other dichotomy, where the self involves the subjectivity and superiority of the white, Western woman and other refers to subaltern women as objects. For many of these women, the extreme emphasis on the expression and development of the individual self is also being critiqued in the deconstruction of this dichotomy. In this instance, community takes precedence over individualized selves.

It is this latter criticism which is most relevant to my own reconstruction of leisure as personal space. For these women the concept would have little meaning in the sense of developing a self that is clearly delineated from others in the community of women, and the idea of self-enhancement without their enhancement as well would be alienating. And here I must confess that my own bias in building up the idea of leisure as personal space throughout the book has been towards individual enhancement. It was not until I began to listen to the voices of these 'other' women that the necessity for them of a communal sense of self became apparent to me. So, in the final analysis there is a need from a postcolonial perspective to break down the self/other dichotomy inherent in my own thinking concerning the self. The 'I' that these women talk about is very much one that incorporates the 'we' of the local African-American, Australian Aboriginal or the Pacific Islander community. As one Australian Aboriginal woman has pointed out (Watson, 1988, video), it is white language which projects 'I', 'I', 'I', 'me' 'me', 'me' and 'take', 'take', 'take'. Aboriginal people talk about 'we' and 'sharing', not 'owning' and 'giving', or even 'lending'. Any concept of leisure as personal space must also incorporate communal spaces for a communal sense of self which can go beyond derogatory racial stereotypes, as well as gendered stereotypes. I need to redefine personal space to go beyond the usual Western definition of 'personal' as referring to a particular, private, individual person, to include personal as a sense of being one of a group or community. There is, then, no reason why leisure as personal space cannot include others of like mind who as a group use leisure to express communal concerns and to enlarge a communal sense of self beyond the constraints of powerful discourses. Nor does this idea exclude the talents such as writing and art that individuals bring to the group. It is the interpretation of that contribution that is different, as Watson points out. She says: 'When we are singled out for a prize for our art or poetry or music we hang our heads and think, but it wasn't just me, it was the whole community and our history that has made this thing' (Watson, 1988, video).

In a similar vein postcolonial theory draws attention to the deconstruction of the private/public, personal/political dichotomies. Socialist feminists will criticize my work for its insistence on the relative power of individuals to make significant changes in the position of women through personal space and individual resistance. Yet women who write from subaltern perspectives see personal action as invariably flowing on to communal and political action and back again to the self. Leisure spaces such as writing, poetry, art, dance, singing, story-telling and humour often begin in the private sphere and very soon become part of the community, frequently leading then to political action. In this manner subaltern women have been able to enlarge the sense of self that they have in worlds which have treated them badly and sought to stamp on their self-esteem. Bell hooks says of her own writing: 'In counter hegemonic race talk I testify in this writing – bear witness to the reality – that our many cultures can be remade, that this nation can be transformed, that we can resist racism and in the act of resistance recover ourselves and be renewed' (hooks, 1996: 7).

The argument that I am presenting here turns on notions from feminist poststructuralist, postcolonial theory which include the deconstruction of the self/other dichotomy, the presence of multiple subjectivities within the self and the ability of women to challenge dominant discourses on woman-hood through alternative discourses. Thus women are able to reach towards becoming more than dominant discourses tell them they should be. In many ways my project is similar to Probyn's in *Sexing the Self* (1993). In this work Probyn presents the gendered self as never fixed or stable like a 'combi-nation of acetate transparencies: layers and layers of lines and directions that are figured together and in depth, only to be rearranged again' (1993: 1). She emphasizes the way that listening to the voices of women whose cul-tural position is different from one's own can introduce alternative dis-courses and enable one to imagine other ways of being women. She attempts to deconstruct the 'I' and 'she', through the imagination and through moving from 'her' experience to 'mine', and 'mine' to 'hers'. Care of self in her terms is more than a personal endeavour, 'it must be consti-tuted somewhere between my self and hers: it must be able to reach beyond "me", beyond who or what "I" am' (1993: 4). Thus Probyn offers 'a geog-raphy of the possible' which is similar to my 'personal space' in that both offer the potential of care for the self and hope for 'becoming' and 'ex-tending' the self through the use of the imagination and interaction with other women (1993: 173). For both of us this is a political project which goes well beyond an individual enterprise.

I contend, then, that the approach offered here has important impli-cations for leisure policy. Policies and procedures need to be put in place at local, state and federal levels to address issues relevant to the positions of women in many and varied circumstances of oppression. Poststructural and postcolonial feminist theories suggest that leisure policies should not try to implement uniform policies for all women, nor try to give women equality with men by treating them the same as men. For example, money spent on football grounds for women would not work. Nor would public swimming pools, which are open to all, be satisfactory leisure spaces for women from Muslim backgrounds. Public leisure facilities and leisure programmes which act in the manner of pre-formed pigeon-holes into which women can be fitted will not be used by many women. They could act as cultural straightjackets for women, instead of spaces for becoming. As was sug-gested in Chapter 8 of this book, the concept of public leisure spaces as 'chora' presents us with possibilities for planning spaces which extend for women, children, older people, disabled and culturally diverse people, as well as for unencumbered males, the horizons of their becoming through interaction with others.

The provision of public spaces in which people from a diversity of back-grounds can interact in ways that enhance the contribution that each can make and at the same time enable a stretching of the self beyond gender, age, racial and ethnic stereotypes is not purely utopian. One example of such a space is the interactive museum. Museums such as the Powerhouse, Mari-time and Australian Museums in Sydney provide multicultural programmes which include people, music, dance, food and artefacts from many cultures and interactive displays which encourage 'chorasters', be they children or adults, to have hands-on experiences. In another example, local councils in multicultural areas such as the inner city suburb of Newtown have closed off the main street for at least one weekend a year for a festival which celebrates, through food, dance, music, art and theatre, the various cultures that reside in that area. There has also been a deliberate attempt to make Sydney's public parks, such as Centennial Park, safe for women, children, older and disabled people through well-lit, wide paths with smooth surfaces, ample seating and specific areas for cycling, rollerblading, horseriding and walking the dog. Money has yet to be spent, however, in the massive amounts that are allocated to football stadiums for the active use of able-bodied young men, on public leisure spaces which are open to the interactive use of other groups in the population.

In leisure management the application of the concept of leisure as personal space providing horizons for extending the self would avoid the provision of set programmes which pigeon-hole women into already created spots appropriate to the cultural construction of female bodies and hegemonic control of womanhood. Programmes would be designed in which individual women could have some input into both the content and the process. There would be a deliberate attempt to tap in to the various 'I's', rather than the socially determined 'me's'. To some extent personal trainers already do this, but at exorbitant prices, and both the goal and the process often fit gendered stereotypes and male oriented competitiveness and task achievement rather than personal perceptions of self-enhancement in a supportive environment. The use of the imagination to extend people's horizons beyond gendered stereotypes yet with sensitivity to cultural differences presents a challenge to men and the limited number of women who hold decision-making positions in leisure management.

Research based on the poststructuralist, postcolonial perspective which has been presented here would examine the ways that men as well as women use leisure to go beyond gender and racial stereotypes. 'How do men and women use repeated performative acts through leisure and sport to resist and transform dominant modes of gendered selves?', 'Do some men and some women interact in leisure spaces with recognition and respect for the other's abilities and contributions, so that each is honoured?' and 'How can these aspects of leisure be fostered?' would be research questions which may be productive for leisure professionals. With recognition of the possibilities for diverse forms of masculinity and femininity as well as multiple subjectivities within one person, such research may move the leisure literature beyond monofocal identity politics to possibilities of coalitions between different groups of people with benefits for each. By opening up the concept of leisure as 'chora' or spaces, both physical and metaphorical, for interaction with diverse others and for becoming more than powerful discourses tell us we should be, leisure research may be able to make a valuable contribution to the quality of individual lives as well as those of oppressed communities. The leisure of women, other than that of the colonizers, has hardly been researched to date. Traditional concepts of leisure may not be appropriate for them. Concepts such as leisure as 'chora' or a space for becoming and persons engaged in leisure as 'chorasters' may be able to tap into leisure experiences in other cultures. Leisure retains, however, its sense of 'heterotopia', that is, a space somehow apart or different from one's routine everyday activities and their associated experiences. Specific programmes and policies may well be suggested by research which has a wider and more flexible approach and is more applicable in the postmodern era.

Massive surveys with pre-coded slots to be ticked and computer analysed will not tap in to this information. Nor will positivistic attempts to statistically correlate independent and dependent variables in order to establish cause and effect. Research which includes insights from the perspectives presented here will focus on qualitative, interpretive methods able to explore the diversities of meanings attached to leisure experience for people from many different cultural situations. Sensitive, open-ended questions may produce results which push thinking concerning leisure into the twenty-first century.

In conclusion, it must become apparent from the evidence presented in this book that feminist theory has made an incontrovertible contribution to leisure theory in the last 30 years. That contribution has included a greater understanding of the phenomenon of leisure when viewed from women's perspectives, but it has also contributed to an understanding of men's leisure. Hopefully, in the future it will contribute to the meanings given to personal spaces for people other than those who have colonized others. My own approach in the book has been impure, eclectic and neo-pragmatic, combining the strongest features of each feminist approach when applied to leisure. It is very much in the vein that Nancy Fraser argues is necessary if feminist theory is not to be stalemated into opposing camps. This approach, she says, 'would encompass the full range of processes by which the sociocultural meanings of gender are constructed and contested. It would maximize our ability to contest the current gender hegemony and to build a feminist counter hegemony' (1995: 158). It is also more likely than singular approaches to cope with the most difficult task for feminist theory of connecting individualized perspectives with structural analyses of institutions and political economy. The future of feminist theory, and hence feminist leisure theory, probably depends on such an eclectic, neo-pragmatic approach which draws on a range of theories, yet rejects those that are inappropriate. These would be those that do not present a perspective that allows the honouring of difference and the deconstruction of binary oppositions which have valorized the ways that men construct their worlds and participate in them. The future project for feminist leisure theory is to continue to open up spaces for women and men to move beyond rigid gender, class, race, age and ethnic definitions of the self which are limiting and oppressive, and to envisage spaces which extend people's horizons and provide the potential for personal and political growth.

Bibliography

Anderson, R. (1975) *Leisure an Inappropriate Concept for Women?* Canberra: Australian Government Publishing Service.

Atichison, C. (1996) 'Patriarchal paradigms and the politics of pedagogy: a framework for a feminist analysis of leisure and tourism studies', *World Leisure and Recreation*, 38 (4): 38–40.

Attwood, A. (1997) 'It's extreme hypocrisy time', *Sydney Morning Herald*, 20 January: 32.

Australian Bureau of Statistics (1990) *The Labour Force.* Canberra: Commonwealth Government Printer, Cat. No. 6203. 0.

Australian Bureau of Statistics (1993) *Women in Australia.* Canberra: National Capital Printing, Cat. No. 4113. 0.

Australian Bureau of Statistics (1994) *How Australians Use their Time* (rev. edn). Canberra: Australian Government Publishing Service, Cat. No. 4153. 0.

Australian Heritage Commission (1992) *What is Social Value? A Discussion Paper.* Technical Publications, Series Number 3, Canberra: Australian Government Publishing Service.

Barrett, M. (1980) *Women's Oppression Today.* London: Verso.

Bartky, S. (1988) 'Foucault, femininity and the modernisation of patriarchal power', in I. Diamond and L. Quinby (eds), *Feminism and Foucault.* Boston: Northeastern University Press. pp. 61–86.

Bathurst, L. (1995) 'Constrained by care: leisure opportunities for the mothers of people with intellectual disability'. MA thesis, University of Technology, Sydney.

Bayer, R. (1981) *Homosexuality and American Psychiatry.* New York: Basic Books.

Beale, V. (1988) 'Men's journey, women's journeys – a different story?', *Journal of Colorado Outward Bound Wilderness School Education*, 4: 7–13.

Beechey, V. (1979) 'On patriarchy', *Feminist Reveiw*, 3: 66–82.

Bell, D. (1978) *The Cultural Contradictions of Capitalism.* New York: Harper Torchbooks for Basic Books.

Bell, D. (1990) 'Aboriginal women, separate spaces and feminism', in S. Grunew (ed.), *A Reader in Feminist Knowledge.* New York: Routledge. pp. 13–26.

Bella, L. (1989) 'Women and leisure: beyond androcentrism', in T. Burton and E. Jackson (eds), *Understanding Leisure and Recreation: Mapping the Past, Charting the Future.* State College, PA: Venture. pp. 159–79.

Bellear, L. (1996) *Dreaming in Urban Areas.* St Lucia, QLD: University of Queensland Press.

Benhabib, S., Butler, J., Cornell, D. and Fraser, N. (1995) *Feminist Contentions.* New York and London: Routledge.

Benjamin, W. (1973) *Charles Baudelaire: A Lyric Poet in the Era of High Capitalism* (translated H. Zohn). London: New Left Books.

Berman, M. (1983) *All That is Solid Melts into Air: The Experience of Modernity.* London: Verso.

Bhabha, H.K. (1983) 'The other question – the stereotype and colonial discourse', *Screen*, 24, November/December: 18–36.

Bialeschki, M.D. (1984) 'An analysis of leisure attitudes and activity patterns of women related to locus of control and perceived choice'. PhD dissertation, University of Wisconsin, Madison, WI.

Bittman, M. (1991) 'Home centred leisure: a trap for women', in P. Brown (ed.), *Women and Leisure: Towards 2000*, proceedings of symposium, University of Newcastle, 11–12 July. University of Newcastle, Newcastle, Australia. pp. 28–36.

Blachford, G. (1981) 'Male dominance and the gay world', in K. Plummer (ed.), *The Making of the Modern Homosexual*. London: Hutchinson. pp. 184–210.

Bly, R. (1991) *Iron John: A Book About Men*. Shaftesbury, Dorset and Rockport, MA: Element Books.

Bock, G. and James, S. (1992) 'Introduction: contextualising equality and difference', in G. Bock and S. James (eds), *Beyond Equality and Difference*. London: Routledge. pp. 1–13.

Bolla, P.A. (1990) 'Media images of women and leisure: an analysis of magazine advertisements, 1964–87', *Leisure Studies*, 9: 241–52.

Bordo, S. (1995) *Unbearable Weight*. Berkeley, CA: University of California Press.

Brace-Govan, J.V.F. (1997) 'Women working on their bodies: a feminist sociological exploration of three active physicalities'. PhD thesis, Monash University, Melbourne.

Braidotti, R. (1993) 'Embodiment, sexual difference, and the nomadic subject', *Hyaptia*, 8 (Winter): 1–3.

Brightbill, C. (1960) *The Challenge of Leisure*. Englewood Cliffs, NJ: Prentice Hall.

Broom, D.H., Byrne, M. and Petkovic, L. (1992) 'Off cue: women who play pool', *Australian and New Zealand Journal of Sociology*, 28 (2): 175–91.

Brown, G. (1992) 'Tourism and symbolic consumption', in P. Johnson and B. Thomas (eds), *Choice and Demand in Tourism*. London: Mansell.

Brown, J. (1985) *Toward the Development of a Commonwealth Policy on Recreation*. Canberra: Australian Government Publishing Service.

Bryson, L. (1987) 'Sport and the maintenance of masculine hegemony', *Women's Studies International Forum*, 10 (4): 349–60.

Bryson, L. (1990) 'Challenges to male hegemony in sport', in M. Messner and D. Sabo (eds), *Sport, Men and the Gender Order*. Champaign, IL: Human Kinetics Books. pp. 173–84.

Bryson, L. (1991) 'A place for women in the Australian sporting ethos', address *Equity for Women in Sport*, Seminar Parliament House, Canberra, ACT, 27–8 February, Hansard Report. pp. 155–61.

Burden, J. and Kiewa, J. (1992) 'Adventurous Women', *Refractory Girl*, 43: 29–33.

Burt, R. (1994) 'Representations of masculinity in contemporary theatre dance', in C. Brackenridge (ed.), *Body Matters: Leisure Images and Lifestyles* (2nd edn), Leisure Studies Association No. 47. Eastborne: LSA Publications. pp. 54–9.

Butler, J. (1990) *Gender Trouble: Feminism and the Subversion of Identity*. New York: Routledge.

Butler, J. (1992) 'Contingent foundations: feminism and the question of "postmodernism"', in J. Butler and S.W. Scott (eds), *Beyond Equality and Difference*. New York: Routledge. pp. 3–21.

Butler, J. (1993) *Bodies that Matter: On the Discursive Limits of Sex*. New York: Routledge.

Caldwell, G.T. (1977) 'Leisure', in A.F. Davies, S. Encel and M.J. Berry, *Australian Society*. Melbourne: Longman Cheshire. pp. 410–39.

Campbell, C. (1987) *The Romantic Ethic and the Spirit of Modern Consumerism*. Oxford: Basil Blackwell.

Carrigan, T., Connell, B. and Lee, J. (1985) 'Toward a new sociology of masculinity', *Theory and Society*, 5 (14): 551–604.

Castells, M. (1977) *The Urban Question: A Marxist Approach*. London: Edward Arnold.

Chodorow, N. (1978) *The Reproduction of Mothering: A Psychoanalysis and the Sociology of Gender*. Berkeley, CA: University of California Press.

Christian, H. (1994) *The Making of Anti-sexist Men*. London: Routledge.

Clarke, J. and Critcher, C. (1985) *The Devil Makes Work: Leisure in Capitalist Britain*. London: Macmillan.

Coalter, F. and Parry, N. (1982) *Leisure Sociology or the Sociology of Leisure?* Department of Leisure Studies, Polytechnic of North London.

Cohen, C.B. (1995) 'Marketing paradise, making nation', *Annals of Tourism Research*, 22: 404–21.

Cohen, E. (1988) 'Authenticity and commoditization in tourism', *Annals of Tourism Research*, 15: 371–86.

Cohen, P. (1968) *Modern Social Theory*. New York: Basic Books.

Cohen, S. and Taylor, L. (1976) *Escape Attempts*. Harmondsworth: Penguin.

Collins, P.H. (1990) *Black Feminist Thought: Knowledge, Consciousness, and the Politics of Empowerment*. New York: Unwin Hyman.

Colton, C.W. (1987) 'Leisure, recreation, tourism: a symbolic interactionist view', *Annals Of Tourism Research*, 14: 345–60.

Connell, R.W. (1987) *Gender and Power*. Sydney: Allen & Unwin.

Connell, R.W. (1990a) 'A whole new world: remaking masculinity in the context of the environmental movement', *Gender and Society*, 4 (4): 452–78.

Connell, R.W. (1990b) 'An iron man: the body and some contradictions of hegemonic masculinity', in M. Messner and D. Sabo (eds), *Sport, Men and the Gender Order*. Champaign, IL: Human Kinetics Books. pp. 83–95.

Connell, R.W. (1991) 'Live fast and die young: the construction of masculinity among young working class men on the margin of the labour market', *Australian and New Zealand Journal of Sociology*, 27 (2): 141–71.

Connell, R.W. (1992) 'A very straight gay: masculinity, homosexual experience and the dynamics of gender', *American Sociological Review*, 57 (6): 735–51.

Connell, R.W. (1995) *Masculinities*. Berkeley, CA: University of California Press.

Craig, S. (ed.) (1992) *Men, Masculinity and the Media*. Newbury Park, CA: Sage.

Craik, J. (1994) *The Face of Fashion*. Routledge: London.

Critcher, C. (1989) 'A communication in response to "Leisure, lifestyle and status"', *Leisure Studies*, 8: 159–61.

Cronin, V. (1995) 'Retirement: less money more husband – a study of the impact of male partner's retirement on the female partner's leisure'. Honours thesis, University of Technology, Sydney.

Cuff, E.C. and Payne, C.C.F. (1984) *Perspectives in Sociology* (2nd edn). London: Allen & Unwin.

Cuneen, C., Findlay, M., Lynch, R. and Tupper, V. (1989) *Dynamics of Collective Conflict: Riots at the Bathurst 'Bike Races*. Sydney: Law Book Company.

Currie, J. (1996) 'Motherhood and stress: a study of the effect of exercise class on the stress levels of mothers'. PhD thesis, University of New South Wales, Sydney.

Cushman, G. and Veal, A.J. (1993) 'The new generations of leisure survey – implications for research on everyday life', *Society and Leisure*, 16 (1): 211–20.

Davidson, P. (1996) 'Women's leisure: the woman's perspective of holidays'. MA thesis, Royal Melbourne Institue of Technology, Melbourne.

de Certeau, M. (1988) *The Practice of Everyday Life*. Berkeley, CA: University of California Press.

de Lauretis, T. (1990) 'Upping the anti (sic) in feminist theory', in M. Hirsch and E. Fox Keller (eds), *Conflicts in Feminism*. Cambridge: Polity Press.

Deary, C.M. (1985) *Designing Places for People: A Handbook on Human Behavior for Architects, Designs and Facility Managers*. New York: Whitney Library of Design.

Deem, R. (1986) *All Work and No Play*. Milton Keynes: Open University Press.

Deem, R. (1987) 'Unleisured lives; sport in the context of women's leisure', *Women's Studies International Forum*, 120 (4): 423–32.

Deem, R. (1988) 'Feminism and leisure studies: opening up new directions', in E. Wimbush and M. Talbot (eds), *Relative Freedoms: Women and Leisure*. Milton Keynes: Open University Press. pp. 5–17.

Deem, R. (1992) 'The sociology of gender and leisure in Britain – past progress and future prospects', *Society and Leisure*, 15 (1): 21–38.

Dempsey, K. (1989) 'Women's leisure, men's leisure', *Australian and New Zealand Journal of Sociology*, 25 (1): 27–45.

Dempsey, K. (1990) 'Women's life and leisure in an Australian rural community', *Leisure Studies*, 1: 35–43.

Denzin, N.K. (1992) *Symbolic Interactionism and Cultural Studies: The Politics of Interpretation*. Oxford and Cambridge, MA: Blackwell.

Department of Planning (1995) *Cities for the 21st Century*. Sydney: New South Wales Government.

Dixey, R. (1988) 'Eyes down': a study of bingo', in E. Wimbush and M. Talbot (eds), *Relative Freedoms: Women and Leisure*. Milton Keynes: Open University Press.

Douglas, S. (1995) *Where the Girls Are: Growing Up Female with the Mass Media*. London: Penguin.

Driver, B. (1990) 'The highlights of the US experiences in recreation benefit measurement'. Papers on recreation benefit measurement presented at a workshop convened by the Department of Leisure Studies, Philip Institute of Technology, Bundoora, Victoria, 18–20 April.

Duncan, M.C., Messner, M., Williams, L. and Jensen, K. (1994) 'Gender stereotyping in televised sports', in S. Birrell and C.L. Cole (eds), *Women, Sport and Culture*. Champaign, IL: Human Kinetics Books.

Dunk, T. (1991) *It's a Working Man's Town: Male Working Class Culture in Northwestern Ontario*. Montreal: McGill-Queens University Press.

Dunning, E. (1986a) 'Sport as a male preserve: notes on the social sources of masculine identity and its transformations', in N. Elias and E. Dunning, *Quest For Excitement: Sport and Leisure in the Civilising Process*. Oxford: Basil Blackwell. pp. 267–85.

Dunning, E. (1986b) 'Social bonding and violence in sport', in N. Elias and E. Dunning, *Quest for Excitement*. Oxford: Basil Blackwell. pp. 224–44.

During, S. (ed.) (1993) *The Cultural Studies Reader*. London and New York: Free Press.

Edmund, M. (1992) *No Regrets*. St Lucia: University of Queensland Press.

Eisenstein, Z. (1977) 'Constructing a theory of capitalist patriarchy and socialist feminism', *The Insurgent Sociologist*, 7 (3): 3–17.

Elias, N. (1986a) 'Introduction', in N. Elias and E. Dunning, *Quest For Excitement: Sport and Leisure in the Civilising Process*. Oxford: Basil Blackwell. pp. 19–62.

Elias, N. (1986b) 'An essay on sport and violence', in N. Elias and E. Dunning, *Quest For Excitement*. Oxford: Basil Blackwell. pp. 150–74.

Elias, N. and Dunning, E. (1986) *Quest for Excitement: Sport and Leisure in the Civilising Process*. Oxford: Basil Blackwell.

Farrell, W. (1974) *The Liberated Man, Beyond Masculinity: Freeing Men and their Relationships With Women*. New York: Random House.

Farrell, W. (1993) *The Myth of Male Power: Why Men are the Disposable Sex*. New York: Simon & Schuster.

Featherstone, M. (1982) 'The body in consumer culture', *Theory, Culture & Society*, 1 (2): 18–33.

Featherstone, M. (1991) *Consumer Culture and Postmodernism*. London: Sage.

Fiske, J. (1989) *Reading the Popular.* Boston: Unwin Hyman.

Fiske, J., Hodge, B. and Turner, G. (1987) *Myths of Oz: Reading Popular Culture.* Sydney: Allen & Unwin.

Foucault, M. (1978) *The History of Sexuality, Vol. 1.* London: Tavistock.

Foucault, M. (1979a) *Power, Truth, Strategy.* Sydney: Feral.

Foucault, M. (1979b) *The History of Sexuality, Vol. 1,* Introduction. London: Allen Lane for Penguin.

Foucault, M. (1979c) *Discipline and Punish: The Birth of the Prison.* London: Tavistock.

Foucault, M. (1980) *Power/Knowledge: Selected Interviews and Other Writings 1972–77.* Brighton: Harvester Press.

Foucault, M. (1983) 'The subject and power', in H. Dreyfus and P. Rabinow (eds), *Michel Foucault: Beyond Structuralism and Hermeneutics.* Chicago: Chicago University Press. pp. 208–20.

Foucault, M. (1984) 'Space, knowledge and power', in P. Rabinow (ed.), *The Foucault Reader.* Harmondsworth: Penguin. pp. 239–56.

Foucault, M. (1986) 'Of other spaces', *Diacritics,* Spring: 22–7.

Fraser, N. (1995) 'Pragmatism, feminism and the linguistic turn', in S. Benhabib, J. Butler, D. Cornell and N. Fraser, *Feminist Contentions: A Philosophical Exchange.* New York: Routledge. pp. 157–71.

Freund, P. (1990) 'The expressive body: a common ground for the sociology of emotions and health and illness', *Sociology of Health and Illness,* 12 (4): 452–77.

Freysinger, V.J. (1988) 'The meaning of leisure in middle adulthood: gender differences and changes since young adulthood', PhD dissertation, University of Wisconsin-Madison, Madison, WI.

Freysinger, V.J. and Flannery, D. (1992) 'Women's leisure: affiliation, self-determination, empowerment and resistance?', *Society and Leisure,* 15 (1): 303–22.

Friedan, B. (1963) *The Feminine Mystique.* New York: Norton.

Frisby, D. (1989) 'Simmel and Leisure', in C. Rojek (ed.), *Leisure for Leisure.* London: Macmillan. pp. 75–89.

Frow, J. and Morris, M. (eds) (1993) *Australian Cultural Studies: A Reader.* Sydney: Allen & Unwin.

Fullagar, S. (1991) 'From dichotomies to difference: developing a feminist discourse on womon, nature and leisure'. Unpublished honours thesis, University of Technology, Sydney.

Gagnon, N. (1996) 'Sport culture and violence against women', *World Leisure and Recreation,* 38 (4): 28–30.

Galbally, R. (1990) 'Recreation: an integrating concept for health promotion outcome'. Papers on recreation benefit measurement presented at a workshop convened by the Department of Leisure Studies, Philip Institute of Technology, Bundoora, Victoria, 18–20 April.

Gamman, L. and Marshment, M. (1988) *The Female Gaze: Women as Viewers of Popular Culture.* London: The Women's Press.

Gatens, M. (1988) 'Towards a feminist philosophy of the body', in B. Caine, E. Grosz and M. de Lepervanche (eds), *Crossing Boundaries: Feminism and the Critique of Knowledges.* Sydney: Allen & Unwin. pp. 59–70.

Gatens, M. (1996) *Imaginary Bodies.* London: Routledge.

Gershuny, J. and Thomas, G. (1980) *Changing Patterns of Time Use Data and Some Preliminary Results, UK 1961–74/5.* Brighton: University of Sussex, Science Policy Research Unit.

Gerth, H.H. and Wright Mills, C. (eds) (1948) *From Weber: Essays in Sociology.* New York: Routledge & Kegan Paul.

Giddens, A. (1984) *The Constitution of Society.* Cambridge: Polity Press.

Giddens, A. (1989) *Sociology*. Cambridge: Polity Press.

Giddens, A. (1991) *Modernity and Self-Identity: Self and Society in the Late Modern Age*. Cambridge: Polity Press.

Gilligan, C. (1982) *In a Different Voice*. Cambridge, MA: Harvard University Press.

Godkin, M.A. (1980) 'Identity and place: clinical applications based on notions of rootedness and uprootedness,' in A. Buttimer and D. Seamon (eds), *The Human Experience of Space and Place*. London: Croom Helm.

Goffman, E. (1961) *Encounters*. Indianapolis, IN: Bobbs-Merrill.

Goffman, E. (1963) *Stigma*. Englewood Cliffs, NJ: Prentice Hall.

Goffman, E. (1967) *Interaction Ritual*. Chicago: Aldine.

Goffman, E. (1969) *The Presentation of Self in Everyday Life*. Harmondsworth: Penguin.

Goffman, E. (1974) *Frame Analysis*. New York: Harper & Row.

Goffman, E. (1976) *Gender Advertisements*. London: Macmillan.

Gordon, C. (1980) *Michel Foucault, Power/Knowledge: Selected Interviews and Other Writings 1972–1977*. Brighton: Harvester Press.

Grace, D. (1994) 'Postmodernism and Foucault'. Unpublished paper, School of Social Work, University of New South Wales, Sydney.

Gramsci, A. (1978) *Selections From Political Writing: 1921–1926* (trans. Quintin Hoare). New York: International Publishers.

Gramsci, A. (1985) *Prison Notebooks: Selections*. New York: International Publishers.

Graveline, M. (1990) 'Threat to rural women's well-being: a group response', in V. Dhruvarajan (ed.), *Women and Well-Being*. Montreal: McGill-Queen's Press.

Green, E., Hebron, S. and Woodward, D. (1987) 'Women's leisure in Sheffield: a research report'. Department of Applied Social Studies, Sheffield City Polytechnic.

Green, E. and Woodward, D. (1990) ' "To them that hath . . .". Inequality and social control in women's leisure'. Paper presented at the XIIth World Congress of Sociology, Madrid, Spain.

Green, E., Hebron, S. and Woodward, D. (1990) *Women's Leisure, What Leisure?* London: Macmillan.

Griffin, S., Hobson, D., MacIntosh, S. and McCabe, T. (1982) 'Women and leisure', in J. Hargreaves (ed.), *Sport, Culture and Ideology*. London: Routledge & Kegan Paul.

Griffiths, V. (1988) 'Stepping out: the importance of dancing for young women', in E. Wimbush and M. Talbot (eds), *Relative Freedoms: Women and Leisure*. Milton Keynes: Open University Press. pp. 115–25.

Grosz, E. (1986) 'Conclusion: what is feminist theory?', in C. Pateman and E. Grosz, *Feminist Challenges*. Sydney: Allen & Unwin. pp. 190–204.

Grosz, E. (1987) 'Notes towards a corporeal feminism', *Australian Feminist Studies*, 5: 1–16.

Grosz, E. (1989) *Sexual Subversions*. Sydney: Allen & Unwin.

Grosz, E. (1994) *Volatile Bodies: Towards a Corporeal Femininism*. Sydney: Allen & Unwin.

Grosz, E. (1995a) 'Women, *chora*, dwelling', in S. Watson and K. Gibson (eds), *Postmodern Cities and Spaces*. Oxford: Blackwell. pp. 47–58.

Grosz, E. (1995b) *Space, Time and Perversion: The Politics of Bodies*. Sydney: Allen & Unwin.

Gruneau, R. (1983) *Class, Sports and Social Development*, Amherst, MA: Unversity of Massachusetts Press.

Guha, R. (ed.) (1981–9) *Subaltern Studies: Writings on South Asian History and Society*, vols I, II and III. Delhi: Oxford University Press.

Hall, L. (1991) *Hidden Anxieties: Male Sexuality, 1900–1950*. Cambridge: Polity Press.

Hall, M.A. (1985) 'Knowledge and gender: epistemological questions in the social analysis of sport', *Sociology of Sport Journal*, 2: 25–42.

Hall, M.A. (1995) 'Bodies resisting and resisted: women and physicality'. Keynote presentation to the International Conference on Women and Leisure, University of Georgia, Athens, Georgia, USA.

Hall, S. and Jefferson, T. (eds) (1976) *Resistance through Rituals*. London: Hutchinson.

Hamilton-Smith, E. (1990) 'Preliminary thoughts about directions for recreation benefit measurement in Australia'. Papers on recreation benefit measurement presented at a workshop convened by the Department of Leisure Studies, Philip Institute of Technology, Bundoora, Victoria, 18–20 April.

Hamilton-Smith, E. and Robertson, R. (1981) 'Recreation and government in Australia', in D. Mercer and E. Hamilton-Smith (eds), *Recreation Planning and Social Change in Australia*. Malvern, VIC: Sorrett.

Hargreaves, J. (1987) 'The body, sport and power relations', in J. Horne, D. Jary and A. Tomlinson (eds), *Sport, Leisure and Social Relations*. London: Routledge & Kegan Paul. pp. 139–59.

Hargreaves, J. (1989) 'The promise and problems of women's leisure and sport', in C. Rojek (ed.), *Leisure for Leisure*. London: Macmillan. pp. 130–49.

Hargreaves, J. (1994) *Sporting Females: Critical Issues in the History and Sociology of Women's Sports*. London and New York: Routledge.

Harman, E. (1983) 'Capitalism, patriarchy and the city', in C. Baldock and B. Cass (eds), *Women, Social Welfare and the State*. Sydney: Allen & Unwin. pp. 104–29.

Harvey, D. (1985) *Consciousness and the Urban Experience*. Oxford: Basil Blackwell.

Hayden, D. (1980) 'What would a non-sexist city be like? Speculations on housing, urban design, and human work', *Signs*, 5 (3), supplement S170–S187.

Hayden, D. (1984) *Redesigning the American Dream: The Future of Housing, Work and Family Life*. New York: Norton.

Haywood, K.M. (1988) 'Responsible and responsive tourism planning in the community, tourism management', *Tourism Management*, 9: 105–18.

Hearn, J. (1987) *The Gender of Oppression: Men, Masculinity, and the Critique of Marxism*. Brighton: Wheatsheaf.

Hearn, J. (1994) 'Research in men and masculinities: some sociological issues and possibilities', *Australian and New Zealand Journal of Sociology*, 30 (1): 47–70.

Heaven, P. and Rowe, D. (1990) 'Gender, sport and body image', in D. Rowe and G. Lawrence (eds), *Sport and Leisure: Trends in Australian Popular Culture*. Sydney: Harcourt Brace Jovanovich. pp. 59–73.

Henderson, K.A. (1983) 'The motivation of men and women in volunteering', *Journal of Volunteer Administration*, 1 (3): 20–9.

Henderson, K.A. (1990) 'The meaning of leisure for women: an integrative review of the research', *Journal of Leisure Research*, 22 (3): 228–43.

Henderson, K.A. and Bialeschki, D. (1986) 'Outdoor experiential education (for women only)', in M. Gass and L. Bluell (eds), *Proceedings Journal*. Moodus, CT: Association of Experiential Education 14th Annual Conference. pp. 35–41.

Henderson, K.A. and Bialeschski, M.D. (1987) 'Qualitative evaluation of a women's week experience', *Journal of Experiential Education*, 10 (6): 25–9.

Henderson, K.A. and Rannells, J.S. (1988) 'Farm women and the meaning of work and leisure: an oral history perspective', *Leisure Sciences*, 10: 41–50.

Henderson, K.A., Bialeschki, M.D., Shaw, S. and Freysinger, V.J. (1989) *A Leisure of One's Own: A Feminist Perspective on Women's Leisure*. State College, PA: Venture.

Henderson, K.A., Bialeschki, M.D., Shaw, S. and Freysinger, V.J. (1996) *Both Gains and Gaps: Feminist Perspectives on Women's Leisure*. State College, PA: Venture.

Heycox, K. (1997) 'The personal is political is personal: the older women's network in the 1990s'. PhD thesis, University of New South Wales, Sydney.

Hiller, H.H. (1990) 'The urban transformation of a landmark event: the 1988 Calgary Winter Olympics', *Urban Affairs Quarterly*, 21 (1): 118–37.

Hochschild, A.R. (1979) 'Emotion work, feeling rules, and social structure', *American Journal of Sociology*, 85: 551–75.

Hochschild, A.R. (1983) *The Managed Heart: Commercialization of Human Feeling.* Berkeley, CA: University of California Press.

Hochschild, A.R. (1989) *The Second Shift.* Berkeley, CA: University of California Press.

Hochschild, A.R. (1994) 'The commercial spirit of intimate life and the abduction of feminism: signs from women's advice books', *Theory, Culture & Society*, 11: 1–24.

hooks, b. (1984) *Feminist Theory: From Margin to Center.* Boston, MA: South End Press.

hooks, b. (1989) *Feminist Theory: From Margin to Center.* Boston, MA: South End Press.

hooks, b. (1993) *Sisters of the Yam: Black Women and Self-Recovery*, Boston, MA: South End Press.

hooks, b. (1996) *Killing Rage: Ending Racism.* London: Penguin.

Huggins, J. (1994) 'A contemporary view of Aboriginal women's relationship to the white women's movement', in N. Grieve and A. Burns (eds), *Australian Women: Contemporary Feminist Thought.* Melbourne: Oxford University Press. pp. 7–91.

Hunter, P.L. and Whitson, D.J. (1992) 'Women's leisure in a resource industry town: problems and issues', *Society and Leisure*, 15 (1): 223–43.

Huxley, M. (1994) 'Space, knowledge, power and gender', in L.C. Johnson (ed.), *Suburban Dreaming: An Interdisciplinary Approach to Australian Cities.* Geelong, VIC: Deakin University Press. pp. 181–92.

Huyssen, A. (1990) 'Mapping the postmodern', in L.J. Nicholson (ed.), *Feminism and Postmodernism.* New York: Routledge. pp. 234–77.

Irigaray, L. (1985[1974]) *Speculum of the Other Woman*, trans. by G.C. Gill. New York: Cornell University Press.

Irigaray, L. (1986) 'The sex which is not one', trans. C. Reeder, in E. Marks and I. de Courtivron (eds), *New French Feminisms.* Brighton: Harvester Press. pp. 99–106.

Jagtenberg, T. and McKie, D. (1997) *Eco-Impacts and the Greening of Postmodernity.* Thousand Oaks, CA: Sage.

James, W. (1952 [1891]) *The Principles of Psychology.* Chicago: William Benton.

Johnson, L.C. (1994) 'The postmodern Australian city', in L.C. Johnson (ed.), *Suburban Dreaming: An Interdisciplinary Approach to Australian Cities.* Geelong, VIC: Deakin University Press. pp. 51–72.

Jolly, M. (1991) 'The politics of difference: feminism, colonialism and decolonisation in Vanuatu', in G. Bottomley, M. de Lepervanche and J. Martin (eds), *Intersexions: Gender/Class/Culture/Ethnicity.* Sydney: Allen & Unwin. pp. 52–74.

Kauffman, M. (1990) 'A framework for research on men and masculinity', *Men's Studies Review*, 7 (3): 14–19.

Kellner, D. (1992) 'Popular culture and the construction of postmodern identities', in S. Lash and J. Friedman (eds), *Modernity and Identity.* Oxford: Blackwell. pp. 141–77.

Kelly, J.R. (1982) *Leisure.* Illinois: Prentice Hall.

Kelly, J.R. (1983) *Leisure Identities and Interactions.* London: Allen & Unwin.

Kelly, J.R. (1987a) *Freedom to Be: A New Sociology of Leisure.* Macmillan: New York.

Kelly, J.R. (1987b) *Peoria Winter: Styles and Resources in Later Life.* Lexington, MA: Lexington Books.

Kelly, J.R. (1990) 'Social benefits of leisure'. Papers on recreation benefit measurement presented at a workshop convened by Department of Leisure Studies, Philip Institute of Technology, Bundoora, Victoria, 18–20 April.

Kelly, J. (1994) 'The symbolic interaction metaphor and leisure: critical challenges', *Leisure Studies*, 13: 81–96.

Kelly, J.R., Steinkamp, M. and Kelly, J. (1986) 'Later life leisure: how they play in Peoria', *Gerontological Society of America*, 26 (5): 531–7.

Kimmel, M. (1996) *Manhood in America: A Cultural History.* New York: Free Press.

Kimmel, M. and Messner, M. (1989) *Men's Lives.* New York: Macmillan.

Kleiber, D.A. and Kane, M.J. (1984) 'Sex differences and the use of leisure as adaptive potentiation', *Society and Leisure*, 7: 165–73.

Labone, M. and Wearing, S. (1994) 'Family leisure decisions and national parks: a sociological perspective', in D. Mercer (ed.), *New Viewpoints in Australian Outdoor Recreation Research and Planning.* Melbourne: Hepper, Marriot. pp. 52–74.

Langford, R. (1988) *Don't Take Your Love to Town.* Ringwood, VIC: Penguin.

Larbalestier, J. (1994) 'Imagining the city: contradictory tales of place and space', in K. Gibson and S. Watson (eds), *Metropolis Now.* Sydney: Pluto.

Lefebvre, H. (1974) *The Survival of Capitalism.* London: Allen & Unwin.

Lloyd, G. (1989) 'Woman as other: sex, gender and subjectivity', *Australian Feminist Studies*, 10, Summer: 13–22.

Lynch, K. (1960) *The Image of the City.* Cambridge, MA: MIT Press.

Lynch, R. and Veal, A.J. (1996) *Australian Leisure.* Melbourne: Longman.

Lyng, S. (1990) 'Edgework: a social psychologial analysis of voluntary risk taking', *American Journal of Sociology*, 95 (4): 851–85.

Lyon, D. (1994) *Postmodernity.* Buckingham: Open University Press.

MacCannell, D. (1992) *Empty Meeting Grounds.* London: Routledge.

Marks, E. and de Courtivron, I. (eds) (1986) *New French Feminisms,* Brighton: Harvester Press.

Mason, J. (1988) 'No peace for the wicked: older married women and leisure', in E. Wimbush and M. Talbot (eds), *Relative Freedoms: Women and Leisure.* Milton Keynes: Open University Press. pp. 75–85.

Mason-Cox, S. (1992) 'Challenging gender mythologies through an Outward Bound standard programme'. Honours thesis, University of Technology, Sydney.

Massey, D. (1994) *Space, Place and Gender.* Cambridge: Polity Press.

Mattelart, M. (1986) 'Women and the cultural industries', in R. Collins, J. Curran, N. Garnham, P. Scannell, P. Schlesinger and C. Sparks (eds), *Media, Culture and Society.* London: Sage.

Matthews, J.J. (1995) 'Dancing modernity', in B. Caine and R. Pringle (eds), *Transitions: New Australian Feminisms.* Sydney: Allen & Unwin. pp. 74–87.

McCrohan, P. (1993) 'Time out boys: it's time to refocus: masculinist literature in the 1990s'. Paper presented to the Australian Sociological Association, Annual Conference, Macquarie University, 13–15 December.

McKay, J. (1990) 'Sport, leisure and inequality in Australia', in D. Rowe and G. Lawrence (eds), *Sport and Leisure: Trends in Australian Popular Culture.* Sydney: Harcourt Brace Jovanovich. pp. 125–60.

McKay, J. (1991) *No Pain, No Gain? Sport and Australian Culture.* Brunswick, VIC: Prentice Hall.

McNeill, P. and Coulson, M. (1994) *Women's Voices: Refugee Lives.* Woonona, NSW: Book People.

McRobbie, A. (1978) 'Working class girls and the culture of femininity', in *Women Take Issue.* London: Hutchinson.

McRobbie, A. (1993a) 'Feminism, postmodernism and the real me', *Theory, Culture & Society*, 11 (4): 127–42.

McRobbie, A. (1993b) 'Shut up and dance: youth culture and changing modes of femininity', *Cultural Studies*, 7 (3): 406–26.

Mead, G.H. (1972 [1934]) *Mind, Self and Society.* Chicago: University of Chicago Press.

Mera Molisa, G. (1978) Speech to the First Conference of Vanuaaku Women, Efate, Ts (translation).

Mera Molisa, G. (1987) *Colonised People.* Port Vila: Black Stone Publications.

Mercer, D.C. (1985) 'Australians time use and preferences: some recent findings', *Australian and New Zealand Journal of Sociology*, 21 (3): 371–94.

Messner, M. (1987) 'The meaning of success: the athletic experience and the development of male identity', in H. Brod (ed.), *The Making of Masculinities*, Boston: Allen & Unwin. pp. 193–210.

Messner, M. (1990) 'Boyhood, organised sports, and the construction of masculinities', *Journal of Contemporary Ethnology*, 18 (4): 416–44.

Messner, M. (1992a) 'Boyhood, organised sports, and the construction of masculinity', in M. Kimmel and M. Messner (eds), *Men's Lives* (2nd edn). New York: Macmillan: 176–82.

Messner, M. (1992b) *Power at Play: Sports and the Problem of Masculinity*. Boston: Beacon Press.

Messner, M. and Sabo, D. (1990) *Sport, Men, and the Gender Order*. Champaign, IL: Human Kinetics Books.

Mieli, M. (1980) *Homosexuality and Liberation*. London: Gay Men's Press.

Miller, L. and Penz, O. (1991) 'Talking bodies: female body-builders colonize a male preserve', *Quest*, 43: 148–63.

Miranda, W. and Yerks, R. (1985) 'Women outdoors – who are they?', *Parks and Recreation*, 20: 48–51.

Moffat, G. (1961) *Space Below My Feet*. London: Hodder & Stoughton.

Moor, R., Goltsman, S. and Iacofano, D. (1987) *Play for All Guidelines: Planning, Design and Management of Outdoor Play Settings for All Children*. Berkeley, CA: MIG Communications.

Moorhouse, H.F. (1983) 'American automobiles and workers dreams', *Sociological Review*, 31: 403–26.

Moorhouse, H.F. (1989) 'Models of work, models of leisure', in C. Rojek (ed.), *Leisure for Leisure*. London: Macmillan. pp. 15–35.

Moraga, C. and Anzaldua, G. (1983) *This Bridge Called My Back: Writings by Radical Women of Color*. New York: Kitchen Table, Women of Color Press.

Morgan, D. (1993) 'You too can have a body like mine: reflections on the male body and masculinities', in S. Scott and D. Morgan (eds), *Body Matters: Essays on the Sociology of the Body*. London: Falmer Press.

Morgan, S. (1987) *My Place*. Fremantle, WA: Fremantle Arts Centre Press.

Mowl, G. and Towner, J. (1995) 'Women, gender, leisure and place: towards a more "humanistic" geography of women's leisure', *Leisure Studies*, 14 (2): 102–16.

Mulvay, L. (1975) 'Visual pleasure and narrative cinema', *Screen*, 16 (3): 6–18.

Neumeyer, M.H. and Neumeyer, E.S. (1958) *Leisure and Recreation*. New York: Ronald Press.

Nicholson, L. (1995a) 'Interpreting gender', in L. Nicholson and S. Seidman (eds), *Social Postmodernism*. Cambridge: Cambridge University Press. pp. 39–67.

Nicholson, L. (1995b) 'Introduction', in S. Benhabib, J. Butler, D. Cornell and N. Frazer, *Feminist Contentions*. New York and London: Routledge. pp. 1–16.

O'Connor, B. and Boyle, R. (1993) 'Dallas with balls: televised sport, soap opera and male and female pleasures', *Leisure Studies*, 12: 107–19.

O'Malley, P. and Mugford, S. (1991) 'Crime, excitement and modernity'. Paper presented at the American Society of Criminology, San Francisco, CA.

O'Shea, K. (1995) *Person in Cosmos: Metaphors from Physics, Philosophy and Theology*. Bristol, IN: Wyndham Hall.

Oglesby, C. (1990) 'Epilogue', in M.A. Messner and D.F. Sabo (eds), *Sport, Men and the Gender Order: Critical Feminist Perspectives*. Chamapaign, IL: Human Kinetics Books. pp. 241–5.

Orbach, S. (1979) *Fat is a Feminist Issue*. New York: Berkeley Books.

Park, R. (1952) *Human Communities: The City and Human Ecology*. New York: Free Press.

Parker, S. (1983) *Leisure and Work*. London: Allen & Unwin.

Parker, S. (1988) 'Recent developments in leisure theory in Britain'. Paper presented to the World Congress on Free Time, Culture and Society, Lake Louise, Alberta, Canada, 16–22 May.

Parker, S. and Paddick, R. (1990) *Leisure in Australia.* Melbourne: Longman Cheshire.

Parsons, T.P. (1954) *Essays in Sociological Theory.* New York: Free Press.

Parsons, T.P. and Bales, R.F. (1955) *Family, Socialisation and Interaction Process.* London: Routledge & Kegan Paul.

Pearce, P. (1990) 'Social impact of tourism', in Griffin, T. (ed.), *The Social, Cultural and Environmental Impacts of Tourism.* Sydney: NSW Tourism Commission. pp. 31–8.

Pearson, K. (1979) *Surfing Subcultures of Australia and New Zealand.* St Lucia, QLD: University of Queensland Press.

Pettman, J. (1991) *Living in the Margins: Racism, Sexism and Feminism in Australia.* Sydney: Allen & Unwin.

Pfeiffer, E. and Davis, G.C. (1971) 'The use of leisure time in middle life', *The Gerontologist,* 3 (13): 187–95.

Pollock, G. (1988) 'Modernity and the spaces of femininity', in *Vision and Difference: Femininity, Feminism and the Histories of Art.* London; Routledge.

Poovey, M. (1988) 'Feminism and deconstruction', *Feminist Studies,* 14 (1), Spring: 51–65.

Prakash, G. (1994) 'Postcolonial criticism and Indian historiography', in L. Nicholson and S. Seidman (eds), *Social Postmodernism: Beyond Identity Politics.* Cambridge: Cambridge University Press. pp. 87–100.

Probyn, E. (1993) *Sexing the Self: Gendered Positions in Cultural Studies.* London: Routledge.

Ram, K. (1993) 'Too "traditonal" once again: some poststructuralists on the aspirations of the immigrant, Third World female subject', *Australian Feminist Studies,* 17: 5–28.

Rapoport, R. and Rapoport, R.N. (1975) *Leisure and Family Life Cycle.* London: Routledge & Kegan Paul.

Roberts, G. (1986) 'Visitor use information and its implications for park management planning: centennial park case study', in *Developing Communities into the 21st Century.* Belconnen, ACT: Royal Institute of Parks and Recreation.

Roberts, K. (1983) *Youth and Leisure.* London: Allen & Unwin.

Roberts, K. (1997) 'Same activities, different meanings: British youth cultures in the 1990s', *Leisure Studies,* 16: 1–15.

Roberts, K., Parsell, G. and Chadwick, C. (1991) 'Unemployment and young people's leisure in Liverpool and Swindon', *Leisure and Society,* 14 (2): 513–30.

Rojek, C. (1985) *Capitalism and Leisure Theory.* London: Tavistock.

Rojek, C. (1986) 'Leisure and legitimation'. Keynote Address, XI World Congress of Sociology, New Delhi, August 18–22.

Rojek, C. (1989) 'Leisure and recreation theory', in E. Jackson and T.L. Burton (eds), *Understanding Leisure and Recreation: Mapping the Past, Charting the Future.* State College, PA: Venture. pp. 71–88.

Rojek, C. (1993a) *Ways of Escape: Modern Transformations in Leisure and Travel.* London: Macmillan.

Rojek, C. (1993b) 'After popular culture: hyperreality and leisure', *Leisure Studies,* 12: 277–89.

Rojek, C. (1995) *Decentring Leisure: Rethinking Leisure Theory.* London: Sage.

Rojek, C. (1996) 'The West House: domestic leisure and the English murder'. Address given to the Ontario Research Council on Leisure at the Eighth Canadian Congress on Leisure Research, Ottawa, Ontario.

Roman, L. (1988) 'Intimacy, labour, and class: ideologies of feminine sexuality in the punk slam dance', in L. Roman, I. Christian-Smith and E. Ellsworth (eds), *Becoming Feminine.* London: Falmer Press. pp. 143–84.

Rowe, D. (1995) *Popular Cultures: Rock Music, Sport and the Politics of Pleasure.* London: Sage.

Rowe, G.P. (1966) 'Developmental conceptual framework to the study of the family', in F.I. Nye and F.M. Berado (eds), *Emerging Conceptual Frameworks in Family Analysis.* New York: Macmillan.

Ryan, J. (1994) 'Women, modernity and the city', *Theory, Culture and Society,* 11 (2): 35–63.

Saegert, S. (1980) 'Masculine cities and feminine suburbs: polarized ideas, contradictory realities', *Signs,* 5 (3): supplement S96–S112.

Samdahl, D. (1988) 'A Symbolic Interactionist model of leisure: theory and empirical support,' *Leisure Sciences,* 10 (1): 27–39.

Samdahl, D. (1992) 'The effect of gender socialization on labeling experience as "leisure"'. Paper presented at the SPRE Leisure Research Symposium, Cincinnati, Ohio.

Samuel, N. (1986) 'Free time in France: a historical and sociological survey', *International Social Science Journal,* 107: 49–63.

Sandercock, S. and Forsyth, A. (1992) 'A gender agenda: new directions for planning theory', Signs, 58 (1), Winter: 49–59.

Savage, M. and Warde, A. (1993) *Urban Sociology, Capitalism and Modernity.* London: Macmillan.

Scherl, L.M. (1988) 'The wilderness experience: psychological and motivational considerations of a structural experience in a wilderness setting', PhD thesis, James Cook University, Queensland.

Scherl, L.M. (1990) 'Wilderness benefits from an interactionist perspective'. Papers on recreation benefit measurement presented at a workshop convened by the Department of Leisure Studies, Philip Institute of Technology, Bundoora, Victoria, 18–20 April.

Schulze, L. (1990) 'On the muscle', in J. Gaine and C. Herzog (eds), *Fabrications: Costume and the Female Body.* New York: Routledge. pp. 59–78.

Scott, H. (1982) *Sweden's Right to be Human.* London: Allison & Busby.

Scott, S. and Morgan. D. (1993) *Body Matters: Essays on the Sociology of the Body.* London: Falmer Press.

Scraton, S. (1994) 'The changing world of women and leisure: feminism, "postfeminism" and leisure', *Leisure Studies,* 9: 249–61.

Scraton, S. (1995) 'Continuities and change – challenges for a feminist leisure studies'. Paper presented at Women and Leisure: Towards a New Understanding, International Conference, Athens, Georgia, USA.

Scraton, S. and Talbot, M. (1989) 'A response to "Leisure, lifestyle and status: a pluralist framework for analysis"', *Leisure Studies,* 8: 155–8.

Segal, L. (1990) *Slow Motion: Changing Masculinities, Changing Men.* London: Virago.

Seidler, V. (1989) *Rediscovering Masculinity: Reason, Language and Sexuality.* London: Routledge.

Seidler, V. (1994) *Unreasonable Men: Masculinity and Social Theory.* London and New York: Routledge.

Shaw, S.M. (1985) 'Gender and leisure: an examination of women's and men's everyday experience and perceptions of family time', *Journal of Leisure Research,* 17 (4): 266–82.

Shaw, S.M. (1994) 'Gender, leisure, and constraint: towards a framework for the analysis of women's leisure', *National Recreation and Park Association,* 26 (1): 8–22.

Sheridan, S. (1995) 'Reading the women's weekly: feminism, femininity and popular culture', in B. Caine and R. Pringle (eds), *Transitions: New Australian Feminisms.* Sydney: Allen & Unwin. pp. 88–101.

Simmel, G. (1936) *The Web of Group Affiliations,* trans. by Reinhard Bendix. New York: Free Press.

Simmel, G. (1950) *The Sociology of Gorge Simmel*, trans. by K.H. Wolff. Glencoe, IL: Free Press.

Simmel, G. (1964) 'The metropolis and mental life', in K. Wolff (ed.), *The Sociology of Georg Simmel*. New York: Free Press. pp. 409–24.

Simmel, G. (1965) 'The adventure', in K.H. Wolff (ed.), *Essays on Sociology, Philosophy and Aesthetics by Georg Simmel* (2nd edn). New York: Harper & Row. pp. 243–58.

Simmel, G. (1978) *The Philosophy of Money*. London: Routledge & Kegan Paul.

Smith, D.E. (1988) 'Femininity as discourse', in L.G. Roman and L.K. Christian-Smith (eds), *Becoming Feminine: The Politics of Popular Culture*. London: Falmer Press. pp. 37–59.

Soja, E. (1993[1989]) 'History, geography: modernity', in S. During (ed.), *The Cultural Studies Reader*. London and New York: Routledge. pp. 135–50.

Spivak, G.C. (1988a) 'Can the subaltern speak?', in C. Nelson and L. Grossberg (eds), *Marxism and the Interpretation of Culture*. Urbana, IL: University of Illinois Press. pp. 271– 313.

Spivak, G.C. (1988b) *In Other Worlds: Essays in Cultural Politics*. New York: Methuen.

Stebbins, R.A. (1982) 'Serious leisure: a conceptual statement', *Pacific Sociological Review*, 25 (2): 251–72.

Stebbins, R.A. (1997) 'Casual leisure: a conceptual statement', *Leisure Studies,* 16: 17–25.

Stedman, L. (1997) 'From Gidget to Gonad Man: surfers, feminists and post-modernism', *Australian New Zealand Journal of Sociology*, 33 (1): 75–90.

Summers, A. (1994) *Damned Whores and God's Police*, 2nd edn. Ringwood, VIC: Penguin.

Sydney City Council (1995) *Sydney Spaces*. Sydney: Sydney City Council.

Sydney Morning Herald (1994) Weekend magazine, 30 July: 14.

Sydney Morning Herald (1995) 'Pretty on paper: Sydney is poised for redevelopment on a grand scale', Monday, 21 August: 10.

Szalai, A., Converse, P.E., Feldham, P., Scheuch, E.K. and Stone, P.J. (1972) *The Uses of Time: Daily Activities of Urban and Suburban Populations in Twelve Countries.* The Hague: European Co-ordination Centre for Research and Documentation.

Talbot, M. (1988a) 'Beating them at their own game? Women's sports involvement', in E. Wimbush and M. Talbot (eds), *Relative Freedoms: Women and Leisure*. Milton Keynes: Open University Press. pp. 102–14.

Talbot, M. (1988b) ' "Their own worst enemy"? Women and leisure provision', in E. Wimbush and M. Talbot (eds), *Relative Freedoms; Women and Leisure*. Milton Keynes: Open University Press. pp. 161–76.

Tenhouten, W.D. (1996) 'Introduction: sociology of emotions', *International Journal of Sociology and Social Policy*, 16 (9/10): 1–20.

Thompson, E.P. (1980 [1963]) *The Making of the English Working Class.* Harmondsworth: Penguin.

Thompson, S. (1992) ' "Mum's tennis day": the gendered definition of older women's leisure', *Loisir et Société/Society and Leisure*, 15 (1), Spring: 271–89.

Thomson, M. (1995) *Blokes and Sheds*. Sydney: Angus & Robertson for Harper-Collins.

Thornton, S. (1996) *Club Cultures: Music, Media and Subcultural Capital*. Hanover, NH: University of New England Press.

Tomkins, J. (1994) 'The football discourse: the generation and control of the male and female body and its impact on the football world', in C. Brackenridge (ed.), *Body Matters: Leisure Images and Lifestyles*, 2nd edn. Leisure Studies Association No. 47. Eastborne: LSA Publications. pp. 283–91.

Turner, B. (1984) *The Body and Society*. Oxford: Basil Blackwell.

Turner, B. (1991) 'Recent developments in the theory of the body', in M. Feather-stone, M. Hepworth and B. Turner (eds), *The Body*. London: Sage.

Turner, B. (1996) *The Body and Society*, 2nd edn. London: Sage.

Van de Water, S. (1993) *Parks, Play and People*. Surry Hills, NSW: Network of Community Services.

Van Gyn, D., Raddulph, J. and Bell, R. (1989) 'Body image of active women as related to age', in Proceedings of the *Jyvaskyla Congess on Movement and Sport in Women's Life*, 17–21 August 1987. Jyvaskyla, Finland, vol. 1: pp. 465–75.

Veal, A.J. (1987) *Leisure and the Future*. London: Allen & Unwin.

Veal, A.J. (1989) 'Leisure, lifestyle and status: a pluralist framework for analysis', *Leisure Studies*, 8: 141–53.

Veal, A.J. (1993) 'Leisure participation in Australia: 1985–91, a note on data', *Australian Journal of Leisure and Recreation*, 3 (2): 37–45.

Walby, S. (1990) *Theorising Patriarchy*. Oxford: Blackwell.

Walby, S. (1992) 'Post-post-modernism? Theorising social complexity', in M. Barrett and A. Phillips (eds), *Destabilising Theory: Contemporary Feminist Debates*. Cambridge: Polity Press.

Walker, J.C. (1988) *Louts and Legends: Male Culture in an Inner City School*. Sydney: Allen & Unwin.

Wallace, M. (1993) 'Negative images: towards a black cultural criticism', in S. During (ed.), *The Cultural Studies Reader*. London and New York: Free Press. pp. 118–31.

Walter, A. (ed.) (1980) *Come Together*. London: Gay Men's Press.

Waters, M. (1989) 'Patriarchy and viriarchy: an exploration and reconstruction of constructs of masculine domination', *Sociology*, 23 (2): 1171–89.

Watkins, B. (1991) 'Marginalisation and self-sufficiency: women in a northern interior town'. Paper presented at the Canadian Sociology and Anthropology Association, Kingston.

Watson, M. (1988) (video) *Koorie Out Tapes: Maureen Watson – Storyteller* (producers T. Woolmer and L. Hewson). Sydney: Cluster Productions.

Watson, S. and Gibson, K. (eds) (1995) *Postmodern Cities and Spaces*. Oxford: Blackwell.

Wearing, B.M. (1984) *The Ideology of Motherhood*. Sydney: Allen & Unwin.

Wearing, B.M. (1990a) 'Beyond the ideology of motherhood: leisure as resistance', *Australian and New Zealand Journal of Sociology*, 26 (1): 36–58.

Wearing, B.M. (1990b) 'Leisure and the crisis of motherhood; a study of leisure and health amongst mothers of first babies in Sydney, Australia', in S. Quah (ed.), *The Family as an Asset: An International Perspective on Marriage, Parenthood and Social Policy*. Singapore: Singapore Times Academic Press. pp. 122–55.

Wearing, B.M. (1992a) 'Leisure and women's identity in late adolescence', *Society and Leisure*, 15 (1): 323–43.

Wearing, B.M. (1992b) 'Leisure and health for men and women over 55'. Preliminary report, School of Social Work, University of New South Wales, Sydney.

Wearing, B.M. (1995) 'Leisure and resistance in an ageing society', *Leisure Studies*, 14: 263–79.

Wearing, B.M. (1996) *Gender: The Pain and Pleasure of Difference*. Melbourne: Longman.

Wearing, B.M. and Wearing, S.L. (1988) ' "All in a day's leisure": gender and the concept of leisure', *Leisure Studies*, 7: 111–23.

Wearing, B.M. and Wearing, S.L. (1990) ' "Leisure for all? Gender and leisure policy" ', in D. Rowe and G. Lawrence (eds), *Sport and Leisure: Trends in Australian Popular Culture*. Sydney: Harcourt Brace Jovanovich.

Wearing, B.M. and Wearing, S.L. (1992) 'Identity and the commodification of leisure', *Leisure Studies*,11: 3–18.

Wearing, B. and Wearing, S. (1996a) 'The Olympic city 2000: phallic fallacy in accessing leisure spaces'. Paper presented at World Leisure and Recreation Association Congress, Cardiff, UK.

Wearing, B.M. and Wearing, S.L. (1996b) 'Refocusing the tourist experience: the flâneur and the choraster', *Leisure Studies,* 15: 229–43.

Wearing, B.M. and Wearing, S.L. (1996c) 'The hegemonic construction of tourist spaces: place, space and otherness'. Paper presented at the Australian Sociological Association Annual Conference, Hobart.

Weber, M. (1970) *From Max Weber* (eds H. Gerth and C. Wright Mills). London: Routledge & Kegan Paul.

Weedon, C. (1987) *Feminist Practice and Poststructuralist Theory.* Oxford: Basil Blackwell.

Williams, C. (1981) *Open Cut.* Sydney: Allen & Unwin.

Williams, R. (1983) *Keywords: A Vocabulary of Culture and Society.* London: Flamingo.

Wilson, E. (1989) *Sex, Politics and Society.* London: Longman.

Wilson, E. (1991) *The Sphinx in the City.* London: Virago.

Wilson, E. (1995) 'The invisible flâneur', in S. Watson and K. Gibson (eds), *Postmodern Cities and Spaces.* Oxford: Blackwell, pp. 59–79.

Wilson, J. (1988) *Politics and Leisure.* Boston, MA: Unwin Hyman.

Wimbush, E. (1988) 'Mothers meeting', in E. Wimbush and M. Talbot (eds), *Relative Freedoms, Women and Leisure.* Milton Keynes: Open University Press. pp. 60–74.

Wimbush, E. and Talbot, M. (eds) (1988) *Relative Freedoms: Women and Leisure.* Milton Keynes: Open University Press.

Winship, J. (1983) 'Options for the way you want to live now, or a magazine for superwoman', *Theory, Culture and Society,*1 (3): 44–85.

Wirth, L. (1938) 'Urbanism as a way of life', *American Journal of Sociology,* 44: 1–24.

Wolff, J. (1985) 'The invisible flâneuse; women and the literature of modernity', *Theory, Culture & Society,* 2: 37–45.

Woodberry, N. (1995) 'The social value of coastal leisure, recreation and tourist settings: incorproating community knowledge into coastal land use planning'. Individual research project for Masters of Coastal Resource Management, University of Technology, Sydney.

Woodward, D. and Green, E. (1990) 'In celebration of women's friendships: collusion, catharsis or challenge?'. Paper presented to the XIIth World Congress of Sociology, Madrid.

World Leisure and Recreation Association (1975) *Beyond Survival: Leisure and Recreation in Human Settlements: A Global Survey.* New York: World Leisure and Recreation Association.

Yeatman, A. (1993) 'Voice and representation in the politics of difference', in S. Gunew and A. Yeatman (eds), *The Politics of Difference.* Sydney: Allen & Unwin. pp. 228–45.

Yeo, E. and Yeo, S. (1981) *Popular Culture and Class Conflict 1590–1914: Explorations of the History of Labour and Leisure.* Brighton: Harvester Press.

Young, I. (1990) *Throwing like a Girl.* Bloomington and Indianapolis, IN: Indiana University Press.

Young, N. (1994) *The History of Surfing,* rev. edn. Angourie, NSW: Palm Beach Press.

Zakus, D. (1995) 'Production, consumption, and sport: use of the body in women's elite sport', *International Review for the Sociology of Sport,* 30 (1): 81–95.

Index